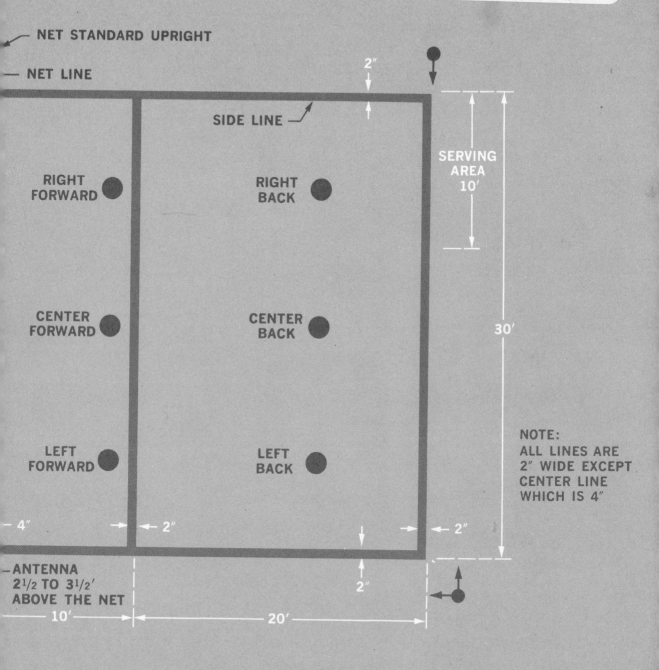

NET STANDARD UPRIGHT

NET LINE

2"

SIDE LINE

SERVING
AREA
10'

RIGHT
FORWARD

RIGHT
BACK

CENTER
FORWARD

CENTER
BACK

30'

LEFT
FORWARD

LEFT
BACK

NOTE:
ALL LINES ARE
2" WIDE EXCEPT
CENTER LINE
WHICH IS 4"

4"

2"

2"

2"

ANTENNA
2½ TO 3½'
ABOVE THE NET

2"

10'

20'

WINNING VOLLEYBALL.

Second Edition

ALLEN E. SCATES

Elementary Physical Education Specialist
Beverly Hills School District

Head Coach, UCLA
NCAA Volleyball Champions, 1970, 1971, 1972, 1974, 1975

Head Coach, U.S. Pan American team, 1971

Head Coach, U.S. Olympic Volleyball team, 1972

Allyn and Bacon, Inc.
Boston • London • Sydney • Toronto

To my loving wife, Sue
Thank you for your patience.

Photographs appearing on the following pages are works of these photographers:

Stan Abraham (page 6), Jim Haberlin (page 138), Barry Schreiber (pages 20, 90, 140, 168, 238), Norm Scindler (page 58), Stan Troutman (pages 4, 36, 116), Bob Van Wagner (pages 190, 216)

Copyright © 1976 by Allyn and Bacon, Inc.
Copyright © 1972 by Allyn and Bacon, Inc.
470 Atlantic Avenue, Boston, Massachusetts 02210.

Library of Congress Cataloging in Publication Data

Scates, Allen E
 Winning volleyball.

 Bibliography: p.
 Includes index.
 1. Volleyball. I. Title.
GV1017. V6S28 1976   796.32'5   75-26723

ISBN 0-205-04875-7

Fourth printing . . . July, 1977

Contents

Foreword

The Allyn and Bacon Sports Education Series
Arthur G. Miller, *Consulting Editor*

Sports play a major role in the lives of almost everyone—the players, the coaches, the officials, and the spectators! Interest in sports is the result of several factors.

There is increased emphasis on *personal physical fitness*. Formal exercises or calisthenics, while worthwhile, are not as popular nor as motivating for the promotion of fitness as participation in sports is. Through *sports participation*, children and adults gain fitness but also develop skills, group and personal satisfactions, and enjoyment.

Another factor in the growing interest in sports is the increase in television and radio broadcasts of sporting events. Team sports, such as baseball, football, basketball, soccer, and hockey, are seasonally covered by major networks. Lifetime sports, including bowling, golf, tennis, and skiing, are also receiving more air time. Activities such as gymnastics, swimming, and other aquatic sports continue to receive expanded coverage. Analysis of the skills and strategies of each sport by knowledgeable commentators using instant video replay and stop-action techniques makes a game or activity more interesting to the viewer.

The *Allyn and Bacon Sports Education Series* has been created to meet the need for players, coaches, and spectators to be informed about the basic and advanced skills, techniques, tactics, and strategies of sports. Each book in the Series is designed to provide an in-depth treatment of a selected sport or activity. Players find the individual skills and accompanying picture sequences very valuable. Coaches gain basic and advanced knowledge of individual and team play, along with techniques of coaching. Sports fans are provided information about the activities and are thus able to become more knowledgeable about and appreciative of the basic and finer aspects of sports.

The authors of the *Sports Education Series* have been carefully selected. They include experienced teachers, coaches, and managers of college and professional teams. Some books represent the combined effort of two or more authors, each with a different background and each contributing particular strengths to the text. For other books, a single author has been selected, whose background offers a breadth of knowledge and experience in the sport being covered.

Among the authors and titles of some of the team sport books is George Allen, successful coach of the Washington Redskins, who collaborated with Don Weiskopf on *Handbook of Winning Football*. Weiskopf also wrote, with Walter Alston of the Los Angeles Dodgers, *The Complete Baseball Handbook* and *The Baseball Handbook*. *Basketball: Concepts and Techniques*, by Bob Cousy and Frank Power, presents the game for men. *Women's Basketball*, by Mildred J. Barnes of Central Missouri State University, covers the "new" five-player game for girls and women. Dr. Barnes also wrote *Field Hockey: The Coach and the Player*. *The Challenge of Soccer* is by Hubert Vogelsinger, coach of the Boston Minutemen, and *Winning Volleyball* was written by Allen E. Scates of UCLA. A group of authors including general managers Jack Kelley of the New England Whalers and Milt Schmidt of the Washington Capitals collaborated on *Hockey: Bantam to Pro*.

Books covering individual sports in the series are: *Advantage Tennis: Racket Work, Tactics, and Logic* by Jack Barnaby of Harvard University, *Modern Track and Field for Girls and Women* by Donnis H. Thompson of the University of Hawaii, and *Women's Gymnastics* by Kitty Kjeldsen, formerly of the University of Massachusetts.

Thomas Tutko and Jack Richards collaborated on the meaningful book, *Psychology of Coaching*, and Patsy Neal of Brevard College also collaborated with Dr. Tutko on *Coaching Girls and Women: Psychological Perspectives*.

The Sports Series enables readers to experience the thrills of the sport from the point of view of participants and coaches, to learn some of the reasons for success and causes of failure, and to receive basic information about teaching and coaching techniques.

Each volume in the series reflects the philosophy of the authors, but a common theme runs through all: the desire to instill in the reader a knowledge and appreciation of sports and physical activity which will carry over throughout his or her life as a participant or a spectator. Pictures, drawings, and diagrams are used throughout each book to clarify and illustrate the discussion.

The reader, whether a beginner or one experienced in sports, will gain much from each book in the Allyn and Bacon Sports Education Series.

Arthur G. Miller
*Chairman, Department of Human
    Movement and Health Education
Boston University*

Preface

Volleyball is played in 120 countries using standard international rules. The Athletic Institute reports 60 million volleyball participants in the United States alone. Volleyball is a physically demanding game with plays and patterns that rival basketball for intricacy and imagination. Within the last decade, the AIAW, NAIA, NCAA, and NJCAA have all adopted volleyball as a championship event. In 1975, volleyball became the first professional team sport where men and women competed together.

This book is the complete guide for the player, teacher, and coach who want a comprehensive insight into the many changes in fundamentals, tactics, and strategy that have occurred in volleyball during the last few years. It is the most readable, well-illustrated book on American volleyball. Unless specifically noted, this book is designed for both male and female players.

Six of the twelve chapters are devoted to helping the beginner master the latest fundamental techniques used at all levels of competition. A new chapter on volleyball for children has been added for teachers and coaches of this age group. Step-by-step learning sequences and drills are included to improve performance. Hundreds of easy-to-follow sequence and action photographs of All-American and Olympic men and women clearly illustrate techniques. The coverage of the serve, pass, set, spike, block, and individual defensive techniques gives everyone from the prospective player to the established coach insight into the basic principles required for successful play. These fundamental techniques should not be considered too advanced for the average player.

Detailed sections are presented on duration and intensity of practice sessions, selection of offense and defense, and scouting and game plans. All standard offenses and defenses and serve reception patterns are covered. This material is more advanced than any text being offered by American authors. It is a necessity for serious students of the game. After studying this book, the reader should be qualified to become a teacher or coach at any level of play.

ACKNOWLEDGMENTS

I wish to express my thanks to the contributing photographers, Barry Schreiber; Dr. Leonard Stallcup; the Official USVBA Photographer; Stan Troutman of UCLA; Bud Fields; Bob Van Wagner; Gary Adams of the *Beverly Hills Independent*;

Norm Scindler of UCLA; Lurline K. Fujii; Andy Banachowski; Jim Haberlin; Dennis Keller of Excel Sport Products; Richard Mackson; and Stan Abraham.

Special appreciation is also extended to the players on the UCLA Bruins, the men and women of the United States Volleyball Association, and the students of the Beverly Hills School District. My thanks also go to Esther Goldfarb, who typed much of the original manuscript.

This book is dedicated to the memory of Coach Harry E. Wilson.

Allen E. Scates
Los Angeles, California

Introduction

ORIGIN AND DEVELOPMENT

In 1895 William G. Morgan, a YMCA physical director in Holyoke, Massachusetts, devised the game of volleyball (first called mintonette) by stringing a lawn tennis net across a gym at a height of 6 ft 6 in and using the inside of a basketball for a ball.[1] The game was invented to provide an activity for middle-aged businessmen that was competitive, fun, and not too strenuous. In 1896 Morgan put on a demonstration for a conference of YMCA physical directors at Springfield, Massachusetts, and Professor Alfred T. Halstead of Springfield College renamed the game *volleyball*.[2] Mr. Morgan's volleyball rules were published in 1897 in the *Handbook of the Athletic League of YMCAs of North America*.[3] During the next several years, YMCA physical directors introduced the game throughout the United States and in many foreign countries. In 1913, volleyball was included in the Far Eastern Games at Manila by Elwood S. Brown, the International YMCA Secretary. In 1916 the *Spaulding Volleyball Rule Book* was published at the request of the YMCA, and the NCAA was invited to help promote the game. In 1916 it was estimated that 200,000 persons in the United States played volleyball.[4] During World War I, "more than 16,000 volleyballs were distributed in 1919 to the American Expeditionary Forces alone."[5]

The United States Volleyball Association (USVBA) was formed in 1928, and the previously closed National YMCA Championship became open to teams

[1] Harold T. Friermood, "Volleyball Reflections," in the *1970 Official Volleyball Guide* (Berne, Indiana: United States Volleyball Association, 1970), pp. 144–49.
[2] *Ibid.*
[3] *See* Harold T. Friermood (ed.), *When Volleyball Began: An Olympic Sport* (Berne, Indiana: United States Volleyball Association, 1966). A complete reproduction of the *1916 Spaulding Volleyball Guide* and selected highlights of the sport of volleyball.
[4] *See* Friermood, "Volleyball Reflections."
[5] *See* Friermood (ed.), *When Volleyball Began*.

from other organizations. To this day, USVBA Open Championships are held in conjunction with YMCA championships. The first senior championship for men 35 years or older also began in 1928.

Members of the United States Armed Forces often stretched a rope or net between supports and played volleyball during rest periods in World War II. The sight of American soldiers playing volleyball helped the sport's growth and worldwide popularity.

It was estimated that within two years after the close of the war the number of volleyball players doubled and some five to ten million participants were active in the United States alone.[6]

The International Volleyball Federation (FIVB) was formed in 1947 with the USVBA as a charter member. In 1948 the USA volleyball team made a goodwill tour of Europe. The USVBA sponsored separate college and women's divisions in the 1949 championships held in Los Angeles. The University of Southern California won the Collegiate Division and Houston, Texas, won the Women's Division competition.[7] Los Alamitos Naval Air Station won the first Interservice Volleyball Championship held at Columbus, Ohio, in 1952.[8] Volleyball was included in the 1955 Pan American Games in Mexico City. Mexico won and the USA placed second. In 1964 volleyball took a monumental step forward when it was included in the Olympic Games held in Tokyo, Japan.

In 1969 the National Association of Intercollegiate Athletics (NAIA) adopted volleyball as an official NAIA championship event and held its first tournament at George Williams College in Chicago. In 1970 the National Collegiate Athletic Association (NCAA) and Division of Girls and Women's Sports (DGWS) held national championships. The Association for Intercollegiate Athletics for Women (AIAW) was formed in 1971 by the DGWS to provide leadership for women's intercollegiate athletic programs and to conduct all championship events formerly conducted by the DGWS.

The first AIAW Junior College / Community College Championship was held at Miami Dade Community College in 1973. In 1974 the National Junior College Athletic Association (NJCAA) joined the bandwagon and held its first volleyball championship at Schoolcraft College in Livonia, Michigan. All national collegiate sports governing bodies now conduct championship events in volleyball.

THE MODERN GAME

The status of volleyball has increased tremendously since it was adopted as an Olympic sport in 1964. The sensational performance of the 1964 Gold Medalist Japanese Women's team opened the door to mass exposure of the sport via television, film, and tours of foreign teams throughout the world.

Japanese men and women use the greatest individual and team defenses known to the game. Japanese women have perfected the *rolling dig*, which en-

[6] See Carl M. McGowan (ed.), *It's Power Volleyball* (Berne, Indiana: United States Volleyball Association, 1968).
[7] Harold T. Friermood, "Cumulative Record of Volleyball Championship Winners," in the *1969 Official Volleyball Guide* (Berne, Indiana: United States Volleyball Association, 1969), pp. 105–21.
[8] See Friermood, "Volleyball Reflections."

ables them to go to the floor and retrieve a hard-hit spike and then roll to their feet in time for the next play. Japanese men have perfected the spectacular *diving save*, which provides even greater court coverage and makes their defense almost impenetrable.

Volleyball was slow to develop in this country because of its image as a game that was not strenuous in which a ball was lobbed back and forth across a low net. Today the game of "power" volleyball demands a player who can dive or roll to the floor to recover his opponent's attack and jump high above the net to block or spike a moving ball into his opponent's court. Power volleyball requires more organization of team strategy than recreational volleyball. The athlete playing power volleyball must master the individual skills of the game in order to perform with quickness, alertness, coordination, and stamina in complex playing situations.

During the past few years, new standards of volleyball training and performance have emerged to test the speed, strength, endurance, and coordination of the best athletes. The sport has begun to assume a position of importance in the eyes of students and athletic departments throughout the country.

A majority of the better teams are using a three-hitter offense, which features a variety of sets and spikes designed around fast patterns of attack. There is increased emphasis on the defensive techniques of diving and rolling to the floor to dig or retrieve balls; these tactics, in turn, have led to longer rallies. Recent rule changes and interpretations have allowed officials to silence their whistles and let the players determine the outcome of the game.

Volleyball is a universal game easily adapted to the needs and abilities of all participants. For younger players, the net can be lowered, and for recreational and coeducational play, rules can be modified. Volleyball appeals to people of all ages at different levels of skill.

Volleyball is played in 120 countries and about 30 countries recognize the game as a major sport. In the United States, volleyball is the most popular participant sport and is fast becoming a popular spectator sport as well. The game is very popular in East Europe and the Far East. In the last decade, the USSR and Japan dominated men's and women's international competition. Young players from these countries participate in 100 to 150 international matches before they become a starter on the national team. Japan and the USSR host 60 to 70 international matches a year.

I

Fundamentals

1

Serving

A well-developed serving technique puts the opposing team on the defensive. Accurate placement, unpredictable movement, and high velocity of the ball—or a combination of these factors—are crucial elements for an effective serve. Varsity players should be able to deliver their strongest serves to their opponents' court in at least nine out of ten attempts. In strong competition, there is less than a 5 percent chance of scoring an ace on the serve. There is a much greater chance of scoring when the opponent passes the serve inaccurately.

SERVING TACTICS

Players should serve to score a point, not only to put the ball into play. The serve should be directed to a player who: 1) is a weak receiver; 2) has just made an error; 3) is a substitute; 4) is upset over the last play; or 5) is tense. The server should aim for a spot that is: 1) in the seam of receiving responsibility between two players; 2) open; 3) requires a back set to a strong attacker; 4) requires the best attacker to receive the ball or alter the approach; or 5) in the setter's path. Another tactic is to pick a key player and to constantly serve to that player in an attempt to wear him out.

The serve should be extra strong when the server's team is far ahead or behind in scoring; in the beginning or near the end of a game; and when the server's team has not scored for a long period of time. The serve following a time out, a substitution, or a serving error by a teammate should be served easy to ensure that there will be no serving error. The serve following should be strong.

SERVING RULES

The service area is located in the right third of the court behind the end line. The server cannot touch the lines bounding this area or the floor outside the service area until the ball is contacted. However, the server's arm or body may be extended in the air over or beyond these lines. If the playing area does not extend to a minimum depth of 6 ft beyond the end line, the server is allowed to step into the court to whatever distance is necessary to provide the minimum service area.

With the hand, fist, or arm, the server hits the ball over the net into the opponents' area of the court. The right back player on the serving team is the first server of the game. This player continues to serve until his team committs a foul or the game is completed. If a member of the serving team commits a foul, a side out is called by the referee, and the ball is awarded to the opposing team, whose members rotate clockwise one position to the position of server. The player rotating from the right front position is always the next server.

UNDERHAND SERVE

The underhand serve is the easiest to learn and to control. It requires very little

a   b

Figure 1–1 *The Serve.* Servers sometimes stand 20–30 ft behind the end line in order to hit the ball with great force and still keep the serve in their opponents' court. Here, both women toss the ball above and in front of their serving shoulder and transfer their weight from their back to front leg before contacting the ball. (Dr. Leonard Stallcup)

a   b

Figure 1–2   *The Underhand Serve.*   Striking the ball on its right side will cause it to travel to the server's left or cross court (*a*). Notice that the player's serving arm follows-through at a slight angle (*b*). When the ability to strike the ball on its right or left side has been mastered, the position of the player's body can remain the same, regardless of where he intends to direct the ball. This principle also applies to serves. (Los Angeles City Unified School District)

strength in comparison to the other serves and can be mastered by most elementary school children. The exceptionally weak or uncoordinated child should be allowed to serve in front of the serving line during games and gradually move back to the regulation 30-ft serving line as his skill and confidence improve.

Unlike the overhand serve, the underhand serve is not a strong weapon. When accurately placed and carrying a "floating" motion, however, it can threaten the opposition.

The server places her left foot forward and bends both knees slightly. She takes a long backswing with her striking arm and contacts the ball below its midline with the heel of her hand (if the hand is open) or with the heel and knuckles (if the hand is closed). If the server prematurely takes her eyes off the ball, she may contact the ball above its midline and serve into the net. The server's weight shifts from the back leg to the forward one at the moment of contact. Follow-through occurs in the direction of flight.

When follow-through does not occur in a straight line, i.e., when the armswing is across the body or away from the body, the ball travels past the side lines and out of bounds. Flexing the ball-holding arm just prior to contact causes the ball to be contacted too far below its midline. Beginners, especially, tend to raise their ball-holding arm when extending their knees before hitting the ball.

OVERHAND SERVE

Overhand Floater Serve

The overhand floater serve, which has no spin, moves in an erratic path as it approaches the receiver, making it difficult for the opponent to pass. To achieve the desired floating action, the ball is hit with only a momentary point of contact and very little follow-through. This quick contact just below the center of the ball causes it to travel with a "wiggle" type of motion—rising, dropping, or moving from side to side—similar to a knuckleball in baseball. At recent USVBA, NCAA, NAIA, and AIAW championships, about 95 percent of the serves were overhand floater serves.

a

b

Figure 1–3 *Floater Contact.*   The ball should be contacted with the heel of the hand below the midline of the ball, with the wrist held firm. There is little follow-through. (Dr. Leonard Stallcup)

a

b

c

d

e

Figure 1–4   *Overhand Floater Serve.*   Olympian Patti Bright demonstrates the overhand floater serve. (Los Angeles City Unified School District)

If the floater serve does not have any "action," or wiggle-type movement of the ball, the server has usually contacted the ball with too large an area of the hand, snapped the wrist, or used too much follow-through. The majority of servers hit the ball with the heel of the hand. Some, however, strike the ball with the heel of the hand and closed fingers or a closed fist (*see* Figure 1–3). Players generally prefer to bend their arm slightly on contact. For additional power, many servers take a short step forward with their front foot just prior to contact.

In Figure 1–4, Olympian Patti Bright holds the ball about shoulder height, directly in line with her back foot. Her feet are in a stride position and her weight is evenly distributed. She tosses the ball about 3 ft in the air, above and in front of her right shoulder. Her right arm extends from a cocked position to contact the ball a few inches below its midline with the heel of her hand. Patti is short; therefore, she fully extends her right arm upon contact with the ball so that it will travel in a low trajectory and still clear the net. Notice that her wrist is stiff and that there is little follow-through.

The area of the ball housing the valve stem is heavier than the rest of the ball, which causes an uneven distribution of weight. Since the official volleyball only weighs about 9 ounces, the valve stem usually causes the ball to change its direction during the floater serve. Many coaches believe that the air hits the valve as the ball travels along its flight, causing the ball to wobble and move about.

Regardless of which theory or combination of factors are at work, the placement of the valve upon contact does have an effect on the flight of the ball. Ex-perience has shown that if the valve is pointed toward the center of the serving target, the ball will break from side to side. When the valve is pointed down, the ball will drop; when the valve is pointed up, the ball will travel a greater distance.

When using the common serving strategy of serving the "seams" of two receivers' area of responsibility, many servers place the valve on the weaker receiver's side so that the serve will break in that direction. Of course, the toss must be perfected to place the valve stem in the proper position.

Figure 1–5 *Valve Placement.* Aiming the valve of the ball toward the opponents' court will help the floater serve to move from side to side with a dropping motion. (The Ealing Corp.)

Many players disregard the location of the valve stem and consequently lose some accuracy during the serve. Players should experiment with valve placement during practice sessions to make their serves harder to receive.

Overhand Spin Serve

The overhand spin serve results in a fast dropping action, which gives the opposition less time to react. Although quite effective when used against inexperienced competition, better players find the flight of the ball very predictable (due to its spinning action) and usually have little trouble in passing the serve. It is difficult for most servers to control the spin serve, and it is not popular because of the increased chance of a serving error.

During the past decade, Gene Selznick, Mary Jo Peppler, and Larry Rundle were the only outstanding players in this country to develop the accuracy and speed needed to score frequently with this serve in important competition.

To serve an overhand spin, the right-handed player places his left foot in front and stands in a stride position. He tosses the ball about 4 ft in the air (one foot higher than the toss for the floater). The server's left arm should be fully extended as his right arm, hand held open, cocks behind his head. Shoulders rotate so that the left shoulder faces the net and weight is on the back foot. As the ball starts to descend, the shoulders twist forward, and the elbow leads the way as the arm begins to straighten. The ball is contacted in the center of the lower midsection, the heel of the server's hand first contacts the ball, and then the wrist snap rolls his hand over the ball, imparting a topspin as weight shifts to the forward foot.

Figure 1–6 *Overhand Spin Serve.* This serve results in a fast dropping motion that gives the passer less time to react. All-World Gene Selznick prepares to contact the ball slightly on its right side to impart a curving motion. (Dr. Leonard Stallcup)

The server may contact the ball on the left or right side, causing the ball to curve. Since the server must stand behind the right third of the court, right-handed players usually strike the ball on the right side so the ball will not fly beyond the near side line.

ROUND HOUSE SERVE

In 1960 the Japanese Women's team introduced the round house floater serve in international competition at the World Volleyball Championships in Brazil. Because their opponents did not have an opportunity to practice receiving the hard, fast-floating action of this serve, it was an instant success. After the Japanese Women's team won the Gold Medal in the 1964 Olympic Games in Tokyo, they made numerous tours in the United States to compete against our top women players. After attempting to field the superior serves of the Japanese for six years, the United States National Women's Team began a serious attempt to copy their serving technique during practice for the 1970 World Volleyball Championships in Bulgaria.

In 1969 a Japanese student, Toshi Toyoda, arrived in the United States to study and to play volleyball at UCLA. He came with a mastery of the round house floater serve and was the most effective server in the 1969 and 1970 USVBA National Championships. In 1969 he was one of the few men at the USVBA Championships to use the round house floater; in 1970 a few more players began to use the round house floater but had not yet perfected it.

a   b

Figure 1–7 *Toss for Round House Serve.* As the player tosses the ball, he leans over his back leg, extending his serving arm downward. His arm moves in a windmill motion, contacting the ball directly over the hitting shoulder. (The Ealing Corp.)

Round House Floater Serve

The round house floater serve is currently the most effective serve for local, regional, and national competition because of its unique dropping and side-to-side movement. Few players in the United States have mastered this serve, so there has been little opportunity to practice receiving it.

Better players are reluctant to try a new serving style because they are forced to endure a temporary loss of serving effectiveness while they are struggling to learn the new technique. Until the round house floater serve becomes common in this country, it will remain the most effective serve in local, regional, and national competition. Because it can be delivered with great force and with a dropping side-to-side movement that has proven unpredictable to receivers, more players should try this technique.

To accomplish the round house floater serve, the player stands with his body perpendicular to the net, feet shoulder-width apart, and knees slightly flexed. He tosses the ball about 3 ft in the air, slightly in front of and above his forward shoulder. During the toss, his body leans backward as both legs bend. His hitting arm swings upward from the area of his right knee in a fully extended windmill motion. As the ball starts to descend, he shifts his weight forward and extends his legs. He contacts the ball with the *heel* of his hand, directly above the right shoulder. (If the ball is contacted *behind* the shoulder, it usually has a high trajectory and travels out of the opponents' court. If the ball is contacted *in front of* the shoulder, it usually travels in a very low trajectory and hits the net.)

The weight of the player's body should be supported by his front leg when the ball is hit. After contact, the server pivots on his front foot and faces the net, ready to move to his defensive assignment.

Round House Spin Serve

The round house spin serve, used by several male members of Asian and European teams, is a very fast serve that drops rapidly but cannot be directed with the same accuracy as the overhand floater serve. Once the ball leaves the server's hands, the receivers can predict its flight; thus, members of our national men's teams have passed this serve well and have not attempted to copy the round house spin serve.

The outstanding difference between the round house spin serve and the round house floater lies in the technical execution of contacting the ball with the striking hand. For the spin serve, the ball is struck with the entire cupped hand in the same manner as the overhand spin serve.

TYPES OF SERVES USED IN COMPETITION

The underhand serve is still used by the majority of players participating in recreational volleyball in this country. Athletes participating in "power" volleyball, where a refined application of team strategy and individual skills are required, overwhelmingly prefer the overhand floater serve. Europeans participating in power volleyball generally use the round house and overhand spin and only recently have the majority switched to the overhand floater serve.

Figure 1–8 *Round House Floater Serve.* All-American Toshi Toyoda prefers to move far behind the endline so that he can contact the ball with great force and still direct it into the opponents' court. (The Ealing Corp.)

Figure 1–9 *Round House Spin Serve.* Contact is first made below the midline of the ball with the heel of the hand. As the wrist snaps forward, the palm and fingers impart a topspin to the ball, making it drop. The arm follows through in the direction of the flight. (Andy Banachowski)

Until a few years ago the serve was the only fundamental part of the game in which American teams consistently outperformed European teams in international competition. Recently, the improved technique of the forearm pass used by Europeans has negated the slight serving advantage that the Americans once enjoyed. United States national teams have not experienced any great difficulty receiving the fast and predictable round house and overhand spin serves of the Europeans. Consequently, our players have not used these serves.

SERVING DRILLS

In serving drills and in competition, players should be able to serve to a specific spot on the court nine times out of ten. The top international teams only make serving errors 5 percent of the time, while the majority of international teams have a 10 percent serving error.

Serving practice should be held at the beginning, middle, and end of practice sessions to simulate game conditions when players are fresh, tired, or exhausted. When serving to targets on the floor, the court should be cleared of receivers and the players divided along the end lines of the available courts so they can serve back and forth across the net. When the ball lands out of bounds, the player recovering the serve should signal how far the ball landed out of bounds so the server can adjust the force or direction of the serve. The server should always serve from the serving area behind the right third of the court, unless practicing a straight-ahead, or line, serve. When practicing line serves, each player might have a partner who stands on the opposite side of the net serving the ball back and forth from any position behind the end line. The best position to serve crosscourt is near the sideline. When serving down the line, the best position is 9 ft from the sideline.

Since serving is probably the dullest fundamental to practice, it is best to make the drills competitive by placing towels, chairs, or other markers on the floor for players to hit. The coach can keep a practice serving chart to record the players' scores. Players should not ease up when using targets but deliver their toughest serves during all drills.

It is often beneficial to combine serving and receiving drills. Each player should receive from 50 to 100 serves during every practice session. If the drill is server-oriented, the receiver can be placed in position at the discretion of the server. For example, if the server wishes to serve cross court, the receiver takes the right-front or right-back position.

A simple game can provide competition between two players by allowing the receiver to score one point each time the ball is passed to a designated target area and by giving a point to the server each time the receiver fails to pass the ball accurately. Balls that are served out—into the net or away from the receiver's area—are scored for the receiver.

Another server–receiver game incorporates some of the pressure that occurs during actual competition. To win this game, either the server or the receiver must score 3 straight points. For example, if the server has 2 points and the receiver has passed the ball perfectly, the receiver takes the lead, 1 to 0. As soon as the opponent scores, the other player's score automatically returns to 0.

A third player can be added to act as the passing target for the receiver. When one of the players wins, the third player exchanges positions with the winner and the loser remains in the same position. In this manner, the weakest player gets the added work that is needed to improve performance. It is surprising how readily a coach can detect from such a simple game which performers will do well in pressure situations.

The most time-consuming, although effective, way for the server to practice is to direct serves against the type of actual team-receiving formation that will be faced in competition. Weaknesses inherent in the formation can be pointed out to the server and attacked.

2

Passing

Passing simply refers to the act of hitting the ball to another teammate. Typically, a player passes the ball to another teammate who hits the passed ball into the air. Or, a player sets the passed ball into position for another teammate to attack it above level of the net and spike or dink it into the opponents' court. Occasionally, the pass is spiked or dinked to confuse the opponents' block. A passer in highly competitive or power volleyball should attempt to receive the serve or the spike in an underhand manner in order to strike the ball with both forearms simultaneously.

FOOTWORK AND BODY POSITION

Every coach looks for size when selecting squad members, but size without quickness will be neutralized by a well-trained, fast-moving, opposition. Quickness and coordination are the most important physical assets in receiving the serve, in digging, and in setting. In order to pass the ball accurately, players must take small, quick steps while maintaining a low center of gravity. For all passing techniques, the player's weight should be evenly distributed on the inside balls of the feet and the heels should be off or barely touching the floor. The feet should be placed wider apart than the shoulder width, with one foot set slightly ahead of the other. Knees should be bent at a 90° angle for smaller players and at a smaller angle for taller players. Hips are bent at approximately 90° and the back is straight. The elbows are held in front of the knees and the knees are bent forward in front of the toes. The hands are held in front and apart about waist high, and the weight is forward. The head should be held upright.

Most of the footwork in serve reception and digging is to the side. The two patterns of movement are the side step and the crossover and run step.

Side Step

The side step is performed by sliding the lead foot laterally and following it with the trailing foot. The steps are small and quick, with the trailing foot moving to within 6 in. of the forward foot. When the player arrives at the desired area, the front foot hits the floor first and points in the direction of the intended pass. It is very important to maintain a low body position in order to stop with good balance. The stop is made with the lead foot slightly forward and the trailing foot closing the gap between the feet to approximately shoulder-width.

After this movement is perfected without the ball, the coach should lob the ball to the left and right of the player and receive a return pass from him. When moving to the left or right, the passer's lead foot should face the coach before the ball is contacted. The coach or partner should feint in several directions before releasing the ball to enable the passer to make slide steps in different directions before receiving the ball.

Crossover and Run Step

The crossover and run step is used to cover greater distances when moving laterally. The crossover and run is accomplished with the inside foot as the passer takes as many successive running steps as necessary to approach the desired area. When the player has time to stop and pass, the front foot should hit the floor first and point in the general direction of the target area. The trailing or outside foot completes the movement as it swings in front of the planted foot and points directly at the target area. The

feet are approximately shoulder-width apart, in a stride position.

OVERHAND PASS

The overhand pass is not recommended for receiving serves or spikes because players who use this method are frequently called for illegal hits. A total of 1,500 serve receptions charted at the USVBA National Championships in Grand Rapids, Michigan, showed that 96 percent of the serves were played with the forearm pass and 4 percent with the overhand pass. The referees called 30 percent of the overhand receptions illegal

Figure 2–1 *Overhand Pass.* The player faces in the direction of the intended target area and cups her fingers to contact the ball directly in front of her face. She follows-through with a synchronized movement of legs, body, and arms. (Dr. Leonard Stallcup)

hits.[1] Since 1966, an even greater percentage of serve receptions in USVBA competition have been played with the forearm pass.

Players in the front line stand 15 ft or more from the net to receive the serve. If the ball is above their waist, they usually let the ball travel to a backcourt player. The backcourt players stand deep in their court so that any ball above their waist will travel past the back line and out of bounds.

FOREARM PASS

At one time, the forearm pass was only used to receive serves by players who had "bad hands" and did not want to risk a rule infraction, or by players who were not in position to use the overhand pass. The restrictions placed on the serving area, removal of the serving screen (created by the server's teammates who stood in front of him to block the view of the receiver), and new techniques for the forearm pass have enabled players to use the forearm pass with better accuracy than with the overhand pass. In fact, directives from the International Volleyball Federation and United States Volleyball Association encouraging the return of the overhand pass are not heeded by players and coaches.

The forearm pass is also used to handle low balls and spikes. When used to recover the opponents' attack, it is called a *dig*. Up to 70 percent of a team's practice can be devoted to this fundamental technique. (The defensive technique of

digging will be covered in chapter 6 along with the *dive* and *roll*.)

HAND POSITIONS

The ball *must not* be played with the open palms in the underhand position because the referee will call a foul. There is no written rule prohibiting the use of the open hand in underhand play, but the universal interpretation of officials is that the ball cannot be clearly hit using this technique.

The hands should be clasped in a manner that is comfortable and effective for the individual player. Beginning players readily learn the popular *clenched-fist* position. This hand position presents a good rebounding service for balls that

Figure 2–2 *Forearm Bump Pass.* The forearm pass is the most common way to pass a serve to the setter. The ball is hit off the forearms. (Bob Van Wagner)

[1] Janis Robins, "A Statistical Comparison, Duluth '61—Grand Rapids '66," in *International Volleyball Review* (April–May 1967): 46.

cannot be reached with the forearms and must be struck with the hands.

The *curled-finger* position allows for more of an outward rotation of the fore-arms. The *thumb-over-palm* position enables the player to achieve a maximum outward rotation of his forearms, which creates a very favorable flat rebounding

Figure 2–3 *Waiting for the Serve.* While anticipating the serve, the player's body should be in a low position, her feet placed more than shoulder-width apart, and her arms relaxed. The player should closely study the server in order to anticipate her actions. When the passer receives the ball, she faces the setter and points her outside foot directly at the setter. When receiving the serve from the left side of the court, the left foot should be pointed ahead. When receiving from the right side of the court, the right foot should be ahead. (Barry Schreiber)

The newer forearm passing technique is called the *elbow snap*. Before contact with the ball, the arms are held in a relaxed manner with the elbows bent. Immediately before contact, elbows are extended and wrists and forearms are brought close together. On a fast serve, the elbow snap requires considerably less leg action because the arms snap forward to contact the ball.

Both the elbow lock and elbow snap require the hands to be clasped together with the thumbs parallel. Prior to contact, elbows should be completely extended and rotated outward, exposing the flat inner surface of the forearms. Thumbs and wrists should be pointed toward the floor, and the ball should contact the internal part of the forearms *above* the wrist. The speed and movement of the arms depend on the speed of the approaching ball and the distance the pass must travel.

PASSING TECHNIQUES

Players who are successful serve receivers anticipate the flight of the ball and quickly position their body in its path

a

b

Figure 2–7 *Forearm Pass.* Reception of an overhand serve forces almost total reliance on the forearm pass because of strict interpretation of thrown balls. The greater area of the forearms allows the receiver to misjudge the flight of the ball by 3 or 4 in. but still make an accurate pass. (Barry Schreiber)

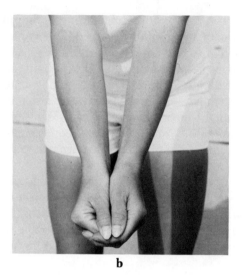

a

b

Figure 2–8 *Contact Area.* Some players are flexible enough to create an ideal rebounding surface in the area from their wrists to elbows (*a*). Others must be satisfied to extend their arms and hold them close together and to contact the ball on the lower forearm or wrist (*b*). (Los Angeles City Unified School District)

a

b

Figure 2–9 *Elbow Lock.* Upward coordinated movement of legs and arms is important when the ball is moving slowly. There should be no upward arm movement when receiving fast serves; if there is, the pass will travel too far. The ball should contact both forearms simultaneously. (The Ealing Corp.)

before contact. The body is lowered or raised so that the ball can be contacted between the legs. The receiver leans slightly forward, with the back straight, arms fully extended, and elbows rotated outward to form a flat rebound surface with the forearms. The player watches the ball before, during, and after contact.

Poor serve receivers splay their elbows instead of locking them at the time of contact. They twist their waist instead of moving their feet to receive the ball between the legs and are forced to bat at the ball with their arms. Probably the most common error is standing up to pass the ball, rather than passing it from a low position.

Follow-through of the arms and knees depends on the speed of the approaching serve and the intended placement of the ball. If the ball moves over the net slowly or must be passed a long distance, the player's arms and legs should move upward as contact is made, which gives greater impetus to the flight of the ball.

Generally, hard overhand floater serves require little follow-through. A hard overhand or round house spin serve requires no follow-through at all. In fact, front row receivers often "cushion" a hard spin serve by leaning back when the ball is contacted, thus preventing the pass from rebounding over the net.

Squatting should be practiced. American players naturally react to low balls by lowering themselves from the waist instead of lowering their bodies with their legs, as is the custom of the Asians and Europeans.

The Japanese teams use the fastest pass in volleyball to build their offense. They have developed a quick, low pass

a   b

Figure 2–10 *Elbow Snap.* When low, fast passes are desired, the elbow snap is recommended. The coordinated leg-and-arm action shown here is used to pass slow-moving balls. (Los Angeles City Unified School District)

Figure 2–11 *Passing the Serve.* Feet are placed shoulder-width apart; their placement can vary from a perpendicular to a stride position. Knees are bent and the trunk is inclined forward. The passer moves directly in front of the ball and makes contact with the ball between the knees. (Bud Fields)

Figure 2–12 *Passing the Low Serve.* The technique for passing a low serve is mastered by players who can maintain control of their body in a low position. (Barry Schreiber)

Figure 2–13 *Japanese Low Pass Technique.* The pass travels in a fast, low arc. To achieve a low trajectory, the ball is contacted with the arms pointing toward the floor and the back held straight. Notice that all players are watching the serve receiver in case they may have to help out with a bad pass. (Dr. Leonard Stallcup)

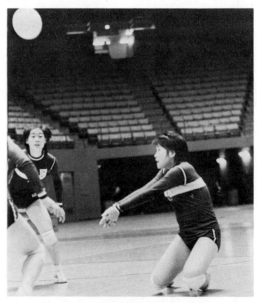

Figure 2–14 *Lining Up the Ball.* The player moves the upper part of his body behind the ball by taking a long slide step and squatting to the height of the ball while extending one leg. (Andy Banachowski)

Figure 2–15 *Screw-Under Step.* The ▶ passer executes a screw-under step to position the upper part of his body behind the ball just prior to contact. Beginners rarely are capable of making this split-second adjustment and usually rely on a lateral arm movement to compensate for poor body position. (Barry Schreiber)

a

b

Figure 2–16 *Jump Chest Pass.* This passing technique is used to pass balls that travel in a high trajectory. Notice that the players keep their eyes on the ball. (Barry Schreiber)

a   b   c

Figure 2–17 *Changing Direction.* Changing direction with the elbow-lock technique is recommended to provide greater control over the ball and to enable the forearms to remain in contact with the ball for a longer period of time. Prolonged contact with the ball is maintained by lateral rotation of the body and arms. Lateral rotation of the body should only be used to pass a slow-moving ball. (The Ealing Corp.)

that gets to the setter before the opposing blockers have a chance to observe the attack patterns of the spikers. The Japanese consider the pass to be the most important part of the offense and spend over 50 percent of their practice time passing serves and spikes. Instead of passing the ball above the net, they concentrate on passing in a low trajectory into the path of the oncoming setter. This pass is particularly advantageous in a fast three-hitter attack.

MOVING TO THE BALL

Good footwork greatly enhances the likelihood of an accurate pass. Players must

◄ **Figure 2–18** *Low Lateral Pass.* The inside shoulder dips forward to turn the interior part of the forearms toward the ball. The player leans toward the ball with a lateral tilt, and with his weight over his front leg. (Stan Troutman)

move quickly toward the flight of the ball. Backcourt receivers should stand close to the backline so they will not have to move backward to receive the ball. When players reach the receiving area, they should plant their feet and pivot toward the target with their outside foot ahead and pointed toward the setter.

If the ball suddenly breaks to one side, the receiver may position his body behind the ball by taking a long slide step and squatting on the sliding leg while extending the other leg. This maneuver has become commonly known as the *screw under step,* for lack of a more descriptive term.

Changing Direction

When passing a slow-moving ball from a lateral position, prolonged contact and

a

b

Figure 2–19 *High Lateral Pass.* Often players must extend their legs completely or jump to orient the interior part of their forearms toward the ball to pass at shoulder height. (Dr. Leonard Stallcup, *a*; Barry Schreiber, *b*)

better control of the ball can be maintained by rotating the upper body toward the target area while the ball is being passed (*see* Figure 2–17). Players should not twist their waists when receiving a serve or hard-driven spike.

LATERAL PASS

The passer must reach laterally to contact the ball when there is not enough time to position his body for the regular forearm pass. When both arms are used, this technique is called a *lateral pass.*

Figure 2–20 *Lateral Pass.* This player is making the common error of not dipping his shoulder far enough inside; consequently, the ball skids off his arms and rebounds backward. (Dr. Leonard Stallcup) *Above*

Figure 2–21 *One-Arm Pass.* The one-arm pass is frequently used in competition, but often neglected in practice sessions. With this technique, contact with the ball can be made with the forearm, the wrist, or the fist. (Bud Fields) *Below*

Figure 2–22 *Backward Pass.* Immediately before contact is made with the ball, the shoulders shrug upward and the player leans backward. (Dr. Leonard Stallcup)

Figure 2–23 *Passing a Dink Shot.* The player drops behind a full squatting position to field a dink shot looped behind the blockers. (Bud Fields)

ONE-ARM PASS

When the ball is too far away to contact with the lateral pass, a one-arm pass, or dig, is used. The dig is an attempt to recover a spiked ball with a one- or two-armed pass. Volleyball lore tells us that the term *dig* originated from beach play: Players would scoop low balls inches from the sand, using their fists and a bent elbow. Today, most players use the forearm to contact the ball whenever possible. The fist is used on balls that are harder to reach.

BACKWARD PASS

The backward pass is often used by a backcourt player to recover balls hit off the top of the blocker's hands. Occasionally, players amaze their teammates by making perfect sets from the back line area or farther with this technique.

The elbow lock technique used in Figure 2–22 is recommended because it gives the ball enough power to reach the net at distances of 30 ft or more. On closer plays, the player rarely must turn his back and run the ball down.

PASSING FROM UNUSUAL POSITIONS

During a game the player will often be called on to pass the ball from unusual positions. Players who have been thoroughly drilled to react to the ball do not hesitate to place themselves in whatever position necessary to pass the ball. To prevent injury, the player must maintain proper flexibility by performing stretching exercises to meet the strenuous demands of competition.

3

Setting

The *set* is an overhand or forearm pass that places the ball in position for a spiker to attack it. The set is usually performed by a specialist called the *setter* who uses the overhand pass whenever possible. The *overhand pass* is a more precise method of delivering the set, and it gives the spiker a better opportunity to analyze the flight of the approaching ball. The fingertips of both hands are used to contact the ball with the overhand pass. If the ball has not been clearly hit or has visibly come to rest, the setter has committed an error.

Setting specialists should stand with their inside foot forward with a slight backward lean of the hips when setting close to the net. This posture does not allow the middle blocker to determine whether the setter intends to deliver the ball forward or backward.

The basic offense employs two setters and four spikers. Beginning setters need superior speed, mobility, and anticipation to move quickly after the pass and deliver a *normal set* in a high arc that

Figure 3–1 *Setting Close to the Net.* The setter should position her inside foot forward and lean her body backward slightly at the waist. (San Diego State University News Bureau)

37

drops about 2 ft from the net at either corner of the net.

Good setters require superior reactions and ball-handling skills to place the ball at any spot along the net at any height. Better setters possess the mental alertness and control to take advantage of the blocker's weaknesses and their spikers' strengths. They know the individual preferences of their spikers and are capable of watching the spiker's approach, the ball, and opposing blockers when moving into position to receive a good pass. They have the competitive spirit to bolster their teammates' play and to perform well in tense situations.

FRONT SET

When the ball is passed, the setter must anticipate its flight and move quickly under it. He must be in a stationary, relaxed position when the ball arrives, with his feet in a stride position, shoulder-width apart. The foot closest to the net should

a   b

Figure 3–2 *Basic Position for Setting.* The setter positions herself directly in front of the ball and holds her hands about 6 in. in front of her face (*a*). The ball must be contacted simultaneously with the fingers and thumbs of both hands, or it will be called a foul. (Barry Schreiber, *a*; Los Angeles City Unified School District, *b*)

Figure 3–3 *The Set.* No. 54 delivers a back set to an approaching spiker. (Stan Troutman)

remain flat on the floor until contact. The forward foot should be pointed in the direction of the set. The setter's nose should be in line with the descending ball, and his hands should be cupped about 6 in. in front of his face prior to contact.

Beginners should be coached to "form a window" in front of the face. When the ball is about to be contacted, weight shifts over the front foot and the back foot rests on its toes. The setter should be directly behind the ball, his elbows close to the sides of his body, and his upper arms horizontal to the floor. His hands should be held approximately 6 in. in front of his head, wrists cocked and fingers spread. He contacts the ball with his fingertips and second joint of the thumb, index and middle fingers, and extends his entire body in a synchronized movement.

BACK SET

The back set is used to confuse the block. For this reason, the setter must be careful not to arch his back too soon because experienced middle blockers will "read" the play and get an early jump on the ball. The back set uses the same initial body position as the front set. The hands contact the ball above the forehead and extend up as the back arches. The head should be raised as the arms follow-through.

a   b   c

Figure 3–4 *Front Set.* The ball's force causes the player's fingers to bend back-ward and come within 3 or 4 in. of his face (*a*). Index and forefingers supply most of the force as the fingers and wrist spring forward (*b*). Smooth follow-through helps to ensure a well-directed pass (*c*). (The Ealing Corp.)

LATERAL SET

The lateral set should be attempted in game conditions by superior ball handlers only. Average setters should employ the safe strategy of facing the direction to which they intend to set and using an occasional back set to confuse the blocker. Generally, referees on the local level carefully scrutinize the lateral set, which is a relatively new technique developed to complement three-hitter offenses.

Some outstanding Japanese and East European setters prefer to receive passes with their backs to the net and to deliver their sets laterally for greater deception. This technique allows the setter to keep his fingers on the ball for a greater period of time; consequently, the ball is placed with greater accuracy.

At this time, referees from other countries in the FIVB, unlike United States National Referees, are more liberal in their interpretations of what constitutes a legal set. At the USVBA Championships, there are still some referees who insist that the setter release the ball with a flick of his wrist and fingers, directly forward of or opposite to the direction in which he is facing. Successful setters are flexible enough to adapt their style to the philosophy of the referee on the stand. Generally, referees of regional and national status on the West Coast allow setters to use the lateral set, which makes the three-hitter attack function so effectively. Some referees in the rest of the

a   b   c

d   e

Figure 3–5. *Setting a Low Pass.* The player's buttocks are close to the floor and his hands are held in front of his face. His back is straight and his weight is centered behind his back foot when the ball is contacted. He follows-through with his arms as he drops to the floor. (The Ealing Corp.)

a.   b.   c.

Figure 3–6. *Back Set.* Contact is made above the forehead; the palms are held up and back throughout the release and follow-through. Olympian Patti Bright delivers the back set here. (Los Angeles City Unified School District)

country, however, prefer the traditional front-and-back setting style, which favors relatively limited contact of the fingers on the ball.

Traditionalists argue that we in the United States, who invented the game, do not have to change our interpretations merely to conform to the newer throwing style of setting used by the most successful teams in world competition. Players on national USA teams and American referees of international stature point to

◀ **Figure 3–7** *Lateral Set.* Movement of the arms is to the side, rather than forward or backward. (Dr. Leonard Stallcup)

the handicaps that American teams face in international competition when opposing setters who have mastered the lateral set.

In Figure 3–8, Larry Rundle takes a long squatting step to the side with his right leg while extending his left leg. He lowers his body until his face is even with the ball's height (*a*). He then quickly pivots on his right foot as he releases the ball to the left so that his body, head, and arms are turned in the direction of the ball's flight (*b*). He extends his arms, wrists, and fingers as he falls toward the floor. After the set, his squatting leg remains flexed and his buttocks and lower and upper back touch the floor. When his shoulder blades touch the floor, the player rocks forward and regains a standing position.

TRADITIONAL SETTING POSITION

The pass is directed to a designated target area about 2 to 4 ft from the net. This area is usually the middle of the court in the two-hitter attack; it is 10 ft from the passers' right side line in the three-hitter attack. The instant the server contacts the ball, the setter should move toward the designated target area, at the same time watching the serve receiver to anticipate the flight of the pass.

If the pass is good, the traditional strategy is for the setter to position his body sidewise toward the net with his knees bent and hands up—thus forming a window in front of his face. As the ball travels across the center of his body, contact occurs about 6 in. in front of his eyes. The setter moves in the direction of

a

b

Figure 3–8 *Low Lateral Set.* The low lateral set is difficult to execute because the player must pivot quickly on his squatting leg until his body faces the direction of the set. (The Ealing Corp.)

Figure 3–9 *Good Tactical Setting Position.* When the setter positions her body, face, and arms in a direct line with the approaching ball, the opposing blockers have no clue as to the intended direction of the set ball. (Los Angeles City Unified School District)

Figure 3–10 *Long Set.* The setter must move quickly to contact the ball by planting and pivoting her inside foot toward the target. (Los Angeles City Unified School District)

the set to "back up" the spiker in the event the spike is blocked.

When the pass is short of the target area, the setter must hurry to get behind the ball so the set will not have to be made on the run. Traditional strategy calls for the setter to face the corner of the net where the set will be delivered. Of course, two blockers will probably be waiting at that point before the setter touches the ball. Better setters learn to set the ball laterally to the other side of the net if the middle blocker leaves early in anticipation of a normal set.

Most beginners make a mistake when setting the type of pass shown in Figure 3–10. They try to set this kind of pass on

Figure 3–11 *Saving a Long Pass.* All-American Dane Holtzman leaps into the air to prevent a high pass from traveling into the net with a back set. He makes contact with the ball above his forehead. (Stan Troutman)

the run instead of actually stopping slightly beyond the ball, thereby allowing contact to be made in a direct line between setter and target area. Notice how Patti Bright in Figure 3–10 has followed through and extended her arms and legs to ensure the proper height and distance of the set.

For greater power and distance, long passes or sets should be executed with the body in a forward leaning position. When setting at the net, the body should have a slight backward tilt.

The *jump set* is used to place the setter in position to save a long pass that will drop over or hit the net. It is also a means of confusing the block. Better front-court setters in the two-hitter attack may jump in the air and decide to spike or set the ball according to the reaction of the opposing block. If the blockers remain on the ground, the setter gets a free spike; if the blocker or blockers jump with the setter, they cannot react fast enough to chase the set to another attacker. Back-row setters in the three-hitter attack use the jump set to confuse inexperienced blockers, although they cannot spike unless they take off from behind the 10-ft line.

Figure 3–12 *Set or Spike.* Number 21 (behind the net) has drawn the complete attention of the opposing middle blocker and is about to attempt a one-handed set to another spiker. A high percentage of one-handed sets are called thrown balls by the referee. (Jim Haberlin)

STRATEGY

Setters should decide what type of setting strategy will best work against their opponents. They should know who are the strongest and weakest blockers on the opposing team and observe their blocking switches so that they are prepared in the event that continual setting in front of the weaker blocker is necessary. When the opposition is in the habit of stacking its strongest blockers on the star spiker, it may be advisable to set a less capable spiker against a weaker block.

Setters should be familiar with the referee's style as well as their opponents'

style. Although the same USVBA rules are in effect in all USVBA, NCAA, AIAW, NAIA, AAU and other major organizational play, interpretation of those rules may vary considerably from one referee to another. Usually, the average setter is not overly concerned with the referee's interpretation of a thrown ball, since most of his sets are high and wide and are delivered in the traditional manner. Better players, capable of setting in a three-hitter attack and delivering the ball from a variety of body positions, are very concerned.

Better setters can cause blockers to move in the wrong direction or move too late to block effectively. Faking a back

a

b

Figure 3–13 *Confusing the Blocker.* Larry Rundle draws the blocker on a ball passed close to the net. He sets the ball in front of his face in the usual manner. The blocker cannot touch the set unless an obvious attempt is made by the setter to score a point or a side out. (The Ealing Corp.)

set by stepping backward but arching the back and thereby contacting the ball high above the forehead to deliver a front set is a technique used to deceive blockers. The opposite ploy is to step forward without arching the back and then delivering a back set. The latest technique is to wait for the pass with the back to the net and set the ball laterally.

When beginners use these techniques, it is called bad form and a poor grasp of the fundamentals of setting. When expert setters use them and deliver the set cleanly and accurately, they are classified as players with an exciting and innovative style.

Good setting techniques are developed by learning to set the ball from every conceivable position. Training for the set is accomplished by having someone toss the ball to the setter from every conceivable angle and speed. In competition, about 40 percent of the passes are set while running, jumping, or diving.

A very talented setter who had developed the style described above lost an important match for his team in the USVBA National Championships because he would not deliver the ball in the traditional manner demanded by the referee—that is, from in front of his face in the direction in which he was facing or directly opposite the way in which he was facing. He often set the ball laterally with his back to the net. His team would have won handily if he had delivered a normal set and allowed his spikers to provide the deception necessary to defeat the block by varying the spike. Deception is a good goal for the setter and worth striving for, but he must be flexible enough to quickly evaluate the limits the referee establishes for him and to change his style if necessary.

Figure 3–14 *Setting a Blocked Ball.* Toshi Toyoda sets a blocked ball in the off-blocker position. One knee touches the floor as Toshi lowers his body so that he can contact the ball directly in front of his face. (Dr. Leonard Stallcup)

Sets from the right back should normally be delivered in a high arc to the left front of the court, as shown in Figure 3–15. Smaller players may have to squat halfway to the floor and extend their legs in a synchronized motion upon contact to ensure the necessary height and distance for this type of set.

Since almost all balls that the spikers will set originate from the four corners of the court, the crosscourt setting drills in the following section should be used in the majority of practice sessions. When setting from the backcourt, the ball should be delivered to an area about 5 ft from the antenna and about 2 ft from the net. The ball should be set high and have the illusion of dropping straight down from the ceiling. Low sets from the backcourt do not allow the spiker to look at the blockers.

TEACHING PROGRESSION

The following teaching progression has been used successfully with secondary school players:

1. Demonstrate the hand position for the overhand set. Instruct the players to form a window with their hands, 6 in. in front of the face with fingers spread and elbows close to the body. Check each member of the group individually.

2. Divide the group into partners and have them face each other at a distance of 5 ft. Distribute one leather volleyball for every two people. Assign one partner as a tosser and the other as a volleyer. From a distance of 5 ft, demonstrate a two-hand underhand toss that falls in an arc on a partner's forehead. Instruct the volleyers to return the ball in an arc that will land on the tosser's forehead. Stress contacting the ball with the fingertips. After 10 tosses, partners should exchange roles. To provide motivation, the volleyer scores one point every time the pass drops in an arc over the tosser's head. The first partner to score 15 points wins.

3. Demonstrate a three-quarter squat, with the back held straight, and simulate an overhand pass. Stress keeping the "window" in front of the face. Have the class squat and simulate a pass with you while you verbally correct individual form. Repeat drill number 2, using a low underhand toss that drops at the waist.

4. Demonstrate the slide step by instructing the tossers to lob the ball from side to side to make the volleyers take a lateral step to get behind the ball. Stress moving the outside foot ahead so the volleyer is facing in the direction of the set. Increase the difficulty by instructing the tosser to lob the ball so that the volleyer must take several slide steps.

5. Demonstrate the technique for setting a low pass to either side. Take a long slide step and squat on the same leg to the level of the toss while fully extending the other leg. Body weight is over the squatting leg. Body, head, and arms turn toward the tosser and simulate a set. Turn your back to the class and instruct them to move with you. Check individual form and then give each partner 10 tosses

Figure 3–15 *Setting from the Right-Back Position.* The left-front spiker (No. 10 in right background) is the only player who can watch the flight of the ball while using a proper approach to attack the set. (The Ealing Corp.)

before changing roles. Stress the pivot and turn toward the tosser.

6. Instruct the partners to rally from a distance of 5 ft. Use all of the techniques in preceding drills 2 to 5 to keep the ball in play.

7. Increase the distance between partners to 10 ft. Show the class how to bend their legs and to extend them to gain additional power and distance in the set. Instruct the tosser to lob the ball in an arc that falls near the volleyer's head. Change roles after 10 tosses. Stress keeping the hands 6 in. in front of the face because power is lost when contact is made with extended arms.

8. Instruct the partners to rally from a sitting position at a distance of 5 ft. Stress moving the upper part of the body behind the ball by leaning laterally. Point out how difficult it is to set the ball when hands are not in front of the face.

9. Move partners to a standing position, 10 ft apart. Instruct the tosser to lob the ball in a high arc anywhere within a 5-ft radius of the volleyer. The volleyer must move quickly to get under the ball and face the setter before contacting the ball.

10. Divide the players into groups of three. Place them in a straight line at a distance of 5 ft apart. Demonstrate the back set. Have the class simulate a back set. Stress contacting the ball above the forehead and arching the back. Follow-through with hands above the head. Tossers on the end should lob the ball to the middle player, who back sets it to the other tosser. The volleyer turns and repeats the drill. Rotate after 10 back sets. Increase the distance between players to 10 ft and repeat.

11. After players learn the rudiments of the back set, they can be paired off once again and placed 10 ft apart. Demonstrate how to set the ball about 5 ft straight overhead, quickly make a half-turn, and back set the ball to the partner. The partner sets the ball overhead, pivots, and returns the back set. Stress a quick pivot and stationary body position before setting.

12. Demonstrate the lateral set by passing the ball about 5 ft overhead, executing a quarter-turn, and setting the ball laterally to the partner, who will pass directly above the head, make a quarter-turn, and deliver a lateral set back to you. Stress moving the arms and body to the side as the ball is set.

13. Players squat and set from a low position; the bottom of the net is used to force a player into a low position. The player starts on the same side of the net as the coach and runs under the net to set a tossed ball. The player is forced into a low position and must use short, fast steps in order to turn and reach the ball in time to set it back to the coach.

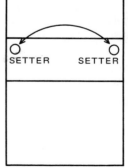

Setting with One Ball to Two Players *Start by overhand passing back and forth in a straight line.*

Partners face each other in a straight line, shoulders at a right angle to the set. They set back and forth from a distance of 15 ft. As they warm up, the distance increases to 30 ft. Setting specialists should always drill by the net.

Return to the 15-ft distance and set the ball laterally. Players drilling by the net should stand facing the net. Halfway through this drill, partners should change positions to practice setting to the left and right. Gradually increase the distance.

Partners once again stand facing each other, shoulders at a right angle to the net. They pass the ball 5–10 ft directly overhead, turn halfway around so that their back is toward their partner, and set backwards. The partner passes to himself (i.e., straight up) and returns the back set. Gradually increase the distance to 30 ft.

Partners stand about 10 ft apart. The tosser lobs the ball at the setter, aiming between the setter's knee and waist. The setter squats and delivers a 15-ft set that drops in the area of the tosser's head. Increase the distance between partners.

The tosser lobs the ball from side to side at a distance of 10 ft. The setter takes short, fast slide steps to reach the area of the toss. Then he takes a long lateral step and squats on the outside leg, pivots, and sets to the tosser.

Crosscourt Set—Three Players *Balls set from the backcourt should travel crosscourt so that the spiker can watch the approaching set. The setter starts in the standard backcourt defensive position that the team uses. The middle back position is a good one from which to drill because this area usually receives many balls that are deflected by the block. One of the spikers lobs balls to the backcourt, and the setter delivers the ball crosscourt. The spiker who receives the set can also practice by setting to the other spiker.*

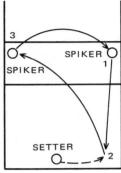

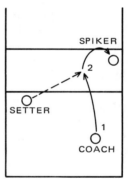

Setting on the Run *Although every setter should strive to contact the ball with his feet in a stationary position, it is necessary to make a great number of sets on the run. The following drill should be introduced during the first week of practice before poor techniques of setting on the run are allowed to develop. The coach lobs the ball 10–15 ft in front of the setter so that the player can just manage to contact the ball using the overhand passing technique. If the setter is close to the spiker, he attempts to set the ball straight up in the air. The forward momentum of the setter's body will cause the ball to travel in a forward arc. The great majority of sets delivered on the run travel too far because the setter attempts to set the ball forward.*

Crosscourt Set—Four Players *When four players are used in the crosscourt setting drill, the ball is kept in continuous motion with the overhand pass.*

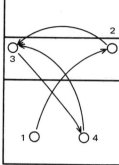

Backcourt Set and Spike *The spiker tosses the ball over his shoulder to the setter in the backcourt and approaches for the spike. A blocker or blockers may be added.*

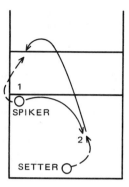

Back Set *Although most coaches prefer their spikers to set the ball in front of them, there are always situations that demand a back set. One player works on a 15-ft set, the middle player on a back set, and the other player on a 30-ft set. Rotate to all positions.*

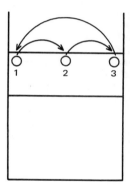

Dig and Set *The coach stands on a table and spikes the ball at either of the two backcourt players. The player who does not dig the ball must set it to one of the two spikers stationed at the corners of the net.*

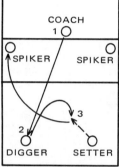

Long and Short Back Sets *The middle player delivers a back set from both directions. The setter can vary the distance between the spikers to practice back sets of varying heights and distances.*

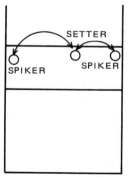

Decision Set *This is a drill for advanced players. Three spikers start 10–12 ft from the net and attack against three blockers. The object of the drill is to spike the ball against one blocker or no block, in the event the blocker does not jump. One spiker sets a teammate; if a two-man block forms in front of the spiker who has received the set, he must set one of his two teammates. If a spiker receives the second set, he must hit it over the net. This drill is very beneficial if spikers are learning the jump set. It can also be used with two attackers against three blockers.*

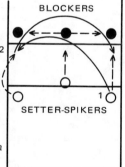

DRILLS FOR SETTING SPECIALISTS

All passes for setting drills should move the setter forward or laterally to simulate game situations.

The low crouch position is difficult for setters to master. The setter must be very quick and adaptable in order to run under the descending ball and squat on one knee while twisting the top of the instep on the floor for stability. This position gives the setter extra time to decide where to deliver the ball and consequently confuses the middle blockers.

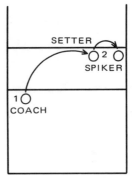

Short Back Set *When a setting specialist is having difficulty with a particular set, the coach should develop a drill to practice overcoming the problem. The setter in the three-hitter attack should receive the set about 10 ft from the right side line and face the left sideline. The setter who often neglects the spiker approaching down the right sideline needs extra practice on the short back set. The coach should pass balls to the setter from various positions on the court and evaluate the placement of each set. After the setter releases the ball, he must quickly turn and cover the spiker to field spikes that rebound off the block.*

Figure 3–16 *Low Crouch Position.* No. 4 has delivered a set from a low crouch position to hold the middle blocker and to prevent her from reaching over the net. This tactic is possible if the pass falls in an arc close to the net. (Andy Banachowski)

Jump Set *Setters who master the jump set can greatly improve the effectiveness of their attack. The coach should attempt to lob balls 1 or 2 ft over the net as the setter runs in from various court positions and attempts to save the pass by reaching above the net and setting the ball before it crosses the tape. Instruct the spiker to stand at various attack positions along the net.*

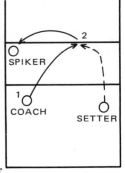

Figure 3–17 *Jump Set.* The setter has approached the net with his body in a spiking position to force the opposing blocker to commit himself. The setter then sets to a teammate who now has only one blocker to defend against him. (The Ealing Corp.)

Figure 3–18 *Punch Set.* When the ball is passed over the net and it is impossible to set the ball with two hands, the back-court setter may elect to punch set the ball to a teammate rather than risk the chance of throwing the ball by contacting it with the fingertips. (Barry Schreiber)

Spike or Set *When the front-court setter approaches a high pass that is close to the net on the on-hand side, he can often spike the ball without opposition from a blocker. Often blockers are concentrating on the spikers and do not expect the setter to spike on second contact with the ball.*

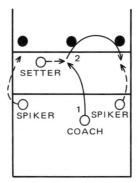

Better setters can jump in the air and, depending on the reaction of the opposing blocker, set or spike the ball. The coach should vary the height and distance of the pass. After the setter learns the fundamental technique of the jump set, the drill should be run against aggressive blockers.

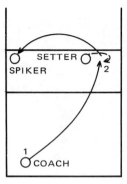

Move Backward and Front Set *Most setters deliver a back set when they take several steps backward to line up the ball. This frequently occurs when they are close to the side line. They must learn to deliver a front set under these conditions, with enough distance and height to reach the spiker on the other side of court. The coach should pass the ball behind the spiker from various positions on the court and instruct the setter to deliver a front set.*

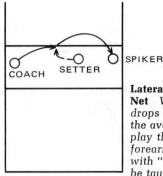

Lateral Set Facing the Net *When a low pass drops close to the net, the average setter must play the ball with the forearm pass. A setter with "good hands" can be taught to squat and face the net to set the ball laterally for best accuracy. The coach lobs low passes at various locations along the net.*

Move Forward and Back Set *Most setters are in the habit of setting forward when they run forward to line up the pass. Pass the ball well in front of the setter from various court positions and instruct the setter to deliver a back set.*

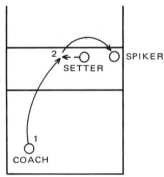

Lateral Set *When a setter must run behind the 10-ft line to line up the pass, he can generally set the ball only in the direction he is facing. Good ball handlers can be taught to set laterally, however. The threat of a lateral set is* important because it will force the middle blocker to stay "honest" and remain in the center of the court until the setter releases the ball. The coach passes the ball around the 10-ft line from various areas of the court and instructs the setter to set laterally.

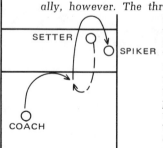

Figure 3–19. *Move Forward and Back Set.* This is a good tactic for an experienced setter because the middle blocker is usually moving with the setter and will have difficulty changing direction to reach the spiker. (The Ealing Corp.)

Lateral Set with the Back Toward the Net
The setter in the three-hitter attack must learn the lateral set, or the middle spiker will only receive the ball on a perfect pass. Pass the ball from various areas of the court while moving the setter off the net to force a lateral set to the middle attacker.

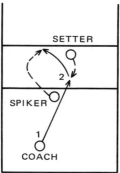

Middle-In Sets to Off-Blocker *The middle-in player has numerous opportunities to set balls looped over or deflected by the block. Often the only attacker who can get in position to spike on the quick change to offense is the former off-blocker. The coach stands on a table and dinks over the blockers. The middle-in player sets the dink to the off-blocker.*

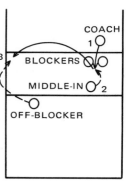

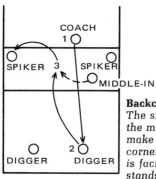

Backcourt Dig and Set
The simplest play for the middle-in player to make is a set to the corner spiker whom he is facing. The coach stands on a table and spikes to a backcourt digger. The middle-in player runs under the dig and delivers a front set to the end spiker.

Dig and Set *The next step is to allow the middle-in player to set any of the attackers.*

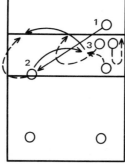

Figure 3–20 *The Quick Set.* A successful completion of the quick, or one-, set rests almost entirely upon the setter. He must place the ball directly in front of the attacker's shoulder for a successful play. (Norm Scindler)

Setting the Attack

The setter must be familiar with the idiosyncrasies of the spikers he will be playing next to in actual competition. Long hours of practice are necessary to refine the attack that has been selected. Teams that use the middle-in defense must give extra setting practice to the players covering the area behind the block. This player is responsible for setting any balls that are dug when his team uses a

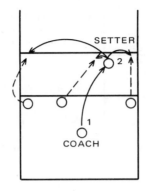

three-hitter attack. The quick reactions and speed of the setter usually make him too valuable a digger to be assigned to the area behind the block. In fact, some coaches place a big, slow spiker behind the block on defense to keep him out of the way. If this player is expected to set when the team switches from defense to offense, much individual coaching attention with special drills is needed.

4

Spiking

Spiking is the act of jumping in the air and hitting a set ball from above the level of the net into the opponents' court. It is an offensive play that usually drives the ball into the opponents' court with great force. Spiking requires coordinating the jump and armswing in order to contact the moving ball.

The *on-hand* side of the court is the side on which the spiker contacts the ball with his predominant hand before it crosses in front of his body. For example, the left-front corner is the on-hand side for a right-handed spiker because the ball is contacted in front of the right shoulder (Figure 4–3a). If the ball is set to the right front corner, it travels across the body to the right side before the spiker contacts the ball. This is more difficult to perform and is known as the *off-hand* spike (Figure 4–3b).

For the left-handed spiker, the on-hand and off-hand sides of the court are reversed—*off-hand* is the left front, *on-hand* is the right front.

Figure 4–1 *Spike-It.* This is a teaching aid that allows the spiker to concentrate on learning the correct approach, takeoff, and ball contact without worrying about the placement of the set. (Dennis Keller)

59

Figure 4–2 *Teaching the Spike.* When instructing children, it is necessary to lower the net to a point where the average child can touch the top of the tape with outstretched fingers. These seventh-grade girls are playing with a 6-ft 6-in. net. (Gary Adams)

APPROACHES FOR THE SPIKE

The preliminary position for the left-front spiker is 8 to 12 ft from the net, near the left side line.

Figure 4–4 shows the following sequence: When the ball is passed close to the net on the spiker's side of the court, he must take a quick straight approach in order to receive a set that will travel a short distance (*a*). When approaching during a good pass, most spikers prefer to swing slightly outside the boundary line and approach the set at a slight angle so that they can keep the ball and blockers in view at the same time (*b*). When a poor pass is directed deep into the court, the primary setter usually cannot reach the ball and a backcourt player becomes the setter. In this situation the spiker should take a wide approach so that he can keep the player setting the ball in full view as he moves toward the net (*c*).

The preliminary position for approaching the off-hand spike is the same as the

a

b

Figure 4–3 *On-Hand and Off-Hand Positions.* From their on-hand side, spikers can usually watch the blockers without taking their eyes off the set (*a*). From their off-hand side, spikers can only observe the blockers closely if the set travels across the spiker's body in front of his attacking arm (*b*). (Dr. Leonard Stallcup)

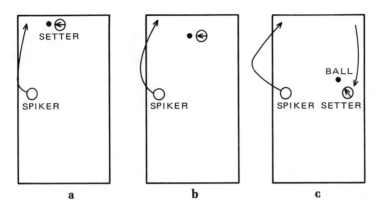

Figure 4–4 *Adjusting the Approach to the Pass.* The spiker must anticipate where the pass will be directed and who will set the ball as he begins the approach for the spike.

on-hand, but from the opposite side of the court. If the setter does not push the ball out to the side line, the hitter should move toward the center of the court to allow the ball to cross his body until it is in front of the attacking arm.

After the spiker reaches his preliminary position, he normally takes three or four steps during his *approach for the spike*. He generally takes the last step with his left leg if he is right-handed. The important point is that the last step should be taken with the stronger leg, regardless of the takeoff used.

Spikers at all levels of competition commonly start their approach too soon. Often they run under the set and cannot see the blockers. Starting the approach too soon also requires the spiker to wait for the set after arriving at the net and to lose several inches off his vertical jump. To correct this situation, the coach should hold the spiker during practice and then push him forward at the last possible moment. After this drill is repeated numerous times, the habit of approaching too early should be corrected.

The *pre-jump takeoff* is similar to the hop a diver takes before leaving the diving board. The spiker starts the approach while the setter is lining up the pass and adjusts his speed to the flight of the ball. The spiker then takes the last step by hopping off the stronger leg to land simultaneously with both heels parallel; next, the weight is shifted to the balls of the feet and the legs bend, then the legs are forceably contracted, forcing the spiker to leave the floor. The pre-jump takeoff is used infrequently in the United States because most coaches believe the step-close takeoff gives players a higher vertical jump.

In the *step-close takeoff*, the spiker takes a long last step by jumping forward, contacting the floor first with the

Figure 4–5 *Normal Approach for the Spike.* The player covers a distance of 10–12 ft in three or four steps. He gradually increases the speed of his approach as he nears his takeoff point. (The Ealing Corp.)

heel of one foot and then with the heel of the other foot; his weight then rolls from both heels to the toes as he takes off. When using this method, there is a tendency to broad jump when the spiker accelerates too quickly during the approach, or when he leans too far forward with the upper part of his body while preparing to jump.

The forward momentum that causes the spiker to broad jump can be overcome by keeping the upper part of the body at a right angle to the floor as the last step is taken. Spikers who prefer to use a rapid approach must jump slightly backward to transfer their forward momentum into a straight vertical jump.

The step-close takeoff approach is used almost exclusively by men and women participating in open and collegiate volleyball in the United States. In both the pre-jump and step-close takeoff, arms are extended backward to approximately shoulder height; they swing down and forward in an arc as the heels hit the floor during the last step. By the time the weight shifts to the toes, the arms should be swinging forward and up above the shoulders as the player's legs and ankles forceably contract, moving him into the air. As the player's hands reach head height, his back begins to arch and his legs bend backward at the knee. His left arm continues to rise until

Figure 4–6 *Pre-jump Takeoff.* This takeoff is performed at a slower speed than the step-close takeoff. A few athletes believe that it gives them better body control.

Figure 4–7 *Step-Close Takeoff.* It is important to contact the floor with the heels of both feet during the last steps of this takeoff so that the forward momentum of the body can be transferred into a vertical, rather than a broad, jump.

it reaches three-quarters to full extension above the shoulder. The right arm moves laterally above and behind the shoulder, and the hand is cocked behind the head. The body twists in the direction of the attacking arm and the left shoulder turns towards the net. The left arm drops quickly as the right arm uncoils toward the ball, with the elbow leading the way. The striking shoulder and upper body torque toward the ball as the body snaps forward from the waist. At contact, the attacking arm is extended and the hand, either cupped or flat and stiff, is held open. As the wrist snaps forward, the heel and palm of the hand simultane-

ously contact the ball, followed by the fingers.

The ball should be hit above and in front of the attacking shoulder, slightly after the apex of the jump. After contact, the striking arm continues down and across the body. As the feet touch the floor, legs bend to absorb the impact.

Occasionally, a player may approach a high pass or set and take off on the leg opposite his attacking arm to spike the ball. *One-leg* takeoff does not allow the spiker the desired balance and control; it is used only to surprise the block on the second touch of the ball. It is also used when the spiker does not have time

a

b

Figure 4–8 *Cocking the Spiking Hand Behind the Head.* This technique is particularly important on sets that are close to the net, where a minimum of body rotation is required. The ball is contacted with a "quick" arm. (Los Angeles City Unified School District, *a*; Bud Fields, *b*)

a   b

Figure 4–9 *Body Torque.* The spiker twists the upper part of his body to deliver maximum power to the spike. This technique is used to hit sets delivered away from the net. (Dr. Leonard Stallcup, *a*; Bud Fields, *b*)

to take a 2-ft takeoff. The player who takes a 2-ft takeoff to set or spike a pass can make his decision while in the air. The player who takes a 1-ft takeoff decides to spike before leaving the floor.

HITTING THE SPIKE

The trajectory of a spiked ball must arc because it is contacted farther away from the net. With deeper sets, the ball must be hit in an arc to land in the opponents' court. Effective spikers can hit the ball with full power at distances of 20 to 30 ft from the net and impart enough of a topspin to drive the ball into the opponents' court. To accomplish this, a spiker hits the ball directly above or behind the attacking shoulder and makes contact below the ball's midline with the heel of his hand; he wraps his palm and fingers up and over the ball, producing a maximum topspin with a vigorous wrist snap.

The height of the spiker's jump loses some of its significance when he can no longer hit the ball at an angle but must

a   b   c

Figure 4–10 *Contacting the Ball Above and In Front of the Attacking Shoulder.* This is perfect form for a straight-ahead spike. (Stan Troutman)

Figure 4–11 *Hitting Over the Block.* Defenders cannot attack-block against high-hitting spikers. (Dr. Leonard Stallcup)

rely on a maximum topspin to put the ball away. A deep set can be contacted below the level of the net and still be hit into the opponents' court with full power if the ball has enough topspin.

Figure 4–13 illustrates the maximum depths to which spikers can hit the ball without imparting a topspin, which causes the ball to drop or travel in an arc. For example, if a player were spiking the ball 10 ft from the regulation 8-ft net, he would have to contact the ball 3 ft above the net to hit a direct angle spike into his opponents' court. In competition, these distances are shorter because balls that are spiked slightly above the top of the net can easily be blocked for a point.

The force of a spiked ball can be increased by arching the back and bending the knees at more than a 90-degree angle. The stomach and hip flexors then con-

a   b

Figure 4–12 *Arm and Hand Positions for the Spike.* This varies according to the distance from which the ball is set at the net. When spiking deep sets (a), the ball should be contacted over the attacking shoulder. When spiking a close set (b), the ball can be contacted up to 2 ft in front of the attacking shoulder by spikers with a superior jump and reach. (The Ealing Corp.)

tract vigorously to snap the upper trunk and legs forward from the waist.

Spikers who contact the ball primarily with the heel of the hand will hit the ball with greater power than spikers who use the palm of the hand for most of the contact. Initial contact with the heel of the hand was popular until the blocking rules were changed in 1968. As soon as blockers were allowed to reach across the net, spiking tactics changed to emphasize placement and deception at the expense

of power; therefore, most spikers favor contacting the ball higher on the hand.

An advantage of 2 to 3 in. in height may be gained by using the palm of the hand. Most players now favor contacting the ball higher on the hand for additional control as well as for extra height.

Experienced hitters with good peripheral vision can see *the hands of the defenders* forming the block while leaping high in the air to spike the ball. Regardless of their approach to the set, they

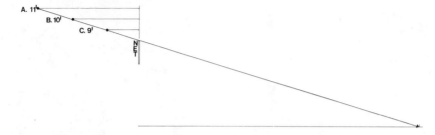

Figure 4–13 *Maximum Distance for Direct Angle Spikes.* The number of feet refers to the point at which the ball is contacted. A = 3 ft above the net at a position 10 ft away from net; B = 2 ft above net at a position 7 ft away from net; and C = 1 ft above net at a position 3 ft away from net. The average player will have to use a lot of topspin and a forceful armswing when spiking the ball more than 8 to 9 ft from the net.

a   b

Figure 4–14 *Power Spiking.* Normal back arch and knee flexion are demonstrated in *a*. Additional knee and back flexion (*b*) add power to the spike, but take away valuable inches from the spiker's vertical jump. The Russian men's team uses this technique frequently. (Stan Troutman)

a   b

Figure 4–15 *Body Snap.* The contraction of the stomach and hip muscles causes the body to snap and increases the power of the spike. (Andy Banachowski)

a   b

Figure 4–16 *Initial Contact with the Heel of the Hand.* Bill Olsson (a) and Al Scates (b) demonstrate. (Bud Fields)

are capable of spiking the ball crosscourt or down the line by rotating their wrist and forearm inward or outward.

This ability to see the block generally takes two to three years of varsity competition, but it can be developed sooner by instructing blockers to move their hands either to the left or right just prior to the spiker's contact with the ball. The spiker will become aware of the blockers and learn to direct his spikes with greater accuracy.

A coach standing behind the spiker can easily signal the blockers to pull their hands left or right or to leave a hole in the middle of the block. If the spiker can successfully direct the ball through a hole in the block, it will seldom be fielded or "dug," since defensive alignments are built around the premise that the front

a

b

Figure 4–17 *Initial Contact with the Palm of the Hand.* This technique allows the spiker greater control, but at the expense of a reduction in power. Palm contact is used almost exclusively by better spikers. (Barry Schreiber)

row defenders will present a solid wall of hands to the spiker.

Spikers should learn to use the blocker's hands to their advantage, particularly on balls set close to the net. Spikers who have the ability to see the blocker's hands can hit or "wipe" the ball off the block into the out-of-bounds area where it cannot be fielded. If the end blocker is small and cannot reach over the net with his outside hand to turn the ball into the court, the spiker should hit the ball hard so that it ricochets off his outside hand. This is an advanced technique and should be taught to experienced players only. Beginners tend to miss the hands and to hit the ball out of bounds.

If the end blocker reaches over the net with his outside hand, the spiker should slow his armswing to confuse the block-

a   b

Figure 4–18 *Placing the Spike.* Capable spikers can use the same approach and armswing to place the spike anywhere on the court with a last-moment turn of the wrist. Outward wrist rotation sends a spike crosscourt (*a*). Inward wrist rotation sends a spike down the line (*b*). (The Ealing Corp.)

Figure 4–19 *Crosscourt Spike.* Horace "Smitty" Duke, All-World Volleyball Player, gives every indication of a straight-ahead spike. He approaches the set with his shoulders parallel to the net and eludes the blockers by contacting the ball before it crosses in front of his shoulder. (Bud Fields)

er's timing and to use his fingertips to impart an "English," or lateral spin, on the ball so that it is wiped off the block-er's hands into the out-of-bounds area. This is accomplished by moving the fore-arm and hand toward the side line at the last possible moment. This technique should be taught only to experienced spikers, who have the ability to watch the set and to block at the same time.

When the spiker is trapped by a close set against tall, aggressive blockers, an effective shot is to hit the ball up, off the middle blocker's fingertips. In both the lateral and vertical wipe-off shots, the spiker runs the risk of having the referee miss the blocker's touch of the ball, awarding his opponent a point or side out if the ball lands out of bounds. For this reason, a spiker must attempt to hit a good "piece" of the block, particularly if he is on the opposite side of the referee's stand.

The vertical wipe-off shot is hit off the blocker's fingertips to prevent the blocker from stuffing a close set back into the spiker's court.

Round House Spike

The round house spike is a valuable weapon in the spiker's attack. It is used

Figure 4–20 *Line Spike.* High-flying spiker demonstrates the line spike by hitting a straight-ahead spike just inside the antenna. (Barry Schreiber)

most effectively on a good set to confuse the opponent's block. In competition, it is usually used when the spiker has run in front of the set or when the spiker is unable to get in position for a normal spike. Few men in this country have mastered the correct technique, and it is rarely attempted by women since the arm action requires more time off the floor than their jumping height normally allows.

To perform the round house spike, the spiker takes a normal approach and jumps with his left arm extended in the usual manner. When his right arm reaches head height, he rotates it downward and backward in a windmill motion while extended (Figure 4–25).

Figure 4–22 *Hitting the Ball Off the End Blocker's Hand.* This technique, which often causes the ball to be hit out of bounds, almost always results in a point for the attacking team. (Bob Van Wagner)

Figure 4–21 *Spiking Between the Blockers.* The end blocker has not placed his inside hand at the point where the ball crosses the net and middle blocker has not moved fast enough to close the hole. Spikers who have the ability to see the block can take advantage of this situation. (Dr. Leonard Stallcup)

Upon contact, the arm is fully extended over the shoulder. The ball is hit with the heel, with the palm and fingers tightly cupped. Since the arm action takes longer than the usual technique, the spiker always contacts the ball after he has reached the height of his jump. Opposing players are usually confused by this maneuver and are not in an optimum blocking position when the ball is hit.

THE DINK

The dink is a soft shot that is used to catch the defense off-guard. It is used most effectively on a good set when the defense is expecting a hard-driven spike. The attacker should cock his spiking arm in the normal manner and swing at a reduced speed to contact the ball with his fingertips (figs. 4–26, 4–27).

Contact is usually attempted as high above the net as possible so that the ball can be tipped over the block. All spikers should master the technique of *dinking over the middle blocker.* It keeps the defense "honest" and prevents it from always being in position to dig hard-driven spikes. The spiker who is skilled in varying his attack is most effective. Shorter attackers may attempt to dink the ball into a tall blocker's forearms in the hope that the ball will roll down the opponent's body on the opposition's side of the net. When the low dink is attempted against a low block, the ball is usually stuffed to the floor.

When three blockers are defending against the attacker, there is a lot of court left open for a well-placed dink shot.

The *two-handed dink shot* is usually used to place the ball deep in the opponents' court or to rebound the ball off the blockers' hands to keep the ball in play.

When a close set drops below the level of the net, it can be punched over with the knuckles. This type of dink is a last resort in the regulation six-man game, used merely to keep the ball in play. In

Figure 4–23 *Lateral Wipe-Off Shot.* Slowing the armswing and contacting the ball with a lateral motion, and then hitting the blocker's outside hand as he is descending, usually prevents the blocker from maintaining the necessary height to keep his hand between the ball and the sideline. (The Ealing Corp.)

a   b

Figure 4–24 *Vertical Wipe-Off Shot.*
This tactic keeps the ball in play and
does not usually score a point or a side
out for the other team. (Stan Troutman,
a; The Ealing Corp., *b*)

two-man volleyball, the open-hand dink
is often interpreted as a throw. Consequently, the closed-fist technique, or
punch, is common in doubles volleyball.

OFF-SPEED SPIKE

The off-speed spike is effective only
when the defense is braced for a hard
kill. If the spiker is off-balance or does
not use a normal approach, the defense
will expect the spiker to hit the ball with
less force. The speed of the striking arm
is reduced just prior to contact to confuse
the defense. If the spiker uses his normal
approach and a slower armswing, the
blockers will lose their timing and the
backcourt defenders will find the ball
losing momentum and landing in front of
them. The off-speed spike is most effective when used infrequently and when
directed toward a definite weakness in
the defense—whether it be an individual
or an open area of the court.

SPIKING THE LOW VERTICAL SET

A well-executed spike of a low vertical set, requiring split-second timing between spiker and setter, is one of the most exciting offensive plays in volleyball. *The low vertical set, or one-set, is extremely important to the success of the three-hitter offense.*

Spiking the low vertical set was popularized by athletes and spectators in the United States by the touring Japanese National Men's and Women's teams shortly after the 1964 Olympic Games. It was perfected by the Japanese to make the small spiker effective and to create one-on-one blocking situations for their strong spikers.

Spiking the low vertical set is performed in this manner: The spiker approaches to within a few feet of the setter as the setter moves into position to receive the pass. If he intends to spike the ball as soon as it rises above the net, he gathers momentum to jump and is in the air before the setter touches the ball. His spiking arm is cocked with little body

Figure 4–25 *Round House Spike.* The ball is contacted as the spiker returns to the floor; the ball usually passes the net as the blocker is also on his downward flight. For this reason, the round house spike is rarely blocked for a point. (Barry Schreiber)

Figure 4–26 *Arm Action.* Arm action of the one-hand dink closely resembles the spike. Most players make the mistake of "telegraphing" their intentions to the defense by straightening their arm too soon. Toshi Toyoda demonstrates the spiking action that he uses when delivering the dink shot. (Dr. Leonard Stallcup)

a   b

Figure 4–27 *Contact.*   Contact with the ball should be made with the fingertips, with the wrist held stiff. (Barry Schreiber, *a*; Dr. Leonard Stallcup, *b*)

a   b

Figure 4–28 *Dinking Over the Middle Blocker.*   This is an effective way to score on the middle-back defense. (Dr. Leonard Stallcup, *a*; Jim Haberlin, *b*)

torque or shoulder rotation, ready and waiting for the setter to deliver the ball in front of his attacking arm. The spiker should be at the apex of his jump just as the ball is clearing the tape at the top of the net. He contacts the ball a few inches above the net.

There is little opportunity for the spiker to consciously direct his spike using this technique. The emphasis is on quickly hitting the ball to the floor with a sharp downward flight—not on power. If the ball is contacted before it crosses his attacking shoulder, he usually hits it to

his right (Figure 4–35a). If the set is contacted in front of or past his attacking shoulder, the spiker generally hits the ball straight ahead or to the left (Figure 4–35b). Better spikers can direct the ball to any area of the court using several different approach patterns.

When a spiker hits the low vertical set just as it leaves the setter's fingertips, the opposing blocker must jump with the attacker to block successfully. Defending against the low vertical set requires the middle blocker to jump with the middle attacker before the ball is set. The play was developed to force the middle blocker to commit himself in this manner so that the other two spikers would have the opportunity to receive a normal set against one blocker. The proficient setter must watch the middle blocker, the ball,

Figure 4–29 *Alternate Tactic.* Occasionally, an experienced attacker jams the ball into the forearms of a tall blocker. The ball will ricochet to the floor on the opponents' side of the court if the blocker's arms are not over the net. (Dr. Leonard Stallcup)

Figure 4–30 *Dinking Against a Three-Man Block.* This is always good strategy because the three remaining backcourt players will find it extremely difficult to cover the entire court. (Bud Fields)

and the approaching spiker while deciding to deliver the ball.

In a three-hitter attack, this places the other two spikers in a one-on-one situation with the end blockers. Since the middle blocker is usually the most proficient, this technique takes on added significance when a weak spiker is able to take the opposition's best blocker out of the play with a feigned attack. When the middle attacker constantly forces the middle blocker to jump with him, the best percentage play is usually a high, wide set to the on-hand spiker. The middle blocker thereby cannot recover fast

enough to join the end blocker if he has left the floor, and the on-hand spiker is given the opportunity to attack from his power side against one blocker.

When a spiker becomes proficient at hitting low sets, the setter may choose to deliver the ball to him even though one defender will always block against him. In this case, the spiker may elect to jump after the ball is released and hit a slightly higher set, generally called a *two-set*.

The spiker contacts the two-set at the top of its flight; consequently, he has enough time to use a normal armswing and body torque to spike the ball in any

a

b

Figure 4–31 *Two-Handed Dink Shot.* Larry Rundle (*a*) and Ed Becker (*b*) attempt to draw a touch of the blockers' fingers as they release the ball toward the opponents' backline. (Dr. Leonard Stallcup, *a*; Bob Van Wagner, *b*)

Figure 4–32 *Keeping the Ball in Play.*
An overhand lob into the block usually
causes the ball to rebound softly into the
attackers' court, allowing the offense to
recover the ball and giving them another
chance to put the ball away. (Bud Fields)

direction. The set should be low enough
to prevent a two-man block and high
enough to allow the spiker to place the
ball accurately. When a valuable spiker
is attacking from the middle, it is usually
good strategy to use a two-set.

Spikers with quick reflexes and good
coordination can hit the ball inches out
of the setter's hands when the setter
jumps to receive a pass that is high and
close to the net.

The low vertical set is almost always
attempted from the on-hand side so that
the setter does not have to push the ball
across the attacker's body in front of his
attacking arm.

The most difficult offensive play in
volleyball is a *back one-set to an off-hand
spiker.* This play is difficult because the
setter can only watch the ball and the
opposing blocker. The spiker's timing
must be perfect because the setter will
only hear his footsteps and can rarely
compensate for a poor approach. Since
this play is rarely attempted, it usually
leaves the blocker standing on the floor
when executed correctly.

SPIKING A SHOOT SET

The shoot set is delivered low and fast to create one-on-one blocking situations. It is usually placed a few feet from the side line and contacted at a height of 1 to 2 ft above the net, depending on the preference and vertical jump of the spiker. The set is extremely difficult for the middle blocker to cover when the ball travels a distance of 10 ft or more from setter to spiker. This is the best method of creating a one-on-one spiking situation in the two-hitter attack. The spiker should start his approach closer to the net and slightly outside the side line. Normal takeoff and spiking technique should be used.

In a three-hitter attack, a shoot set is called a "three" when used by the middle spiker to split the end and middle blockers. It is a very quick, low trajectory set that requires the same split-second timing as the low vertical set.

Ideally, the ball is passed to the setter at a point 2 ft from the net and about 10 ft from the right side line. The spiker quickly moves to a point about 10 ft from the left side line between the end and middle blockers. The spiker should time his approach so that he jumps as the ball is being released from the setter.

SPIKING DRILLS

Most of the following spiking drills can also be used to improve dink shots, off-speed shots, and round house spikes. To

Figure 4–33 *Punching the Ball.* Punching the ball over the net with a closed fist is recommended only if the ball drops below the level of the net prior to contact. (Los Angeles City Unified School District)

Figure 4–34 *Off-Speed Spike.* With a turn of his wrist, player No. 8 directs an off-speed spike through a hole in the block. (Dr. Leonard Stallcup)

increase the difficulty add blockers or an entire defensive alignment.

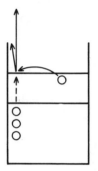

Spikers line up near the left side line, about 12 ft from the net. Work on long and short line spikes. Repeat the drill from the right side line.

Use a straight approach and spike the ball crosscourt. Place a towel on the floor for the spiker to use as a target.

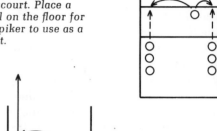

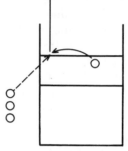

Using an angle approach from the on-hand side, spike the ball down the side line.

a   b

Figure 4–35 *Spiking a Low Vertical Set.* The setter delivers the low vertical set or one-set to the spiker. (Stan Troutman)

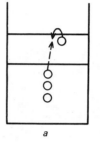

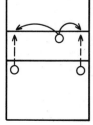

Figure 4–36 *Defending Against the Low Vertical Set.* Unless the middle blocker is quite tall, he must fully commit himself with a maximum jump before the setter delivers the ball in order to stop the play. (Norm Scindler)

Spike a backcourt set crosscourt and down the line. Vary height and placement of the set.

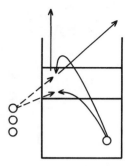

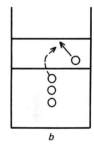

Spikers hit a low vertical set. The setter stations himself 10 ft from the right side line, a foot from the net.

a

The coach passes the ball to the setter at various locations inside the 10-ft line. The spiker must adjust his approach to the pass to get in a favorable position to hit a low, quick set.

b

Using an angle approach from the on-hand side, spike the ball crosscourt.

Using two lines of spikers and one setter, set either side. The spiker should not rotate until he hits.

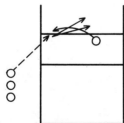

Spikers hit a shoot set from the left side.

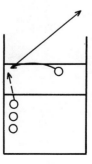

Figure 4–37 *Setting the On-hand Spiker.* Player No. 11 (left rear) approaches from the on-hand side while No. 9 holds the attention of the middle blocker. Toshi Toyoda (No. 1) sets. (Stan Troutman)

◄ **Figure 4–38** *A Maximum Jump by the Middle Attacker.* A jump by the middle attacker is necessary because he never knows whether the setter will deliver the ball to him or to another spiker. The spiker leaps high above the net as teammate No. 1 delivers a set over No. 3 to the on-hand spiker. (Dr. Leonard Stallcup)

Figure 4–39 *Approach for the Two-Set.* ▶
Tom Madison (No. 11) is preparing to
jump for a two-set shortly after Toshi
Toyoda (No. 1) releases the ball. (Bud
Fields)

Figure 4–40 *Spiking the Two-Set.* Left-
handed (No. 5) Kirk Kilgour has just received the set from his teammate (No. 4).
His team passed the ball to the left so
that Kilgour, in the middle position, could
attack from his on-hand side. (Bob Van
Wagner)

Figure 4–41 *Spiking a Jump One-Set.* This play is used when the first pass is delivered too close to the net. Ernie Suwara (right) leaps high above the net to deliver a one-set to Larry Rundle (left) who will hit the ball inches out of Ernie's fingertips. (Stan Troutman)

Figure 4–42 *Back One-Set to the Off-Hand Spiker.* Ernie Suwara (54) sets to Larry Rundle. (Stan Troutman)

Figure 4–43 *Middle Spiker Attacking a Three-Set.* Tom Madision (far left) alertly dinks the ball over the end blocker who has moved from the sideline but has not had time to leave the floor. The middle blocker is late and cannot close in fast enough to touch the ball. After setting, Toshi Toyoda (No. 1) moves forward to back up the spiker. (Bob Van Wagner)

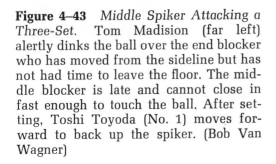

End spikers hit a shoot set *10 ft* from the left side line.

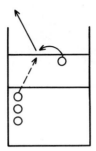

Three spikers work with one setter.

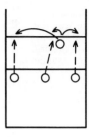

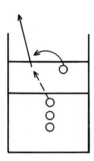

Middle spikers hit a shoot set *10 ft* from the left side line.

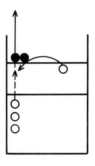

Spikers practice hitting the ball over the blocker's hands. Blockers can stand on a bench to regulate their height.

Middle spikers hit a front two-set.

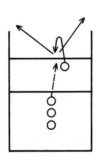

Spikers practice hitting the ball off the end blocker's hand into the out-of-bounds area.

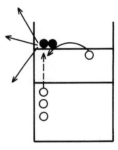

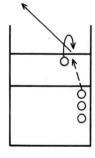

Off-hand spikers hit a back two-set.

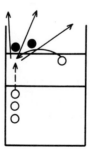

When the ball is in the air, the blockers leave a vulnerable spot in the block. The spiker must hit through the hole in the line of blockers.

A backcourt player passes the ball to the front-row setter, who spikes or jump sets to his teammate.

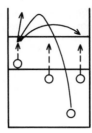

The end spiker attacks weak areas of the man in defense by using dinks, off-speed shots, and spikes.

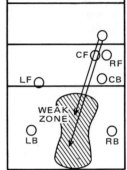

Recover a blocked spike and set the ball to a front-row player. Pass the ball to the setter if he does not field the blocked spike.

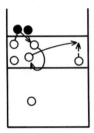

The middle spiker attacks weak areas of the man in defense by dinking and using off-speed shots to the front corners and hitting the ball over or off the blocker's fingertips to the deep corners.

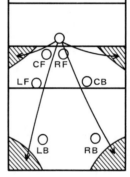

The player simulates a block and, as he is returning to the floor, the coach throws the ball to a teammate who sets him.

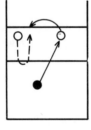

The coach throws balls over the net for players in blocking positions to hit sharply downward or to set.

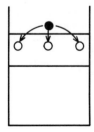

The end spiker attacks weak areas of the man back defense by dinking and hitting off-speed shots into the center of the court and driving long spikes over or off the fingertips of the end blockers.

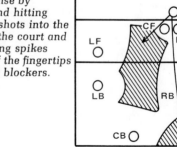

5

Blocking

Blocking is defensive playing by one or more players who attempt to intercept the ball near the net. Any or all of the players in the front line are permitted to block. Blockers are allowed to reach as far over the net as possible, as long as they do not touch the ball before the offense attacks. The most common type of block is a two-man block.

When one or more players participate in the block and make only one attempt to intercept the ball, they may make successive contacts with the ball. A player participating in the block may participate in the next play which counts as the second of the three hits allowed to the team. A team fielding a ball that is blocked may have two additional contacts with the ball before the ball must cross into the opponents' court.

The most effective way to demoralize a team is to prevent the star spiker from hitting the ball over the net. Good spikers find it increasingly difficult to put the ball away because the opposition realizes the importance of aligning its best blockers

against them. Often an aggressive block will score over 50 percent of a team's points—either indirectly (by intimidating opponents to use poor percentage shots to avoid the block) or directly (by blocking the ball to the floor). Aggressive blockers can often force opposing setters to deliver the ball 5 ft back from the net to protect their spikers.

STARTING POSITION

To increase the height of their jump, shorter players and blockers with average jumping ability may need to take a short run or two or three steps while using a full armswing. This approach should be used only if the blocker cannot achieve the necessary height with one step. If blockers start their approach farther from the net, they increase the risk of netting when they attempt to transfer their forward momentum into a vertical jump. Taller players or good jumpers should rarely start their ap-

Figure 5–1 *The Block.* The block is a defensive play in which any or all front-court players place one or two hands above their heads while in a position close to the net. One blocker is shown in *a* and *b*, two blockers are shown in *c* and *d*, and three blockers are in *e*. (Bud Fields, *a*; Barry Schreiber, *b*, *d*, *e*; Dr. Leonard Stallcup, *c*)

Figure 5–2 *Blocking for Points.* Blocking for points can contribute up to 50 percent of a team's total score. (Stan Troutman)

proach more than one arm's length from the net.

In order to determine what degree of leg flexion gives the greatest vertical jumping height, blockers should experiment with the angle of the squat, or gather, used to prepare for the jump. Small players may use a full squat, but taller blockers may be more effective squatting one-third to halfway down.

Exceptional jumpers may use a standing takeoff without a full armswing. By eliminating excessive body movements, the blocker is able to wait for the spiker to commit himself and he can use better body control to counter his opponent's attack.

A few years ago, blockers in international competition were able to stop opponents by jumping as high as eye level to the top of the tape. Now blockers in top international competition must get their armpits over the net to stop high-hitting spikers. Teams now have taller

players in their starting lineups, and these players are increasing their jumps with weight training.

The blocker achieves a vertical jump necessary to stop the attack by starting as close to the net as his height and jumping ability allow.

A simple test to measure a player's jumping reach is administered by chalking the middle fingertips of both hands and measuring the lowest touch mark on a wall after a vertical jump. If a Sargent Jump Board is available, set the zero line at net height for quicker evaluation. This jump test can aid in the determination of the blocking style to be used by a team's blockers. After a thorough warm-up, the player should be tested on the following jumping techniques:

A standing jump with hands held at shoulder height
A standing jump with full armswing
A one-step approach with full armswing
A longer approach if none of the previous techniques have yielded an adequate height

The player should be allowed to flex his knees at the angle of his choice for the first three jumps in every test. Normally, players do not squat low enough to produce maximum jumping height until instructed to do so. Most volleyball players have played basketball since elementary school and consequently have not been trained to use a low squat for added height.

Rebounding does not give a player the necessary time to prepare for the maximum jump used to block the spike of a

a   b   c

Figure 5–3 *Sargent Jump Test.* The player stands flat-footed, feet together, toes and chest against the wall. He places his fingertips underneath the board and pushes the board up until his arms are fully extended (*a*). Then he turns side-wise to the wall and squats at the desired level (*b*). He jumps and reaches, one hand touching as far up on the board as possible (*c*). His score is the difference between his reach while standing and his reach obtained by jumping. (Stan Troutman)

high, wide set. The coach can point this out rather dramatically after he instructs the player being tested to increase his vertical jump by squatting lower; this starting position brings the stronger quadriceps and *gluteus maximus* muscles into play to aid the muscles of the calf.

Unless fatigue becomes a factor, jumping height will increase as the player uses an approach and armswing. Because bet-

ter control is achieved without a full arm-swing and standing takeoff, the point of this test is to determine if an approach and armswing are necessary. The average end blocker starts at an arm's length from the net when blocking smaller players and teams that use quick, low sets. When opposing taller players, a longer approach should be used.

Some end blockers may have to use an

a   b   c

Figure 5–4 *Blocking a Spiker with a Normal Armswing.* Blockers must jump shortly after the spiker leaves the floor. When the ball is set farther away from the net, blockers must hesitate before jumping to give the spiked ball an additional split second to travel the added distance to the net. Here, the middle blocker should have tilted his head slightly forward instead of backward. The forward tilt of the head brings the arms closer to the net, whereas the backward tilt tends to pull the arms away from the net. (The Ealing Corp.)

a   b   c

Figure 5–5 *Blocking a Spiker with a Late Armswing.* Spikers with a slow or late armswing usually contact the ball several inches below the apex of their jump. For correct timing, blockers should jump well after the spiker has left the floor. (The Ealing Corp.)

approach on every block, while outstanding jumpers and taller players may be able to use a standing takeoff with little or no armswing. Smaller players usually jump higher using a two-thirds to full squat, whereas tall blockers generally are more efficient using a half-squat or less.

FOOTWORK

Footwork varies according to the reach and jump of the blocker. The *slide step* is used by blockers close to the net who do not have to travel great distances quickly. End blockers use the slide step most of the time. Middle blockers who are quick and jump well also use the slide step.

The slide step involves moving the lead foot laterally and closing the trailing foot to within 6 in. of the forward foot. When arriving at the blocking area, the front foot hits the floor first and points slightly inward as the trailing foot closes approximately to shoulder-width.

The *run* is used by shorter players or poor jumpers who must start several feet from the net. The run requires greater timing, coordination, and practice than the slide step. The first step in the run uses the inside foot and the last step uses the outside foot. It is particularly important for the end blocker to turn the outside foot toward the center of the court during the last step so the block will not drift toward the sideline. This is a natural movement for most blockers on the left side because the majority of players take the last step with the left foot when spiking. The step-close takeoff should be used for the run. If blockers cannot learn to take the last step with the outside foot on the right side, they will drift toward the sideline while jumping and leave a hole between themselves and the middle blocker.

The popular blocking approach for middle blockers is the *crossover step,* which is faster than the slide step and allows the blocker to gain additional inches during the vertical jump. The first step is a slide with the lead foot; then the trailing foot takes a long crossover step and pivots toward the net so that the blocker's shoulders are parallel to the net as the third step is completed. The foot should be planted slightly inward on the third step to enable the blocker to jump straight up rather than laterally.

The crossover step allows the blocker to use an approach and armswing similar to the one used for the spike, which gives extra lift on the vertical jump. This step is fundamentally sound because it allows the blocker to point the feet toward the net so the arms can be raised straight above the shoulders. If a middle blocker cannot cover at least 12 ft in three steps or starts in the wrong direction, additional steps must be taken to reach sets by the antenna. The important point is to plant the feet at a 90° angle to the net before jumping so the body faces the net when the jump is completed.

A few outstanding middle blockers use a more complicated technique. They take the first step by crossing over with the inside foot, which positions the body at a 90° angle to the net; the second step is long and taken parallel to the net. The third step places the blocker in position for the step-close takeoff used in the spike. At the completion of the second step, the knees should be flexed and the arms extended backward at almost shoulder level. The arms drive downward, pointing toward the floor as the player completes the third step; the arms are then put forward and up as the player leaves the floor. Then the blocker must turn in mid-air and square the shoulders to the net. In other words, the blocker uses a crossover step with a step-close takeoff and a half turn in mid-air. This is the fastest method for the middle blocker and allows for the highest vertical jump. It also requires excellent coordination and timing. Most blockers fail in this technique because they cannot transfer their forward momentum into a vertical jump. Instead, they move laterally and collide with the end blocker.

Generally, a right-handed spiker has a stronger left leg and vice versa. The spiker almost invariably takes the last step in the spiking approach with the strongest leg, which results in greater jumping height. When this principle is applied to blocking, the right-handed middle blocker who masters the techniques of the crossover step should crossover with the first step when moving to his right and crossover with the second step when moving to the left.

While he is getting into position, the blocker must observe the preliminary flight of the ball and then switch his attention to the spiker's approach.

TAKEOFF FOR THE JUMP

The most important point to make about the takeoff is that the player should bend at the knees, not at the waist. The player who bends at the waist tends to swing and bat at the ball, resulting in ineffective blocking. The position of the blocker's feet is also critical: the feet should point slightly inward in a pigeon-toed stance aimed at the attacker. This stance squares the body toward the net. At take-off, the blocker's ankles should be bent at an angle of 80° to 90°, the knees at 100° to 110°, and the hips at 90°.

Most of the time, the blocker should jump shortly after the spiker leaves the floor.

Because spikers use a longer approach, they are able to jump higher and remain in the air longer than blockers. If blockers jump with the spiker on a normal set, they will be too low when the spiker contacts the ball. Blockers must wait even longer when the ball is set deep into their opponents' court. Some spikers create the illusion of hanging in the air by spiking the ball on the way down.

Blockers must constantly remind themselves to hesitate when facing an opponent who spikes the ball on the way down with a late armswing. Figure 5–5 shows how to block a spiker with late armswing. Blockers must discipline themselves to stay on the floor until the spiker nears the apex of his jump. Blockers should time their movement so that they are at the height of their jump as the late-swinging spiker is contacting the ball on his return to the floor. Better spikers can defeat this blocking tactic by switching to a quick armswing and hitting over the blocker's hands.

A short blocker must have perfect timing to block the middle position because his hands cannot remain above the net as long as his taller teammates'. A taller player can jump too soon and still block the spike, but the short blocker must time his jump perfectly.

Short blockers should normally jump after their taller teammates, particularly when facing a very tall spiker. The blocker who has his toes on the floor in

Figure 5–6a is 5 ft 11 in. tall; his opponent spiker, who uses a late armswing, is 6 ft 7 in. tall. The late-jumping blocker leaves the floor just prior to the hit and attempts to contact the spike at the height of his jump.

When the setter delivers a quick, low set to a spiker who is capable of hitting the ball inches out of the setter's hand, the blocker must jump with the spiker (Figure 5–7). In this situation, jumping ability is not as important as agility.

AFTER THE TAKEOFF

As the player jumps, the arms are raised with the elbows out in front and the shoulders locked until the arms are fully extended. The player should be sure to reach straight up from the shoulders; he should not swing or bat at the ball. The back is slightly hunched and, although the head may appear to tilt slightly downward, the eyes are on the spiker— not on the ball. The fingers are spread

a

b

Figure 5–6 *Late Takeoff by Short Middle Blockers.* A late takeoff allows short middle blockers to coordinate their jump with taller teammates as the spike approaches the net. The short blocker is above the net for a comparatively brief period and must time the jump precisely for a coordinated block. (Bob Van Wagner, *a*; Dr. Leonard Stallcup, *b*)

wide apart to cover as much of the ball as possible. The arms are close to the net as the wrists force the ball back into the opponent's court. Some players can extend their forearms from 18 to 24 in. over the net, but the great majority of blockers can only extend their forearms to the top of the net and reach over with their wrists and hands.

Figure 5-7 *Defending Against a Quick Middle Set.* The middle blocker has jumped with the spiker before the ball had left the setter's hand. This is the only way in which to defend against the one-set. (Andy Banachowski)

Tall blockers with a superior jump can crouch with their hands above shoulder level and extend their arms over the net as they jump. The advantage of this technique is added body control, which allows for greater concentration on the intentions of the approaching spiker.

Whatever style is used, the distance between the hands and portions of the arms extended above the net at the moment of contact normally should be less than the circumference of the ball.

The obvious results of leaving a wider space in the block are shown in Figure 5–8. When the ball is set outside the court, the blocker may widen the space between his hands due to the angle of flight the ball must travel to legally pass the sideline markers on the net.

As the blocker descends, his arms and hands draw away from the net and down the sides of his body. The shock of landing is absorbed by the toes, soles, and heels of both feet and then by the legs. If the ball does not rebound into the opponents' court, the blocker turns his head in the direction of the spike as he descends so that he will be ready for the next play.

ATTACK BLOCK

The attack block is an attempt to intercept the ball before it crosses the net. Blockers may reach across the net, but they may not contact the ball until their opponent has attempted to hit the ball across the net.

Blockers should extend their arms above the net and move them downward from the shoulders, tilting their wrists forward while keeping their hands and fingers rigid.

Figure 5–8 *Spiking through a Blocker.* A slight closing of the blocker's (No. 15) arms and hands would have blocked the spike. (Bob Van Wagner)

Ideally, contact with the ball should be made with the heels of the hand just as the body is descending. In competition, spikes are also blocked with forearms, palms, and fingers.

The capable blocker will always attack block when in a good position and when the offense consists of fast, low sets. If the spiker receives a low set close to the net, the blocker should form a "roof" around the ball with his hands, trapping the ball and the spiker.

SOFT BLOCK

Blockers should also master the technique of soft blocking. The soft block

Figure 5–9. *Attack Block.* The attack block has revolutionized the game by forcing setters to place the ball deep in their own court to prevent blockers from rebounding the spike back into the attacking team's court. (Bud Fields)

Figure 5–10 *Teaching the Attack Block.* Seventh-grade girls are playing doubles volleyball with a 6-ft 6-in. net. The lowered net allows them to reach over on the block. (Gary Adams)

Figure 5–11 *Teaching Aid.* The use of the "spike it" enables blockers to concentrate on the approaching spiker rather than watching the flight of the set ball. (Dennis Keller)

Figure 5–12 *Soft Block.* For this technique, blockers may keep their hands above the net longer and cover a greater area above the net. Deep spikes, which are usually not hit with as much force as a close spike, are easier to slow up or to deflect to a teammate. (Andy Banachowski)

is usually used when the ball is set away from the net. It is called a soft block because the blocked ball rebounds back into the opponents' court at a lesser angle or is deflected to the blocker's side of the court. The forearms are held parallel to the net, and hands are held either tilted backward or parallel to the net.

Smaller blockers must use the soft block a majority of the time so that they can reach high above the net to prevent spikers from hitting the ball over their hands. There are many occasions that call for the blocker to attempt to slow up the spike and to deflect the ball to a teammate. A blocker can cover a much greater area above the net by attempting to deflect a spike than he can by reaching over the net. In Figure 5–13, blocker No. 1 has chosen to slow up a crosscourt spike.

When the middle blocker must swing his arms toward the end blocker to shut off the path of the oncoming spike, he often finds himself too far away from the net. To prevent the ball from striking his hands and falling between himself and the net, he should tilt his hands backward to deflect the ball to a teammate. The blocker on the right in Figure 5–14 is using this technique.

Blockers should normally use the soft block to intercept deep spikes. They must jump after the spiker does when the spiker is hitting a ball that is not set close to the net. If blockers jump with the spiker, they will not have the necessary height to block effectively by the time the ball approaches the net. The soft block gives the blocker a greater margin of time to assess the direction and speed of a deep spike.

In Figure 5–14, the middle blocker tries to close the hole between the blockers; he must move his arms laterally and is prevented from reaching over the net if he is slightly late in arriving at the point of attack.

TWO BLOCKERS

In the preliminary position, the right blocker should start about 2 ft from the sideline, the left-end blocker about 4 ft from the other sideline, with the middle blocker splitting the distance between them.

For right- or left-handed spikers, there are easier and more difficult spikes to perform, depending upon which side of the court the ball is set to. These are called "on-hand" and "off-hand" spikes. The on-hand side of the court is the side on which the spiker contacts the ball with his predominant hand before it crosses in front of his body. For example, the left front corner would be the on-hand side for a right-handed spiker because the ball would not cross in front of his body before it could be contacted in

Figure 5–14 *Combination Blocks.* The end blocker is making an attack block and the middle blocker is attempting to close the hole between himself and his teammate by soft blocking. (Stan Troutman)

Figure 5–13 *Attempting to Deflect the Spike.* One blocker is trying to cover a large area of the net. (Bob Van Wagner)

Figure 5–15 *Starting Distance.* A blocker's starting distance from the net is determined by his height, vertical jump, reach, and individual style. The small end blocker in the background is taking a 3-ft approach to combat high-spiking Larry Rundle. (The Ealing Corp.)

front of his right shoulder. Most right-handed spikers are capable of spiking the ball down the sideline by rotating their forearms and wrists inward on the power side. This is the reason why the right-end blocker must start closer to the side-line than his counterpart on the left side when the attackers are right-handed.

When blocking a spiker on his off-hand side, the blocker should start about 4 ft from the sideline; when blocking an on-hand spiker, he or she should start about 2 ft from the sideline. If the spiker demonstrates a good line shot on his off-hand side, the blocker should start closer to the sideline.

When the blocker contacts the ball, his outside hand should be between the ball and the sideline. This prevents the ball from being "wiped off" the blocker's hands into the out-of-bounds area where the backcourt men cannot reach it.

When a blocker senses that the spiker may deliberately hit the ball toward the out-of-bounds area in an attempt to contact his hand, he should quickly drop his hand below the level of the net to allow the spike to travel out of bounds.

The end blocker's primary responsibility is to position the block on wide sets.

The objective of the end blocker on a normal set is to align himself so that he blocks the ball on the inside hand. If middle blockers are late, the backcourt players find themselves continually out of position in attempting to cover their teammates. When the ball is set to the center spiker, the outside blocker from whom the ball is set toward will join the middle blocker. This enables the defense to use a normal four-man digging pattern. Occasionally, all three front court players will be required to block a superior center spiker; however, if the ball gets by the block, there are only three diggers left to cover the entire court.

If a *three-man block* is used, the two end blockers turn the ball in with their outside hands, the other four hands reaching over and parallel to the net.

> The end blocker protects his sideline by placing his inside hand on the ball at the point where it crosses the net and by turning his outside hand toward the ball.

Generally, a right-handed spiker has a stronger left leg and vice versa. The spiker almost invariably takes the last step in his spiking approach with his strongest leg, which normally results in greater jumping height. If this principle were applied to blocking, the right-handed middle blocker would normally use the crossover step when moving to his right; he would use the pivot and drive step when moving to his left.

When blocking the middle position, women may have to use more than three steps to arrive at the point of attack. The first and last steps are the same, but additional steps may have to be added to cover the distance to the takeoff point.

Whatever the movement used to assume a blocking position, it is important to plant the feet at a 90° angle to the net

Figure 5–16 *Turning the Spike In.* The blocker reaches over the net with her outside hand between the boundary line and the ball in order to prevent a wipe-off shot. Turning the spike in is a difficult skill to master; it should be constantly stressed during practice. (Barry Schreiber)

Figure 5–17 *One-Hand Block.* A one- ▶ hand block can be used to increase lateral coverage at the net. This is not a common tactic, but it is useful when the blocker is late and must move fast laterally to fill a hole in the block. (Barry Schreiber)

before jumping in order to squarely face the net. If the feet are not planted at a 90° angle, the blocker must turn in mid-air to square the shoulders—a difficult maneuver for all but the most coordinated players.

BLOCKING STRATEGY

Normally, the most effective blocker switches his rotation to the center, the next strongest blocker to the power, or on-hand, side, and the third blocker to the weak, or off-hand, side.

The middle position allows a mobile blocker to participate in almost all of the blocks against a two-hitter attacker, as well as in the majority of the blocks against a three-hitter attack. Since most teams set the spiker on his on-hand side more often than on his off-hand side, the next best blocker usually switches to his right. This generally leaves the remaining blocker to cover an off-hand spiker. Through the course of the season, the attacks made by many teams become predictable as they try to set the ball to a particular spiker in a certain rotation. A

simple attack chart kept on the opposition will tell the coach how to position his blockers in each rotation.

The coach should instruct his blockers to go after the ball or to protect a given area of the net. For example, the blockers may protect the line and force the spiker to hit crosscourt. The obvious advantage of this tactic is that the backcourt defenders can usually predict where the ball will be hit. The disadvantage is that the blocker becomes less aggressive and does not directly score as many points. A good middle blocker should never be instructed to zone block when playing next to a small or inefficient blocker. Since opposing spikers will continually attempt to hit over the smaller blocker, the middle blocker must have the freedom to key on the ball.

When blockers are instructed to go aggressively after the ball, the backcourt players must constantly adapt to the changing patterns of the block. Unless backcourt players are capable of reacting very quickly, they will not dig as many balls. An additional hazard is that blockers begin to overreact to the ball to such an extent that they begin to interfere

a

b

a   b

Figure 5–18 *Hitting Off the End Blocker.* When end blockers do not place their outside hand between the ball and the sideline, as in *a* and *b*, they are vulnerable to wipe-off shots. (Dr. Leonard Stallcup)

with each other (*see* Figure 5–23). To prevent this from happening, the coach should instruct the players to concentrate on protecting a given area of the net rather than aggressively moving toward the ball.

A *false weakness* in the block is employed occasionally to stop better spikers who like to watch the block closely. A false weakness calls for the blocker to position himself well inside the line and, in effect, to issue an invitation to the spiker to hit outside his position. When the spiker starts his armswing, the blocker quickly closes the unprotected area by moving his arms toward the line. The initial jump brings a blocker to his starting point; through lateral movement of his arms, an effective blocker can protect from 4 to 5 ft of the net.

In Figure 5–24, the blocker in effect issues an invitation to the spiker to hit

Figure 5–20 *Spiking Between the Blockers.* No workable defense can cover a hole between the blockers. Backcourt players are forced to rush to cover the blockers' error. (Barry Schreiber, *a*; Andy Banachowski, *b*)

a

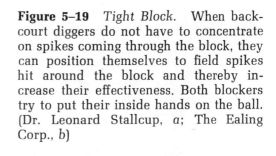

Figure 5–19 *Tight Block.* When back-court diggers do not have to concentrate on spikes coming through the block, they can position themselves to field spikes hit around the block and thereby increase their effectiveness. Both blockers try to put their inside hands on the ball. (Dr. Leonard Stallcup, *a*; The Ealing Corp., *b*)

b

a

b

Figure 5–21 *Forcing the Spiker to Hit Crosscourt.* Blockers Tom Ryan and Dick Montgomery take away the line to enable the digger in the background to be in an excellent position to dig Larry Rundle's spike. Rudy Suwara and Dan Patterson are backing up the spiker. (Bob Van Wagner)

Figure 5–22 *Helping the End Blocker.* Effective middle blockers with good jumping ability learn to reach over their smaller teammates when necessary. (Bud Fields)

to a certain area of the court. Then he attempts to block that area at the last split second. If the blocker does not alert his backcourt teammates as to his intention, they will take themselves out of the play by rushing to fill a hole that the blocker will close.

The same false weakness can be used to draw the spike to the middle or inside of the block. This blocking technique would be futile against beginning players, who simply jump and hit the ball as hard as possible, regardless of where the block has formed.

Figure 5–23 *Overlapping Block Coverage.* This situation should be avoided because it causes net errors and decreases the area of coverage. (Dr. Leonard Stallcup) ▶

READING THE SPIKER

Spikers usually attempt to avoid the block by hitting the ball crosscourt or down the line. A better blocker knows whether the normal spiker plans to hit inside or outside the block. He can judge this by analyzing or "reading" the spiker's approach to the set, his body align-ment, and, most important, his armswing. All spikers give some indication of where they plan to hit the ball, although better spikers try to conceal their intentions until the last split second or until the blockers are in mid-air. The blocker should watch the spiker's waist and then his eyes for last moment split-second adjustments.

The following hints will help the

a   b

Figure 5–24 *Closing the Unprotected Zone.* Experienced blockers use this effec-tive tactic against experienced spikers who watch the block before they con-tact the ball. Andy Banachowski demonstrates proper arm movement (*a*) in the initial position; in *b*, he moves laterally to block. (Stan Troutman)

blocker to "read" or analyze certain types of spikers and situations.

1. The spiker with a right angle or straight approach to the net is in a good position to hit a line shot.

2. An "on-hand" spiker can hit the line shot with greater accuracy and power than an "off-hand" spiker can.

3. Short spikers usually have developed a good line shot.

4. When the ball is set close to the sideline, it is easy for the spiker to hit the ball down the line.

5. Off-hand spikers who begin their approach off the court usually have a weak line shot.

6. The spiker almost always hits the ball crosscourt on a low, quick set.

7. Inexperienced and average spikers hit significantly more crosscourt angle shots than line shots from both the strong and weak sides of the court.

8. As balls are set farther away from the net, the tendency to hit crosscourt is increased.

9. When blocking a taller player or a spiker with a slow or late armswing, the blocker should jump later than he normally does.

10. If the spiker runs under the ball, the blocker should expect a low spike or an off-speed shot.

11. A slow approach or a lack of height on the jump usually indicates an off-speed spike.

12. Tired or off-balance spikers tend to dink or hit off the blocker's hands.

13. Prior to the serve, signals are often exchanged between the spiker and the setter. Close observation of verbal or hand signals often tells the blocker what type of play to expect.

14. A closer starting position prior to the spiker's approach indicates that there will be a play.

Figure 5–25 *Simultaneous Contact.* This play is usually called by the official unless the ball bounces off the players in a legal manner. The blocker must contact the ball with the heels of the hand when the ball is directly over the net or the opponent will force the ball to dribble down the blocker's arms. (Stan Troutman)

15. If the set travels inside the spiker's attacking shoulder, he will probably hit the ball across his body.

16. An average spiker on a poor set should not be blocked.

17. Every opposing spiker has favorite shots. *Learn them.*

COMMON ERRORS

There are several common errors that players make while attemping to block.

Touching the net
Caused by jumping forward or laterally or bending at the waist. Blockers should jump straight up without bending their waist.
Caused by extending arms in front of the body or throwing arms at the ball instead of raising them vertically above the shoulders.
Caused by reaching too far over the net. Blockers must learn their safe range of attack blocking.
Ball bounces down the front of the body on blockers' side of the net
Caused by jumping too far from the net.
Caused by slow arm and hand extension over the net.
Caused by leaving too large a space between hands and forearms.
Constantly missing the spike
Caused by closing the eyes. Blockers should see every ball that goes past the block. The blocker must keep the eyes on the ball after the spiker attacks.
Caused by watching the ball instead of the spiker. Primary attention should be focused on the approaching spiker because the ball comes into view as it nears the spiking arm.

Caused by blockers not moving close enough to each other and thereby creating a hole in the middle of the block (*see* Figure 5–20).
The ball ricochets off the hands and goes out of bounds
Caused by presenting a flat surface of the outside hand instead of keeping it between the ball and the side line.

TEACHING PROGRESSION

Blocking takes longer to teach and is more difficult to perfect than any other fundamental of volleyball.

During the first workout, the coach should instruct his players on blocking techniques and include blocking

Figure 5–26 *Jumping Too Far from the Net.* If the blocker touches the spike, the ball usually will bounce down the front of the body on the blocker's side of the net. This is a common error of beginning players. (Stan Troutman)

drills in every practice session thereafter. All players should learn the techniques of the end and middle blocking positions to give the coach or captain the necessary flexibility to change blocking tactics during the course of a game. Constant individual attention during blocking drills is necessary because players are rarely aware of their mistakes while blocking.

When teaching the block, train the players in the important individual aspects before attempting to perfect the technique as a team effort.

The following are some skills and drills for the coach to use in teaching blocking:

1. Administer the jump and reach test to determine what angle of knee flexion, armswing, and approach each blocker should use.
2. Demonstrate the following and then have players practice the following:
   Slide step and jump
   Slide step and forward one-step approach used to block taller opponents
   Slide step and diagonal one-step approach for blockers who are late in arriving at the proper blocking position
   Crossover step and jump (Note: Alternate to the right and left)
3. Lower net 2 ft
   Explain and demonstrate the arm and hand position used to attack block, soft block, turn the ball in, and close a hole between players to ensure a tight block
   Line up players along the lowered net and have them practice sliding the hands over the net

with the elbows in front of the body rather than on the side. Players should hunch the back to lock the shoulders and keep the eyes focused on the area above the net.

4. Raise net to under one foot of the regulation height.
   Station two players facing each other on opposite sides of a lowered net. One player tosses the ball to himself and spikes it at

Figure 5–27 *Hitting Through the Blocker.* This occurs if the blocker's hands are farther apart than the width of the ball or if the blocker's hands are held too loosely and the ball squirts through rather than rebounds into the spiker's court. (Dr. Leonard Stallcup)

two-thirds speed to the blocker who practices the correct hand and arm motion for the various blocks. The spiker progresses from hitting the ball at two-thirds speed to a predetermined area to hitting the ball at full speed, attempting to drive it by the blocker.

Add a middle blocker and emphasize turning the ball in and coordinating a tight block. The spiker should hit the ball from various angles and depths in the court.

*5. Have two players face each other on opposite sides of a regulation net.

One player simulates a spiking motion while the blocker reaches over the net and attempts to touch the spiker's fingertips.

6. Place a spiker on a 2-ft high bench. He tosses the ball up and spikes it at the blocker. The blocker practices the attack block, soft block, and turning the ball in. Add a middle blocker and coordinate a tight block.

7. Have two players face each other on opposite sides of the net about 3 ft apart. The spiker tosses the ball to himself and jumps straight up to hit it over the net. The blocker uses a slide step to intercept the spike.

8. Pair players of approximate height in two lines on each side of the net. Partners jump and touch hands above the net on the end, middle, and other end of the net. Emphasize a fast slide step and maximum jump. Change the drill by having one player swing his spiking arm as he jumps. His partner must move his arms and hands to intercept the mock spike. Repeat the drill, using the crossover step.

9. Place two benches close to the net, about 3 ft from the sideline and place a third bench near the center of the net. A spiker stands on each bench, tosses the ball up, and spikes it in rotation as the blocker moves from spiker to spiker using the slide or crossover step. To increase the difficulty of this drill, take away the benches and substitute three lines of spikers who hit in rotation to the single blocker.

GAME SITUATION DRILLS

After the blocker develops a blocking style that suits his individual coordination, agility, jump, and reach, drills simulating game situations should be initiated.

A good athlete requires about three years to be able to read the intentions of opposing spikers in top competition. Most players in open competition are still learning after they have passed the peak of their physical ability.

The following drills can be used to practice situations encountered in competition:

1. The spiker passes the ball to a setter who delivers a high, wide set. The blocker attempts to cut off his strongest shot or block the ball. One-on-one blocking situations are becoming more common each year as more teams switch to a three-hitter attack to set up a one-on-one play. Better spikers can usually beat a one-man block. Emphasize taking away the spiker's favorite angle or the best percentage shot for the particular set and approach used by the spiker.

2. Three blockers defend against two hitters. Station the spikers on the end of the net with the setter in the middle. Emphasize a tight, two-man block, with the off-blocker dropping back to the 10-ft line to dig a spike driven inside the middle blocker.

3. Three blockers v. three attackers. Emphasize that the middle blocker stay close to the net if he is late and that individual blockers take crosscourt spiking angles in one-on-one situations.

4. Three blockers v. three attackers. The center spiker hits a quick, low set close to the net, and the outside spikers hit a normal set. Emphasize that the primary responsibility of the middle blocker is the center spiker. Instruct the middle blocker to jump with the middle spiker and to recover and attempt to soft block the end spiker if he is fast enough. If he is out of position to soft block, he should remain close to the net and out of the play.

5. Two end attackers v. three blockers. The middle blocker deliberately moves in the wrong direction and attempts to recover and join the end blocker. Emphasize that the middle blocker should keep his hands close to the net and soft block when late in contacting the ball. The end blocker must take more of a crosscourt angle and attempt to help close the hole between blockers.

6. After the blocker returns to the floor, throw a ball near to him for him to set or to spike.

7. Station two players on opposite sides of the net. Toss a ball about 15 ft high within a foot of either side of the net. Players must decide to spike or block the ball. Empha-

size aggressive attack blocking and the formation of a roof around the ball with the hands. Toss 50 percent of the balls so that they fall directly on top of the net. Emphasize blocking the ball with the heels of the hand when part of the ball splits the net.

8. Instruct the setter to deliver sets outside the court so that the spiker must hit the ball crosscourt. Emphasize soft blocking by the end blocker so that he can turn the ball into the court. Instruct the middle spiker to leave a wide space between his hands so that he can cover more area above the net. Show him that the ball cannot go through his hands (unless he leaves

Figure 5–28 *Turn and Look.* The middle blocker is about to land on his right foot as he twists his body in the direction of the ball to play a dig from his teammate. He will take a step in the direction of the digger as he lands. The end blocker also watches the flight of the ball. (Barry Schreiber)

an extremely wide space) because of the angle of the ball's flight.

9. Construct blocking drills patterned to stop the attack of the chief oppo-nent. Instruct the second team to simulate the opposition's attack to familiarize blockers with their pat-terns.

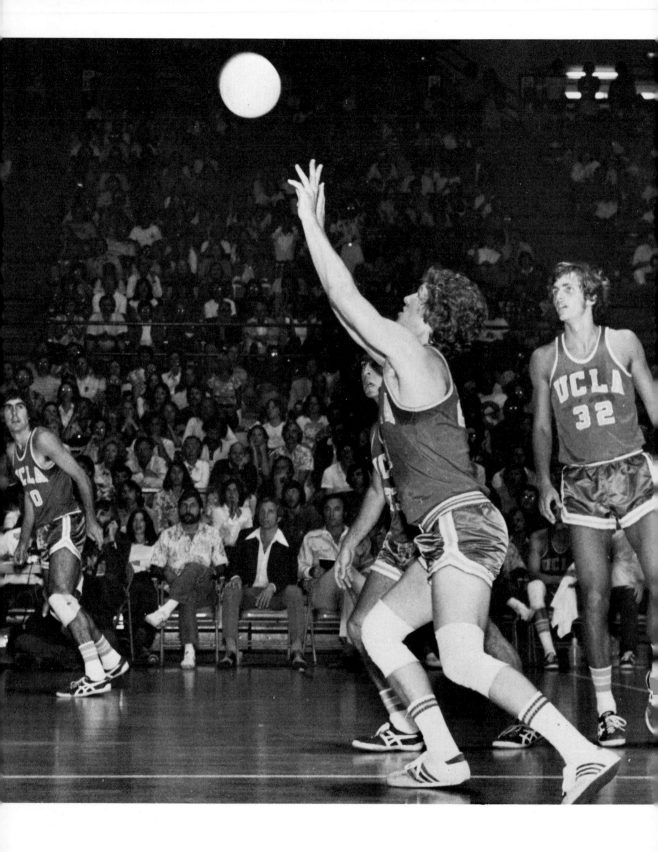

6

Individual Defensive Techniques

THE DIG

The fundamental digger's stance is illustrated in Figure 6–1. In a digger stance, the feet are spread farther apart than shoulder-width, and one foot is planted ahead of the other. The digger's weight is on the inside balls of the feet with the heels off the floor. The knees and hips are bent at approximately 90°. The elbows are held in front of the knees which are in front of the toes. The hands are extended frontally about waist high; the weight is forward.

Most players who do not have good lateral movement do not squat low to the ground or spread their feet farther than shoulder-width apart.

Drills where the player runs under the bottom of the net can be used to train players to maintain a low digger's stance. The digger starts 5 ft from the net and the coach stands 15 ft on the opposite side of the net. The coach throws the ball a few feet from the net on his side of the court and the digger runs under

the net and passes the ball back to the coach. It takes many hours of intensive training for players to learn to react quickly enough to ensure the best possible digging accuracy. The Japanese are the quickest defensive players in the world. To train for the dig, their coaches spike very hard balls at diggers from distances of less than 10 ft. Japanese coaches also have the digger face a wall from a distance of 6 to 7 ft and hit balls at the wall that rebound toward the digger.

When the rules were changed to allow blockers to reach over the net, the status of the quickly reacting player who could "dig" or pass the opponent's spike elevated. Aggressive blockers forced opposing setters to deliver the set 3 ft away from the net so that spikers could avoid the block; consequently, the backcourt defensive player no longer had to defend against "straight-down" spikes and had more time to react to the spike.

Players who are not afraid to go to the floor to recover the attack sufficiently increase their range of effectiveness to the extent that spikers rarely drive the ball directly to the floor.

The forearm pass should be used whenever possible because this technique provides the best possible control of a hard-driven spike under current rule interpretations. A hard spike received by an overhand pass is frequently called a "throw" by the official and is a poor percentage play.

The digger should use whatever stance is necessary to place the upper part of his body directly behind the oncoming ball. It is of little consequence whether the digger is in a balanced or unbalanced position, so long as the body is behind the ball to ensure maximum accuracy at contact.

Slow-moving balls require the digger to move the arms toward the intended

Figure 6–1 *Digger's Stance.* This stance is the same for all defenses. The body is in a semi-crouched position, with the feet spread slightly more than shoulder-width apart. The weight is forward on the balls of the feet, and the hands are held waist-high. (Stan Troutman)

Figure 6–2   *Going to the Floor.*   If players hope to excel, they must accept the responsibility of going to the floor in a dive or roll. Using this approach to dig hard-to-reach balls is as basic to the modern game of volleyball as the spike. (Barry Schreiber)

target area in order to provide the necessary momentum for the ball to travel the required distance. Diggers can attain greater accuracy with slow-moving balls if they use the elbow lock pass to provide prolonged contact with the ball. When digging a hard spike, the arms do not move, although the rest of the body is in motion. If the arms move toward the ball, the dig will rebound a great distance and will not have a controlled flight.

The digger often "cushions" hard-driven spikes so that they do not rebound back over the net. This is accomplished when the digger falls backward in an off-balance position as he contacts the ball. After the dig, the player contacts the floor with his buttocks, the small of his back, and his shoulders. Then he rocks forward to his

Figure 6–3   *Forearm Pass.*   With his elbows fully extended, Toshi Toyoda contacts the ball with the inner part of his forearm, close to his wrist. (The Ealing Corp.)

Figure 6–4 *Moving Behind the Ball.*
Player No. 26 contacts the ball just be-
fore his buttocks touch the floor. (Barry
Schreiber)

a   b   c

feet. His arms and shoulders should move forward as his feet touch the floor to assume a standing position.

A far more effective but little known technique for fielding hard spikes is the *high dig.* Players who use this technique move toward the oncoming ball and contact it while their legs move up from a low squatting position. To enable the dig to travel high in the air on the digger's side of the net, the arms should be held almost parallel to the floor, whenever the flight of the ball permits. Since the dig travels upward rather than forward, the player never has to cushion the ball. The player also has significantly greater body control (Figure 6–7).

ONE-ARM DIG

The one-arm dig is quite common and is usually used to increase the lateral range of the defender. It should be used only when the ball is out of effective range for the forearm pass to be feasible. The ball can be effectively contacted anywhere from the knuckles of the closed fist to the elbow joint. Beginning players should be instructed to contact the ball in the middle of the forearm. If they misjudge the ball and contact it higher on the forearm or lower on the hand, they will not misdirect the pass altogether.

The heel of the hand and the knuckles provide a good rebounding surface for hard-to-reach balls that require full arm extension.

Once players learn to land on the floor without absorbing the force of impact on

Figure 6–6 *Cushioning the Spike.* The digger does not follow-through with his arms or body, but rather contacts the ball as he moves backward. (Dr. Leonard Stallcup)

◄ **Figure 6–5** *Digging Off-Speed Shots.* Olympian Barbara Perry contacts the ball after being forced to move into an off-balance position to get behind it. (Dr. Leonard Stallcup)

Figure 6–7 *High Dig.* This technique eliminates the most frequent digging error: passing the spike back into the opponents' court. (Barry Schreiber)

Figure 6–8 *One-Arm Dig.* The one-arm dig is often used to back up the spiker and to pass block rebounds. The nonstriking arm extends in the other direction for better body control. (Dr. Leonard Stallcup)

Figure 6–9 *One-Arm Dig from the Back-court.* The one-arm dig is often used to field hard-driven spikes while the player moves laterally. (Stan Abraham)

their head, wrist, elbow, or knee, they should be run through vigorous digging drills which require them to leave their feet while fully concentrating on the flight of the ball.

The player should learn to roll to the floor when his body is placed in an off-balance lateral position. This technique allows the force of the fall to be absorbed by a large area of the body rather than allowing the wrist or knee joint to absorb the shock.

Figure 6–14 shows sequence shots of the dig and roll. The digger takes a wide step sideways with her right leg as her left leg extends in an attempt to position her body behind the ball (a). Upon contact, she is already low to the ground (b). After the ball is hit (c), her buttocks, back, and left shoulder contact the ground as knees bend (d). The player's body continues to roll over as the legs remain bent (e). As her toes contact the ground, she pushes her body to an upright position with her hands (e,f).

OVERHAND DIG

Current rule interpretations discourage using the overhand pass to dig a hard-driven spike. Some officials are in the habit of calling every overhand pass of a hard-driven spike a thrown ball. Since the overhand dig is a poor percentage play, coaches have instructed their diggers to stay deeper in the court so that balls spiked above their waist may travel out of bounds. This means that diggers can keep their weight forward to dive for balls in front of them and keep their hands below their waist to use the forearm pass or one-arm dig to field spikes.

Off-speed spikes and dinks can be fielded in the overhand position because officials are far more lenient on slow-

a   b

Figure 6–10 *Forearm Contact for One-Arm Dig.* The inner part of the forearm should be turned toward the ball. Beginners often swing the arm in a strictly vertical plane, which may cause the ball to rebound backward. (Los Angeles City Unified School District)

a

b

Figure 6–11 *Fist Contact for One-Arm Dig.* Fist contact is used when the ball is hard to reach or when the player wishes to pass the ball a greater distance. (The Ealing Corp.)

moving balls. The player should move quickly into position behind the ball and intended target area. Fingers should be spread and cupped, wrists tilted back so the passer can see the ball above the back of his hands. The ball should be contacted above the forehead; knees and arms should extend simultaneously as the wrists straighten.

When an overhand dig of a hard-driven spike is attempted, the player must be positioned directly behind the ball or the referee will probably call a throw. At the same time, the player can achieve longer contact with the ball and consequently greater control by falling backward as the ball is dug. This tech-

c

a   b

Figure 6–12 *Getting to the Ball.* Before players can concentrate on an approaching ball, they must be confident of their ability to fall without injury. (Barry Schreiber)

Figure 6–13 *Eyes on the Ball.* Better diggers keep their eyes on the ball at contact. (Dr. Leonard Stallcup)

nique is known as "cushioning" the spike and is recommended when digging hard-driven balls in the overhand position. During the mid-1960s, it was a popular technique among the better defensive players. However, because of the strict interpretation of a thrown ball when using the overhand dig, it is rarely used now.

DIVING

Diving is a common defense technique used to reach balls that cannot be passed accurately from a standing position. It is also an emergency play for recovering otherwise out-of-reach balls. The ball can be contacted while one foot is still on the ground or while the entire body is in the air. The height of the dive depends upon the height, distance, and speed of the oncoming ball.

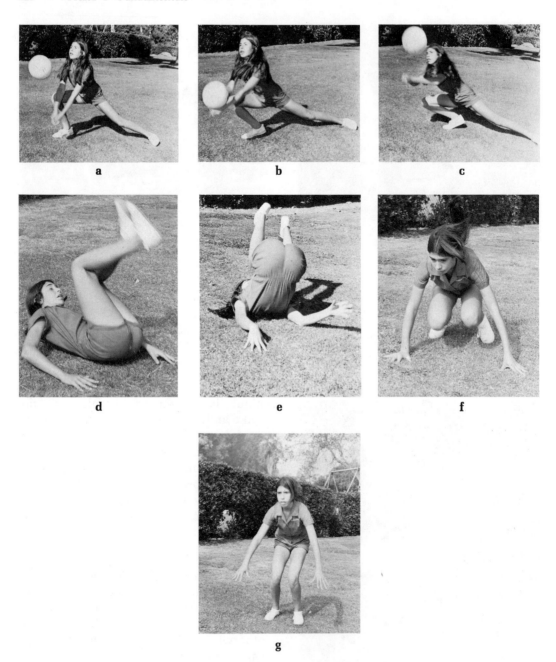

Figure 6–14 *Dig and Roll.* The digger positions herself to hit the ball and then rolls to a standing position. (Gary Adams)

◀ **Figure 6–15** *Overhand Dig.* Although it is still recommended to control slow-moving balls, the overhand dig of a hard-driven spike has become virtually obsolete under current rule interpretations. (Dr. Leonard Stallcup)

Figure 6–16 *Advanced Technique for Overhand Dig.* Olympian Sharon Peterson gains maximum control by moving laterally behind the ball and falling backward to cushion the momentum of the spike. (Bud Fields)

▼

a   b

Figure 6–17 *Low Dive.* The digger dives close to the ground and often uses the back of the hand to hit the ball. For easier landing, the palm is held toward the floor. (Barry Schreiber, *a*; Richard Mackson, *b*)

Many players prefer to play the ball with the back of their hand, particularly when digging a ball close to the floor. This *backhand dig* technique enables the player to keep his palms close to the floor in anticipation of a quick landing.

The higher the body is in the air, the harder it falls to the ground. In landing, it is important to try to absorb the shock with as much body surface as possible. The momentum should not be stopped by the arms; rather, it should be absorbed by the arms, chest, and stomach in that order. Since the movement is usually downward rather than forward, there is little opportunity to slide. Players with poor arm strength will absorb the fall in a jolting bounce.

When diving parallel to the net, it is very difficult to use the two-hand forearm pass and recover in time for a safe landing. Therefore, the one-arm pass is recommended.

In Figure 6–20, Toshi Toyoda crouches before taking the last step. His arms are in front while his forward foot pushes vigorously off the floor (*a*). His thrusting leg moves forward horizontally. He contacts the ball with a forearm pass (*c*) and then rotates his palms toward the floor in preparation for the landing (*e*). As he descends, his legs and feet are higher than his waist, his back is arched, and his head is up. Both arms are extended in order to contact the floor with both hands (*f*). To prevent violent contact with the floor, his body is arched correctly with his knees above his waist. His chest, stomach, and, finally, legs must now contact the floor; his body will spend the momentum by sliding along the floor.

If the ball is traveling slowly, the player must swing his arm across his body to direct it to the intended target area (Figure 6–21*a*, *b*). When digging a hard-spiked ball, the player should merely extend his arm.

Figure 6–21 shows the left-hand dig. The dive to the left should receive a great deal of attention in practice sessions because players dig poorly when they must dive to their left.

BODY POSITION

Defensive strategy currently calls for backcourt players to remain near the

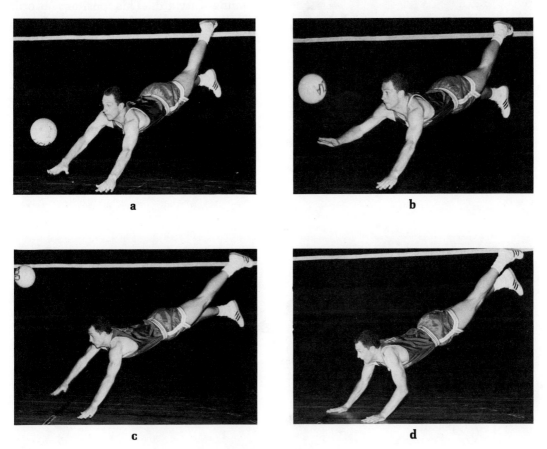

a

b

c

d

Figure 6–18 *Backhand Dig.* Palms are directed toward the floor before contact with the ball, which adds valuable inches to an effective digging range. To bump the ball high into the air, the player usually must flick his wrist upward. (Stan Troutman)

sideline and endline so that they will not have to dig hard-driven spikes in an overhand position. Hard spikes above a digger's waist are usually allowed to travel out of bounds. Therefore, the digger's basic position is a semi-squat in a wide stance with his feet slightly more than shoulder-width apart and his body leaning forward. This position affords quick lateral or forward movement. When expecting a hard spike, the player's hands should be held in an under-hand position at waist level so that they can be joined together quickly for a fore-

Figure 6–19 *High Dive.* Dodge Parker makes an all-out high-diving save. (Richard Mackson)

Figure 6–20 *Front Dive.* Toshi Toyoda demonstrates the front dive. (The Ealing Corp.)
▼ ▶

a   b   c

arm pass and easily raised or lowered to receive a spike. Studies by a Japanese researcher showed that a spiked ball travels from the net to the backline in .33 seconds for men and .50 seconds for women. It takes .39 of a second to move the hands from the shoulders to the knees and .44 of a second to move the hands from the knees to the shoulders.[1]

Often it is necessary for a player to assume a full squatting position to dig low balls. A wide stance should be used to maintain a controlled body position in this case.

[1] Hiroshi Toyoda, "Volleyball Coaching Seminar," in *Technical Journal* 1.1 (1974): 62.

MOVING TO THE BALL

Rather than merely reach for it with their arms, players should always strive to step toward the oncoming ball if time allows. Figure 6–23 shows the low squatting position used to make a dig. American players are somewhat unaccustomed to the low squatting position and require hours of repetitive drills in the low position until movement becomes automatic. A common error is to keep the legs extended and to bend from the waist.

The slide step used in volleyball is similar to the defensive step in basketball. The outside foot points in the direction of movement and the other foot quickly draws parallel to the first. Since legs never cross, the player always faces the ball. When the player must cover the

d

e

f

a

b

 Figure 6–21 *Left-Hand Dig.* The digger should jump off his left foot and contact the ball with the interior part of his forearm. (Stan Troutman)

c

Figure 6–22 *Lateral Recovery.* The digger protects his knees by arching his body after contact with the floor. He must also keep his neck arched upward to prevent his chin from contacting the floor. (The Ealing Corp.)

a

b

Figure 6–23 *Low Body Position.* Olympic captain Jane Ward demonstrates good balance with the center of her body above her back foot. (Dr. Leonard Stallcup)

Figure 6–24 *Moving Laterally.* Sharon Peterson continues to move laterally after digging the spike. (Bud Fields)

required distance in a short period of time, a lateral or forward lean of the body and roll may have to be added to the slide step so that he can get directly behind the ball for maximum passing accuracy.

The roll is used to prevent injuries and to return the player quickly to his feet. The ball is usually contacted just before thigh and buttocks hit the floor. After the buttocks contact the floor, the body continues to roll so that first the entire upper back, forward shoulder, knees, and toes contact the floor as the legs remain bent. The trailing foot contacts the floor as the player's hands push his body to an upright position. If the player contacts the floor too hard or too fast, it is because he has not gradually lowered his body prior to contact. To protect his head, the player's back must remain arched and his chin should remain tucked against his chest during the entire roll.

When speed is required to cover a large area of the court, the player should turn and run, taking short, fast steps. He should gradually lower his body to the height of the ball as he moves. If contact is made in an off-balance position, it is advisable to dive rather than risk an uncontrolled fall to the floor.

LEARNING THE DIVE

Players should not attempt the dive until they develop adequate arm strength. Many women do not have adequate arm strength to slow their landing and, consequently, they hit the floor on their chin. Push-ups and tricep presses develop the necessary arm strength to slow the body's fall to the floor. If a player cannot support his body on outstretched arms

Figure 6–25 *Full Roll.* A well-executed roll is a safe conclusion to off-balance lateral movement. (Dr. Leonard Stallcup)

a

b

Figure 6–26 *Dig and Dive.* The dive is also recommended to recover from off-balance lateral movement. (Barry Schreiber)

and hands while another player holds his feet off the floor in a horizontal position, he is not strong enough to learn the dive.

First, the player lies face down on a mat and arches his body so that his knees and feet are higher than his waist. Next, his partner holds his feet while he extends his arms and lowers his body to the mat. Then the player kneels and falls forward, pushing against the mat as his arms flex. The action is then attempted from a standing position: The player moves off the mat to the floor, falls forward from a standing position, and slides forward with his chest touching the floor. He returns to the mat and dives forward from a squatting position. Next he tries a two-step approach and dives forward.

Finally, the partner lobs a ball to the player who executes a diving save.

When a player learns the correct technique of diving without the ball, he is ready to progress to the backhand dig on the mat. Initially, the coach or partner should lob the ball in a controlled manner and then gradually increase the distance and speed as progress is made. Beginners should be encouraged to field high balls, thereby preventing the common tendency of falling forward and striking the mat with the knees first.

A pepper drill can be used to practice the dig. A coach or partner stands at distances of 10 to 30 ft and alternates hard-driven spikes with off-speed shots and dinks directed at the digger just out of his reach. The digger dives, rolls, and

a   b

Figure 6–27 *Teaching the Dive.* The instructor puts emphasis on keeping the knees and the chin up. (Barry Schreiber)

a

b

c

a

b

Figure 6–28 *On the Mats.* When the player can arch his body and protect his knees, he should practice the long, low dive on the mat. (Stan Troutman)

Figure 6–29 *Pepper Drill.* Pepper Drills should be included in every practice session. (Barry Schreiber)

makes whatever movements are called for according to the height, direction, and speed of the ball.

When the player is learning correct techniques, the coach should frequently stop the drill and comment on his execution. After the dive is mastered, emphasis should be on many repetitions involving diving and rolling saves. When a player automatically goes to the floor to dig the ball without any hesitation, the necessary conditioned reflex for competition has been formed.

Players should also receive plenty of instruction at each defensive court position they will be required to play. The coach can stand on a table and attack from various positions along the net to simulate game conditions.

Other players can retrieve balls and form a supply line to the coach so that the drill never has to slow down for lack of a ball. This concentrated digging drill can send the player to the floor numerous times within a short period. If repeated often enough, diving and rolling saves will become conditioned reflexes.

When individual defense techniques have been covered, players must learn their team defensive responsibilities. The coach can use the table spike technique against three backcourt players and an off-blocker. Once defensive responsibilities are learned, two blockers can be added to field a full defensive team. Finally, the defensive team should practice against a live offense.

II

Team Play

7

Offense

The decision to use a two- or three-hitter attack for the offense depends on the limitations and strengths of the team. A simple two-hitter offense with a few options is the best offense for the majority of high school teams. When a team has four spikers who can hit a high, wide set reasonably well, there is usually no tactical reason to install a three-hitter attack.

Recently, an overwhelming majority of college and open teams have switched to the three-hitter offense. These teams often attempt advanced plays and options which lead to excessive errors. The great variety inherent in the three-hitter attack is successful only if the players have the ability and practice time necessary to pass accurately. It is far better to master the simple two-hitter attack than to be fairly good at the more difficult three-hitter offense.

An offense attempts to hit the ball over the net so that the defense cannot return it. The normal offensive pattern calls for the ball to be passed to a setter close to

the net; the setter then delivers the ball to a spiker to hit into the opponents' court.

PLAY SETS

A team that passes accurately and has good setters should use play sets, which normally create numerous situations in which only one blocker defends against the spiker. Setters should be given the freedom to call their own sets or plays as they see fit. If the coach tells the setter to use only certain sets and plays in particular situations, the opposition will soon be able to predict the offensive strategy. Setters may call for a play at any time during the course of a game, before or after the serve. If the setter is not selecting the plays in an intelligent manner, he should be substituted out of the game to enable the coach to confer with him about the play selection before he returns to the game.

Signals from the setter to the spiker can be given verbally or by hand signs.

Some setters signal by showing a number of fingers that represent a certain play to the spiker. Some coaches prefer to speed up the procedure by using pre-arranged verbal signals. For example, a setter may say "A" to indicate a specific attack pattern to the spiker. It is really not necessary for the setter to be secretive when signaling for the play because the setter has the option of delivering the ball to another spiker when the defense stacks its block on one player.

Play sets are automatically called off if the primary setter cannot reach the pass; otherwise, the spiker or spikers are totally committed to the play. When a back-up setter must step in to deliver the set, a regular set is used. In all other situations, the setter makes the final decision of to whom to deliver the ball. This stipulation motivates each spiker to put forth maximum effort in the approach because each spiker can expect to receive the set. Many coaches stipulate that the setter must always signal one spiker to expect a regular set in the event that the pass is not accurate enough to deliver the play set.

Six play sets and two variations on these sets enable any team to create an imaginative offense: the one-set, two-set, three-set, four-set, five-set, and regular set are standard procedure in most three-hitter attacks. The slow-one and slow-three sets may be added if desired. Even two-hitter attacks can use all of the above sets in their offense.

The most exciting and important play in the three-hitter attack is the well-executed spike of an extremely low set placed only a foot or so above the net. The only way the defender can block this spike is to jump with the spiker before the ball is set, thus placing the entire offense in a one-on-one situation.

The One-Set

Spiking the one-set is a mandatory play in a successful three-hitter attack. The Japanese perfected this play to defeat the block of taller opponents by using split-second timing between setter and spiker.

To perform the one-set, the spiker moves to within a few feet of the setter as the setter is moving into position to receive the pass. The setter must gauge the spiker's approach while watching the pass. If the spiker is late, the setter may drop to a squatting position before contacting the ball in order to give the spiker

Figure 7–1 *Spiking the One-Set.* The spiker relies on the setter to place the ball in front of his spiking arm. (Barry Schreiber)

time to jump. If the spiker is early, the setter must extend his arms or jump-set the ball as quickly as possible. The spiker should jump as the ball touches the setter's hands in order to be at the apex of his jump, with his spiking arm cocked as the ball is rising above the tape.

If the blocker jumps with the spiker, the setter may set to another player; if the blocker does not jump, the spiker can easily put the ball on the floor. If the pass is made more than a few feet from the net, the setter must put more force on the one-set to deliver it in front of the attacking arm of the spiker. If the spiker mistimes the approach, the set will often cross the net. If the pass is off the net, the middle spiker automatically prepares to hit the "one-shoot" instead of the straight up and down one-set. Better setters can deliver the one-set laterally or backward, which tends to leave the middle blocker on the floor. If the setter is close to the net, the attacker (spiker) should jump close to the setter. If the setter is 5 ft away from the net, the spiker should angle the approach so that he arrives 5 ft away from the setter who then delivers the ball to the spiker at a

a

b

Figure 7–2 *Elbow Leads the Way.* When hitting one-, or quick, sets, the elbow should be held high and the ball hit with a quick wrist snap and minimum arm and shoulder movement. (Barry Schreiber, *a*; Andy Banachowski, *b*)

a

b

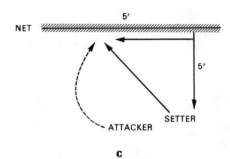

c

Figure 7–3 *One-shoot.* In *a*, the pass has reached the setter about 9 ft from the net so the spiker cannot approach close to the setter. The ball has been passed to the left side of the court because the middle attacker is left-handed. (Norm Scindler)

45° angle. (*See* Figure 7–3*c* for a diagram of the one-shoot.)

The *slow one-set* is used by players who do not have a quick armswing and by players who can beat the middle blocker in a one-on-one situation. The spiker attacks the ball after it reaches its peak, about 2 ft above the net. If the spiker hits the ball after it reaches its peak, he has a better opportunity to direct the spike. The ball is therefore set almost straight up to give the spiker the best opportunity to defeat the middle blocker. There is a disadvantage to the offense on a wide set because the middle blocker does not have to commit himself until after the ball is set and thus has a better opportunity to reach the outside spiker.

The Two-Set

The ball in the *two-set* usually travels from 3 to 4 ft above the net. The two-set play does not require the same split-second timing as the one-set and can be mastered by any good spiker. Because of the extra height on the set, the spiker usually encounters at least one blocker defending against the play. Although the approach is almost completed before the setter touches the ball, the spiker does

Figure 7–4 *The Slow One-Set.* No. 14 (far left of photo) has delivered a slow one-set. He has time to lower his hands to his waist as the spiker cuts the ball away from the middle blocker. The slow one-set can be directed with better accuracy then the quick set, but it will not "freeze" the middle blocker as the quick set will. (Andy Banachowski)

Figure 7–5 *The Two-Set.* The 1974 Los Angeles City Champions use the back two-set in their offense. (Barry Schreiber)

not jump until after the setter contacts the ball. The spiker then hits on its downward flight. The placement of players along the net is determined by the setter's position because the spiker runs to the setter for the play. The two-set can be set forward or backward.

The Three-Set

In the *three-set,* the ball is hit about 10 ft from the left sideline and delivered low and fast to the middle spiker. The

ball should not reach a height of more than 2 ft above the net. The three-set was designed to allow the middle attacker to overcome a slow middle blocker. It is a good play to use after the middle blocker begins to anticipate the one-set. When the middle blocker begins to key on the three-set, he isolates the off-hand spiker in a one-on-one blocking situation. Japanese and Korean teams use a three-set to the left attacker when the middle attacker approaches for a one-set.

The *slow three-set* can be used by the left attacker when the middle spiker is approaching for a one-set. The set is lobbed 10 ft from the left sideline. It is only effective when the middle attacker can "freeze" the middle blocker to allow the left spiker to hit the ball crosscourt. The height of the set depends on the jumping ability of the attacker.

The Four-Set

The "shoot," or *four-set,* is placed about a foot from the sideline, at a height of 1 to 2 ft above the net. The play is very difficult for the middle blocker to cover when the ball travels a distance of 15 to 20 ft from setter to spiker. The play forces the middle blocker to be late on the block, which leaves the crosscourt area open for a hard-driven spike.

The Five-Set

The *five-set* is a back lob set to the spiker on the right sideline. It is designed to create a one-on-one situation for the off-hand spiker. On a perfect pass, the five-set travels about 10 ft before the spiker contacts the ball. If the pass is made away from the net, the ball must be set higher to give the attacker time to see the block and the ball from a more difficult approach.

The Regular Set

The *regular set* should be used in the three-hitter attack when the offense wants to take advantage of a weak blocker. This set can be delivered to either the sideline or the middle of the

a

b

Figure 7–6 *The Three-Set.* This play is used to split the block formed by the middle and end blockers. Delivered 10 ft from the sideline, it is usually spiked away from the middle blocker. (Norm Scindler)

a   b

Figure 7–7   *The Four-Set.*   The four set is used in two- and three-hitter offenses to place the left spiker in a one-on-one situation with the end blocker. (Bud Fields, *a*; Bob Van Wagner, *b*)

court. The ball should travel in a rather vertical path. This is the best percentage set to use when the ball is passed inaccurately.

TWO-HITTER ATTACK

The basic offensive alignment is the *four-two*. The four-two uses four players (spikers or hitters) who are responsible for hitting the ball over the net and two players (setters) who are responsible for setting the ball to the spiker.

M-Formation

The M-formation, the first formation that beginning players should learn, positions

Figure 7–8   *Five-Set.* No. 34 is jumping to hold the middle blocker as the setter (No. 27) back sets the ball to the off-hand spiker. (Norm Scindler)

the setter at the middle-front of the court. Many teachers require each player to set when rotating to the middle-front position in order to give every player an opportunity to develop ball-handling skills. In competition, however, coaches only allow the best setters to set.

In Figure 7–10, the setter is in the middle-front position, ready to receive a pass. The five remaining players are lined up in a receiving formation that resembles the letter "M." The set should travel in an arc at a height of 4 to 10 ft above

the net and drop about 2 ft from the net at the outside right- or left-front corner of the net (see Figure 7–11).

Setter Switch

When the front-row setter rotates to an outside position, he must switch to the center after the serve so that he is in position to receive the pass. The switch starts as soon as the ball is served; the setter can remain in this position until the ball is dead. Before the next serve, the setter must return to his original position.

In Figure 7–12, the setter is in the right-front position. He should start about 5 ft from the sideline to allow the spiker on the right to maintain a normal position for formation, as in Figure 7–13. The rest of the players line up in an M-formation as they did when the setter was in the middle.

When the front-row setter rotates to an outside position (Figure 7–13b and c), a switch to the center of the court should

Figure 7–9 *Regular Set.* A regular set should be delivered to a superior jumper whenever he is opposed by a small blocker. The set ball should be set high enough to allow for a long approach and a maximum jump to enable the spiker to hit over the block. (Bud Fields)

Figure 7–10 *M-Formation.* A high pass is dropping into the center of the court within 2–4 ft of the net. The setter is in a good position to receive the pass. (Los Angeles City Unified School District)

be made to put the setter in a better position to set to either spiker (Figure 7–13a, b). The "switch" is started as soon as the ball is contacted for the serve. The setter must return to the original position in the rotation before the next serve.

The two setters line up diagonally opposite each other, as do the two best spikers, so that one will always be in the front row. As basic fundamentals are learned and as skill and experience increase, the strongest spikers become apparent.

As the setter switches into the middle of the line up from the outside, one of the spikers must switch with the setter. If the best spikers are lined up so that they precede a setter in the service order,

Figure 7–11 *Set.* The setter has placed the ball high in the air for the spiker in the right-front position. (Los Angeles City Unified School District)

Figure 7–12 *M–Formation: Setter in the Right-Front Court.* The team's two best ball-handlers are setters who stand diagonally opposite one another so that one setter is always in the front row. (Stan Troutman)

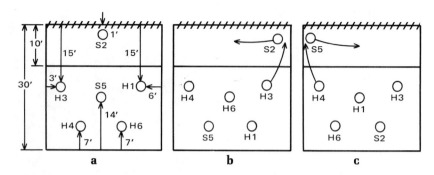

Figure 7–13 *Setter Switch.* The setter (S) is in the middle (*a*); on the right (*b*); and on the left (*c*).

Figure 7–14 *Facing the Strongest Hitter.* By moving as far to the side of the court as possible without overlapping the off-hand spiker's position, the setter (left foreground) can deliver a larger percentage of sets to his on-hand spiker (far right). (Stan Troutman)

they should switch so that they hit twice from their on-hand, or left-front, side; of course, this applies to a right-handed spiker. A left-handed spiker should line up so that he hits twice from his on-hand, or right, side. In Figure 7–13*b*, hitter No. 4, who is in the left-front position, spikes from the on-hand side as setter No. 2 switches into the center. In Figure 7–13*c*, after rotation of setter No. 2 to the back row, the other setter (No. 5) comes to the net. Hitter No. 4 now switches with the setter next to him and hits for the second time from the left-front position.

There is no need to switch when the setters rotate to the middle of the court. The front spikers pull back off the net to about center court, with the left-front player very near the left sideline and the right-front player crowding toward the center of the court, slightly toward the side from which the opponents are serving. The center back player is in the center of the court, even with or slightly behind the front-row spikers, in order to cover the area vacated by the setter who is at the net. The left- and right-back players stand between the front-row players, about 7 ft from the backline.

Facing the Stronger Hitter

If one of the two spikers is significantly stronger than the other, the setter in the middle front rotation may move to the opposite side of the court and face the stronger player. Since forward sets are usually delivered with greater accuracy than over-the-head or back sets, this tactic allows the setter to make a percentage play. Since the setter is still in the middle front position, he may not overlap the right-front spiker.

Backing Up the Passer

When the ball is served, at least one player should back up the passer. If the ball is served to the middle front, as in Figure 7–15, the player behind him moves directly in line with the serve in the event the frontcourt player decides to let the ball go by him. The other backcourt player stands deep in the court in case the ball rebounds backward. Spikers do not begin their approach until they see that the pass will reach the setter. In the event of a bad pass, all 5 players must be ready to step in and set the ball to one of the players at the front corners.

The player in the back row should tell the front-row receiver whether to pass the ball or to let it go by. The back-row passer must accurately judge the height and speed of the serve while evaluating the ability of his front-court teammate to pass the ball. Even though he calls for

Figure 7–15 *Backing Up the Passer.* The right-back player is shown backing up the middle back passer in the four-two formation. (Stan Troutman)

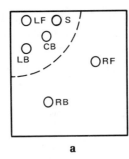
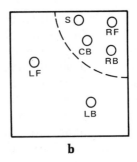

a   b

Figure 7–16 *Four-Two Spiker Coverage.* Covering the spiker should be stressed constantly during practice. A set to the left front is shown in *a*; a set to the right front is shown in *b*.

another player to receive the serve, the backcourt player should always be in a direct line with the ball in case signals are mixed up.

Backing Up the Spiker

After the set, all players back up the spiker to handle *block rebounds*. This means covering the spiker in case the ball rebounds off the blocker's hands back into their court.

If the ball is set to the left-front spiker, the setter and other players move quickly in unison to a designated area. The left back comes in behind the spiker down the line from about 2 to 5 ft behind the spiker—depending on how close the set is to the net and the abilities of the opposing blockers. The center back player stations himself behind the spiker at the same distance as the left back, but between the left back and the setter. The setter completes the half-circle that surrounds the spiker by positioning himself about 2–3 ft from the net. The right-front player pulls back off the net toward the rear of the court, and the right back moves toward the center of the court to the left side near the base line; both are then ready for a ball hit off the block.

If the set is to the right-front player, the coverage is exactly the same on the opposite side of the court. If the ball is set within 18 in. of the net against aggressive blockers, the back-up players should crowd very close to the spiker in anticipation of the ball being blocked straight down. This tactic is not necessary against a small or poor block.[1]

Once the players reach their assigned positions, they should squat close to the floor, with their arms outstretched and weight forward. Even All-American performers sometimes lose their concentration and watch the play. The key to backing up the spiker is *staying low* to give a player more time and distance to react to the block.

[1] Allen E. Scates and Jane Ward, *Volleyball* (Boston: Allyn and Bacon, 1975), p. 46.

THREE-HITTER ATTACK

In the three-hitter attack, all six players can spike. Two spikers are designated as setter–hitters because of their superior ball-handling ability. The three players at the net spike and one back row player sets. This formation offers skilled players an opportunity for multiple offensive plays. Most teams participating in international competition use a three-hitter attack. Because all three players in the front row become spikers, the player who cannot spike adequately usually becomes a backcourt substitute.

Coaches find that players prefer the three-hitter attack over the slower four-two attack because it keeps the team moving constantly and provides a real challenge to players and coaches. Its ob-

Figure 7–17 *The Pass.* The pass is the most important offensive technique in the three-hitter attack. (Barry Schreiber)

vious spectator appeal does much to popularize the sport wherever the offense is introduced. If the offense is executed correctly, spikers have an opportunity to hit the ball with only one blocker with which to cope.

The Pass

> The attack usually functions in direct relationship to the accuracy of the first pass.

Longer practices and concentrated individual and team passing drills are needed to perfect passing techniques. Since there is a great deal more movement in the three-hitter attack, physical and mental endurance must be built and maintained at a high level. A poorly conditioned team may get by using the two-hitter system, but the timing and pinpoint passing required in the three-hitter attack cannot be maintained in long matches and tournaments by poorly conditioned athletes.

Since a poor pass in this system destroys the offensive patterns by forcing the weaker ball-handlers to set and the weaker spikers to hit, it is not beneficial to use this offense unless players can pass accurately. If a team is continually forced into the four-two system by bad passes, it is better to play a straight four-two on the serve reception and allow the best ball-handlers to set the best hitters. A team may elect to use the three-hitter attack only on the "free ball," when it can be passed accurately.

On-Hand Spiking

If the ball is passed within 5 ft of the net and approximately 8 to 12 ft from the

a   b

Figure 7–18 *Setter Facing the Middle-
and Left-Front Spiker.* In this position,
with a flick of his wrist, the setter can
deliver the ball to either spiker. (Dr.
Leonard Stallcup, *a*; Barry Schreiber, *b*)

right sideline, the setter can easily deliver a front set to either the left- or
center-front spikers, who will approach
the set from their advantageous on-hand
side.

Right-handed spikers have an excellent opportunity to boost their spiking
efficiency because they approach the set
from their strongest side in two out of

Figure 7–19 *Back Set to the Open
Spiker.* The setter alertly back sets the
ball to the open player as defending
blockers leave the floor with the middle
attacker (No. 6). (Barry Schreiber)

three rotations. The off-hand spiker, who approaches from behind the setter in the right front, is often relatively ignored by the blockers and can often hit a wide back set unopposed. In Figure 7–19, the blockers have concentrated on No. 6, and the middle spiker has left the off-hand spiker without a blocker.

Back-Row Setter

In the three-hitter attack, the setter always comes from the back row. Most teams only have two players who are capable of setting. They are placed diagonally opposite each other and a setter is assigned to each of the three back row positions. When the setter is in the left-back position, it is difficult for him to run across the court to the right of center, turn, face the two on-hand hitters, and set the ball.

Some teams revert to a four-two play set when their setter is in the left-back position. Most teams use a four-man receiving pattern when the setter is in the left-back position and move both the setter and left-front spiker up to the net. This gives the setter a shorter distance to run to the predetermined passing area and enables the spiker preceding the setter to hit the quick set in the middle when in the left-front and middle-front positions. This type of offensive specialization increases the effectiveness of spikers and setters.

When the setter is in the left-back position, it may be necessary to allow the right-back player to handle the setting. If this is the case, the player preceding the setter in the serving rotation (called the *technique player*) must be a good ball-handler. Technique players must place themselves diagonally opposite one another so that one always plays

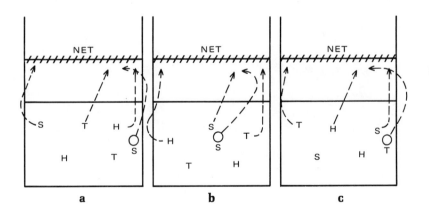

Figure 7–20 *Technique Player.* H= Hitter, S=Setter, T=Technique player, O=Player setting the ball. In *a*, a setter is in the right back of the court; in *b*, the setter is in the middle back; and in *c*, a technique setter is in the right back.

the right-back position when the setter is in the left-back position. The addition of the technique players eliminates the most vulnerable service receiving position of the *six-two* system because the setter now has a shorter distance to travel to receive the pass.

The best formation for the six-two offense is as follows: the two best hitters stand diagonally opposite each other; the technique player and setters stand opposite each other. In Figure 7–20c, the technique player (right back) moves from the right sideline to the passing area in the right side of the court. If the setter moves from the left sideline, his team may become vulnerable to fast sideline serves directed in his path. The three rotations of the six-two are sound, fundamental receiving positions for the three-hitter attack. The basic pattern of the six-two is to pass the ball to the setter in the right-front center of the court.

Six-Two Serve Reception

In lining up to receive the serve, the three front players move away from the net to about midcourt.

The left-front player plays a few feet off the left sideline and the right-front player moves in a direct line between the server and the right-back corner of the court. The middle-front player stands between these players. The left- and right-back players play about 6 ft behind and between the front-row players. Players must assume their positions as quickly as possible so they will not be surprised by a quick serve. Every player must anticipate receiving the serve. The front-row players should ignore the ball if it is above their shoulders. Backcourt players should call "Mine!" when they want to receive the serve. If the ball is above the backcourt players' shoulders, it will be called out. The player closest

a

b

Figure 7–21 *Setter Moving from the Middle-Back Court.* No. 9 moves toward his target area as the server contacts the ball (*a*). All five players watch the passer in case they must set an inaccurately passed ball (*b*). (Stan Troutman)

to the line next to the receiver should yell "In!" or "Out!" on marginal serves.

Receivers should watch the server even before he has the ball. Most servers stand near the sideline when serving crosscourt and 7 to 10 ft from the sideline when serving down the line. Other servers move up to the endline to serve short to a front-row player. Almost all servers point their front foot toward the area to which they intend to serve. A few good teams learn to take advantage of a clue like this by adjusting their position a half step or so toward the area to which the serve is aimed.

Players should move into the ball whenever possible and should never receive the serve while backing up. When balls are served in the seam of two positions, the player moving toward the target area is in the best tactical position to receive the serve. When one receiver is superior to another, the coach may designate the seam to be up to two-thirds of the area toward the inferior receiver, rather than the mid-line between the players. The passer uses a slide step to move toward the ball and points the outside foot to the target area before contacting the ball. When the receiver contacts the ball, all five players turn and watch the passer in case they must set an inaccurately passed ball (Figure 7–21*b*).

In the three-hitter system, the jump set is used effectively by the front-row player, who reacts with split-second timing to the opposing block. If the blocker does not jump with the setter, the setter delivers a one set; if the blocker does jump, he sets the ball to an end spiker and creates a one-on-one blocking situation. The jump set is used by backcourt setters to confuse the block.

Figure 7–22 *Spiking a Jump Set.* No. 1 continues upward after the ball is hit off his fingertips by his spiker. (Stan Troutman)

Figure 7–23 *Forming a Semi-Circle to Back Up the Spiker.* Note the low position of the first three players backing up the spiker. (Norm Scindler)

Backing Up the Spiker

When backing up the hitter in the six-two play, the two spikers who do not receive the set and the setter from the back row must move quickly to form a semicircle around the hitter.

The depth at which the three front players supporting the spiker play depends on the closeness of the set, the ability of the opposing blockers, and the spiking habits of the attacker. Attackers who hit low tend to be blocked straight down and require supporting players to move close to the net in low positions. Small blockers tend to softly block the ball deep into the attackers' court so supporting players should stay deeper in the court.

The two players providing secondary coverage fill the gaps in between the front line players and cover the ball that rebounds deep in the court. The setter is the key player who moves into the area where most of the blocked rebounds fall. Setters must be reminded to follow their set, particularly when setting over their heads.

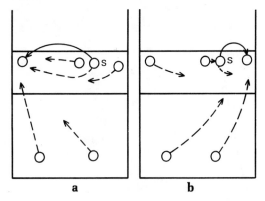

Figure 7–24 *Covering the Normal Set.* In *a*, the set is to the left front; *in b*, it is to the right front.

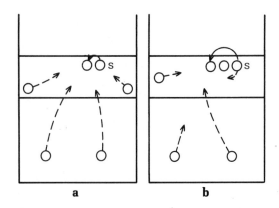

Figure 7–25 *Covering Play Sets.* Supporting players must get close to the spiker because blocked balls tend to rebound straight down (*a*). The right-cross play uses a two-set to the right-front spiker, who crosses behind the middle spiker (*b*).

In Figure 7–24*a*, the ball is set to the left-front spiker; the center front has approached and jumped for the fake set. The center front must now move quickly to assume the "back-up" position about 2 to 3 ft from the net. The setter, in turn, must go around the center-front spiker to get into position behind the spiker and between the left back and center front. The remaining players back up the spiker as they would in the 4–2 system.

In Figure 7–25*a*, the center spiker receives the set. The outside spikers must move in quickly to back up the hitter while the setter moves to get behind the hitter and between the two outside spikers. The two back-row players are deep between the setter and the outside spikers.

In Figure 7–25*b*, the middle attacker is still in the air feigning a one-play when the ball is hit and obviously out of the play. The setter steps toward the attacker as the left-front and right-back players form the rest of the semi-circle. The left-back player covers deep rebounds off the block.

PLAYER SPECIALIZATION

Offensive plays should be based on the physical strengths and qualifications of team members. Until the coach knows who the best six players are, it is impossible to refine the three-hitter attack. Players should be trained to take advantage of their physical capacities in order to perform specific assignments on the offense.

From 1970 to 1975, UCLA won five NCAA Volleyball Championships using a different three-hitter attack with each team. In the 1974 season, UCLA concentrated on three positions: the quick spiker, the power spiker, and the setter. The quick spiker hit the one-set from the left-front and middle positions and played the middle blocker positions. After the quick spiker blocked the middle, he hit a one-set during any scoring opportunity. The power spiker hit in the left front in his left and middle rotations (*see* Figure 7–26*b* and *c*) and blocked on the left side. This player hit from the left during any scoring opportunity. The setter hit left, middle, and right and blocked the right side. During a scoring opportunity, the setter was a right-side specialist. Substitutes were designated for the three positions as quick, power, and setter and picked up the same offensive assignments as the first team when they entered the game. When the UCLA team was on defense, the players were always stationed in their specialty areas, ready for the transition to offense.

Advanced Patterns and Plays

Many different serve reception patterns and plays are used in the six-two attack,

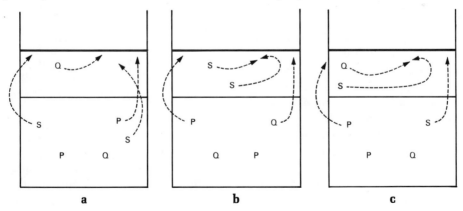

Figure 7–26 *The UCLA System.* S = Setter, Q = Quick spiker, and P = Power spiker. In *a*, the setter is in the right-back position; in *b*, in the middle-back position; and in *c*, in the left-back position.

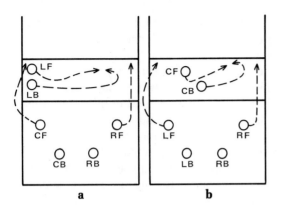

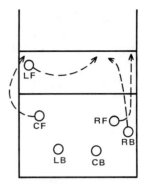

Figure 7–27 *Four-Man Receiving Pattern.* It is not necessary for the setter to run very far when this pattern is used (*a*). If the center-front player is a poor passer, he should move under the net so he is taken out of the receiving pattern and can concentrate on the attack (*b*).

Figure 7–28 *Changing Attack Positions.* This can be easily accomplished by assuming the four-man receiving pattern.

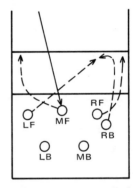

Figure 7–29 *Pass and Switch.* Upon receiving the serve, the middle front player changes assignments with the left-front spiker.

depending upon the personnel, playing rotation, and the opponents' strength. If the middle-front spiker is a good passer, but not quite fast enough to hit the one-set from a normal position, he can start from the spiking line that is 10 ft from the net. When the middle-front player is not a valuable passer, the four-man receiving pattern in Figure 7–27*b* can be used.

Many outstanding national teams use a four-man receiving formation to receive the serve. It is a very efficient method if four superior passers receive the serve because the player approaching for the one-set is divested of serve-receiving responsibilities and can concentrate on the attack.

It may be desirable to use the four-man receiving pattern when the setter is in the right back position if the left-front spiker wants to switch attack positions with the center-front spiker.

Coaches may elect to change attack assignments only when the middle-front player receives the serve in the regular formation. Many middle spikers have great difficulty in passing the ball accurately and in recovering to arrive at the point of attack in time for a quick one-set. By switching outside for a normal high set, they have time to concentrate fully on the accurate placement of their pass (*see* Figure 7–29).

There are many other variations that can be used when the first pass is perfected. The cross, tandem, and thirty-one plays are particularly effective when the opposition begins to block the "one-play." These plays require a great deal of practice before timing is perfected.

If the blocker jumps with the first attacker, the setter has the option of delivering the ball to the right-front spiker who crosses behind the middle attacker and jumps immediately after the first spiker jumps. The second spiker can ask for a slow one- or two-set and approach behind the first spiker's heels or from the middle of the court. (*See* Figure 7–30.) The fake cross should be used after the right cross has been perfected. The right-front player fakes a right cross and returns behind the setter to hit a two-set.

The outside blocker usually jumps with the quick attacker because the middle blocker is assigned to the right-front player during the right cross. The right-front player should contact the ball as the opposing blocker is returning to the floor after defending against the quick attacker. (*See* Figure 7–31).

The USA Men's Volleyball Team recently added a few plays which they use after the one-set to the middle attacker has been used successfully to score or to gain side outs. The right-front attacker crosses in front of the setter to hit a one-

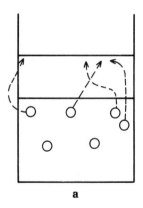

a

b

Figure 7–30 *Right Cross.* The middle attacker approaches for the one-set which he should receive if the blocker remains on the floor. In *b*, No. 14 has held two blockers after faking a quick hit. The spiker has swung around behind him to spike over the blockers on the floor. (Barry Schreiber)

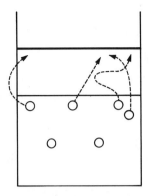

Figure 7–31 *Fake Cross.* This play is used to confuse the block after a series of right crosses have been run.

set (*see* Figure 7–34). The name of the play, thirty-one, is derived from the three-set that is set to the middle attacker or the one-set delivered to the right attacker.

The *thirty-one* is particularly effective when the right spiker is left-handed and can spike a back one-set. The middle spiker runs in for a three-set to draw the middle blocker (No. 6, Figure 7–35) in his direction as the right spiker approaches and jumps for the quick back set. In Figure 7–36, the left-front attacker runs to the setter and hits a two-set in the area vacated by the center blocker, who is usually keying on a possible 3 set to the middle attacker. The left-front attacker should approach straight ahead for a step or two in order to freeze the end blocker before running to the setter to complete the play.

a

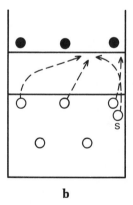

b

Figure 7–32 *Tandem.* In *a*, the middle attacker has faked a quick hit, hoping to draw the middle blocker while the setter delivers a two-set to the left-front spiker who is jumping behind him. The routes of the spikers are shown in *b*. (Barry Schreiber)

When a left-handed spiker is in the middle front, the line-up shown in Figure 7–37 can be used. This arrangement allows the middle attacker to spike the one-set on the power side—a maneuver that confuses the opponents' blocking patterns.

The double quick set is the most difficult play in volleyball. The pass used to accomplish this play must be perfect or the setter will have to deliver the ball to the on-hand attacker who is the safety valve in the play. Both the middle and off-hand attackers converge on the setter

Figure 7–33 *Timing for the Tandem.* The setter can deliver the ball to the first man (No. 14) using the normal timing for the one-set or to the second man (No. 1) who will leave the floor as the middle blocker and attacker are descending. (Barry Schreiber)

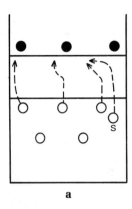

a

b

Figure 7–34 *The Thirty-One.* No. 14 has forced two blockers off the floor; No. 1 is about to take off for a three-set and the on-hand spiker is approaching for a set down the far sideline. (Barry Schreiber)

Figure 7–35 *Spiking the Back One-Set.* This difficult play catches the blocker flat-footed. The play is easier to execute if the spiker approaches from his on-hand side. If the spiker is late in his approach, the setter compensates by dropping to one knee to delay the set. (Bob Van Wagner)

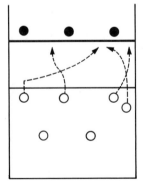

Figure 7–36 *The Left-Inside Play.* This is a good play to trap an aggressive blocker who is jumping with the middle attacker.

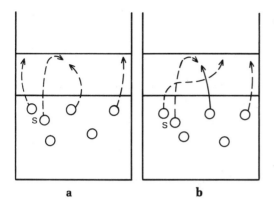

a b

◀ **Figure 7–37** *Pass Left.* The left-hander can spike from the middle position on the on-hand side (*a*). The left cross play (*b*) can be added when opponents start to key on the one-play.

a

b

Figure 7–38 *Double Quick Set.* The Republic of Korea Army Team executes perfect timing in their fast offense (*a*). The USA Women's Team runs a successful double quick against the Japanese Women's Team (*b*). (Barry Schreiber)

for a one-, or quick, set in an attempt to make the middle blocker cover two attackers (*see* Figure 7—38).

FIVE-ONE ATTACK

A five-one offense can add spiking and blocking power to the offense. If only one setter qualifies as one of the top six players on a team, this offense should be considered. The setter must be the type of athlete who can perform reliably during the entire contest. The entire offense bogs down as soon as the setter becomes rattled.

When the setter is in the backcourt, this offense uses a three-hitter attack. When the setter rotates to the front row, a straight four-two or two-spiker attack is used.

The Japanese men's team used a 5 ft 9 in. setter to quarterback their five-one offense in winning the gold medal in the 1972 Olympics. Nakato is considered the best setter in the world and sets over 1,000 balls a day.

When the setter is in the backcourt, this offense uses a three-hitter attack. When the setter rotates to the front row, he can spike a good pass or jump set to another spiker. The setter must be enough of an offensive threat to delay one blocker. Ideally, the setter should be tall and left-handed to be able to block on the right side and have options of spiking the pass from the on-hand side or of jump-setting the other two front-court players on their on-hand side. Whoever plays opposite the setter in the line up should have good hands and serve as the auxiliary setter when the pass is not accurately placed.

UCLA won the 1975 NCAA Championships with a five-one attack.

8

Defense

The two basic defensive alignments used in power volleyball are the *middle back* and the *middle-in*. In both defenses, each player is assigned an area of the court that varies according to the set, block, and intentions of the spiker.

STARTING POSITIONS

The individual's backcourt ready position is the same in all defenses. The body is in a semi-crouch position, with the feet spread about shoulder-width apart. The player's weight is forward and his hands are held about waist high.

Players should assume the team starting position before changing into the middle back or middle-in defense so that their opponents cannot identify their alignments and then attack their weak areas. The defense should remain in the team starting position until after the offense passes the serve. The traditional American defense is the middle back, whereas teams in other countries use variations of the middle back and

middle-in to meet the changing offensive tactics of their opponents.

MIDDLE-BACK DEFENSE

The middle-back defense is effective against teams that spike off the top and over the block without varying their attack with dinks and off-speed shots. After the opponents pass the serve, the defensive players should move to their assigned areas of the court. The tactic of moving after the serve is passed prevents the offense from readily observing the defensive alignment and hinders their attack on weak areas of a particular defense. The middle-back defense is currently the most widely used defensive alignment at all levels of competition in the U. S.

End Blocker

The end blocker should line up even with the spiker in the middle back defense to block the line shot and to encourage the

a   b

Figure 8–1 *Defensive Stance.* The feet should be spread farther apart than shoulder-width, with one foot ahead of the other. The player's weight is on the inside balls of his feet and his heels are off the floor. Knees and hips are bent at approximately a 90° angle. Arms are spread in front about waist high, with the weight forward. (Stan Troutman, *a*; Norm Scindler, *b*)

spiker to hit crosscourt. The average backcourt defender, positioned on the sideline directly in front of the attacking spiker, must move to within 15 ft of the net when the ball is attacked in order to field balls dinked over the block. When this defender rushes in to field the dink and the spiker drives a ball down the line, it is rarely dug. For this reason, it is often good strategy for the end blocker in the middle-back defense to block the line and to try to force the spiker to hit crosscourt. The middle-back defense is particularly strong against crosscourt

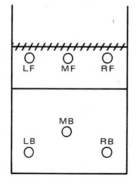

Figure 8–2 *Defensive Starting Position.* Whatever defensive alignment is used, the starting position shown here should be used for all defenses. The middle-back player starts ahead of his backcourt teammates to guard against a quick play on the first or second contact with the ball by the offense.

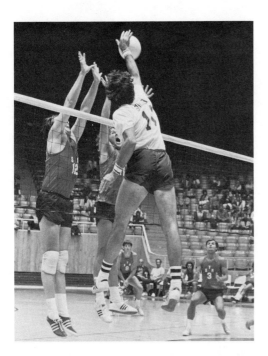

Figure 8–3 *End Blocker Defending Against the Line Shot.* No. 12 places his right hand outside the ball to encourage the spiker to hit crosscourt. (Dr. Leonard Stallcup) *Above*

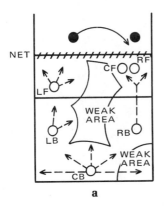

a

Figure 8–4 *Middle-Back Defense.* Two defenders (*b*), Nos. 6 and 10, position themselves in the area of a crosscourt spike that has been hit by the middle blocker. (Stan Troutman)

spikes because two defenders are also in position to dig the crosscourt spike (LF and LB, respectively, in Figure 8–4).

Off-Blocker

The off-the-net blocker (No. 8 in Figure 8–5) has moved about 10 ft away from the sideline and the net to field the spike that has been driven sharply by the middle blocker. This player is also responsible for dinks and off-speed shots hit into the left side of the frontcourt. The off-blocker must concentrate on moving away from the net quickly and stopping before the spiker contacts the ball. When the spiker contacts the ball, the off-blocker's body weight must be forward or he will not be able to move forward quickly enough to field balls hit off the block or to field soft placement shots.

The off-blocker must react quickly to the direction of the set in order to gain a position deep enough in the court to dig the sharp spike angled by the block. The middle blocker who aggressively blocks over the net will force the setter to de-

b

Figure 8–5 *Off-Blocker.* The off-blocker is responsible for spikers and dinks hit sharply inside the middle blocker. (Dr. Leonard Stallcup)

liver the ball about 3 or 4 ft from the net so that most spikers cannot angle hard-driven crosscourt spikes inside the 10-ft line. The off-blocker has a tendency to continue running back beyond the 10-ft spiking line where he might overlap the left-back player who usually has a much better angle on the approaching spike.

Left Back

The left-back defender (No. 2 in Figure 8–6) is stationed in the "power alley" of the volleyball court. Some coaches switch their best back court digger to this

position because most of the time the average on-hand spiker delivers the ball to this area of the court. This position is the key to backcourt defense because most teams set to the on-hand spiker significantly more often than the other hitters in both two- and three-hitter attacks. No. 2 in Figure 8–6 has lined up off the center blocker's left shoulder so that she can watch the ball and spiker when making contact with the ball.

Middle Back

The middle-back player (No. 4 in Figure 8–7) is responsible for balls hit off the top or over the block. Many of the

Figure 8–6 *Left Back.* No. 2 has moved inside the middle blocker's (No. 6) left arm to cover the area between the off-blocker and the middle blocker. (Barry Schreiber)

Figure 8–7 *Middle Back.* No. 4 (foreground) lines up in a good position between the blockers and the point of attack. (Barry Schreiber)

balls he fields are deflected by the block and can be set to one of the end blockers. In the traditional middle-back defense, this player is not responsible for short dink shots.

The middle back must be ready to move forward when he sees that the blockers have not closed in fast enough and have left a hole in the block. When stationed behind a good block, the middle back should be in a direct line behind the blockers and attacking spiker. The middle back starts just inside the endline and moves in the direction of the spike. Setters often play this position, which is comparable to the free safety in football.

Right Back

No. 22 in Figure 8–8 is playing the right-back position. He is responsible for covering balls hit down the line as well as dink shots and soft shots looped over the block. The right-back position requires a player with the ability to "read" the intentions of the opposing spiker. It is extremely difficult for him to recover a soft dink shot that drops at the heels of the blockers when he has ruled out that possibility and has moved close to the floor in preparation for a hard-driven spike. The initial starting position for this player is near the sideline, about 10 ft from the endline.

Figure 8–8 *Right-Back Defender.* Most setters prefer to play this position when their team is using the three-hitter attack because the right-back position enables players to move quickly into a setting position if the ball is dug.

DEFENDING THE CENTER SPIKER

When the center spiker in a three-hitter offense receives a one-set, it is almost impossible to defend the play with more than one blocker. The blocker should normally attempt to stay in front of the spiker's attacking arm to force the spiker to cut the ball back across his body.

If time allows, the off-blockers (LF and RF in Figure 8–10) back away from the net to cover dinks and balls deflected by the blocker. The corner-back players (LB and RB in Figure 8–10) line up outside the blocker's arms so that they can see the spiker contact the ball. The center-back player stays far behind the blocker and reacts to the spike (MB in Figure 8–10). If the blocker does not jump in

Figure 8–9 *Defending the Quick Set.* The lone blocker attack-blocks while the off-blocker and the right back are in a good position to dig the ball. (Norm Scindler)

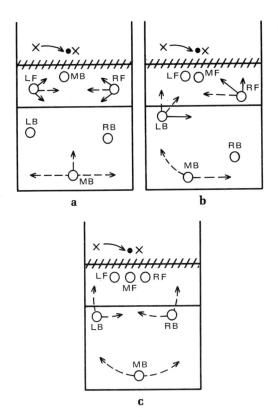

a

b

c

◀ **Figure 8–10** *Center Spiker* v. *the Middle-back Defense.* Only the middle blocker can react in time to stop the quick one-set. If the left- and right-front players can move quickly, they can back away from the net to field dink shots and block rebounds (*a*). The end blocker can easily join the middle blocker when a normal set is delivered to the middle attacker. Blockers with quick reactions may be able to join the middle blocker to stop a two-set. The left-front player should block because most spikers have a habit of dinking the ball across their body. The other blocker drops away from the net to dig a spike hit past the middle blocker and to cover the dink shot (*b*). The three-player block should be used only to stop powerful spikers who rarely dink because the three-player block leaves too much area for the backcourt players to cover (*c*)

time, this player must run forward to dig the straight-ahead spike.

Two Blockers

Two blockers should defend against the center spiker unless the setter delivers a one- or three-set. The corner-back player (LB in Figure 8–10*b*) will approach the 10-ft spiking line if the player in front of him is involved in the block.

Three Blockers

When the middle attacker receives a normal set, it is usually possible to defend with three blockers. This is not considered good strategy most of the time,

Figure 8–11 *Center Spiker* v. *Three Blockers* Three blockers should be used against a spiker who cannot often be stopped by two blockers. (Barry Schreiber)

however, because the three remaining backcourt players cannot cover the court adequately in the event of a dink shot or a soft spike (Figure 8–10).

Using three blockers against an accomplished spiker who has been hitting well against a two-man block can be most effective. This three-man block is also valuable against players who cannot dink well or use a soft spike (*see* Figure 8-11).

MIDDLE-BACK DEFENSE TO VARIOUS OFFENSES

Two-Hitter Attack

If the digger does not pass the ball accurately when fielding the attack, one of the remaining five players who is closest to the pass should set the ball to one of the front-row spikers.

When the pass or dig can be controlled, the transition from the middle-back defense to the two-hitter offense depends on the location of the setter. Normally, the setter is not the strongest blocker in the front row and is not capable of blocking the middle position effectively. When a team has a tall, mobile setter who is talented enough to block the middle position, its transition to offense is very smooth because there is no setter-spiker switch.

Setter Blocking Left

Because the attack usually comes from the opposition's on-hand spiker or from the strong side of the team, the weak blocking setter usually switches to the left to block the attack from the weak

side. This allows the setter to become the off-blocker, with the responsibility of digging crosscourt spikes (S in Figure 8–12*a*).

When a teammate digs a ball, the setter switches with the center blocker and sets to one of the front-row players. This is the best system for defending against the opponents' attack, but it is most inefficient for the middle blocker. The player who blocks the middle position must use a shortened approach if he wants to reach the left-front spiking position in time for the set. He may choose to attack from the middle by verbally signaling the setter while the first pass is in the air. An attack on the middle position has the disadvantage of allowing the opposing blockers to cover 15 ft of the net instead of 30 ft; this means

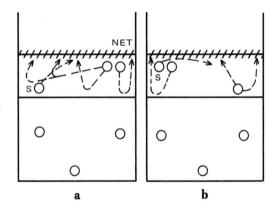

a   b

Figure 8–12 *Setter Blocking on the Left.* If there is not enough time for the middle blocker to run to the left side of the court in order to approach from the on-hand side, the approach for the set can be made from the middle of the court (*a*). If the attack is from the opponents' weak side, the middle blocker can easily approach along the sideline. (*b*).

they should be able to block successfully with two or three players if they so desire. If the first pass is not high, the setter has his back to the on-hand spiker and is not sure of the location of the approaching spiker.

When the attack is from the weak side of the team, the switch is relatively easy (S in Figure 8–12b). The former off-blocker may approach for a play set because the setter is usually facing him.

Setter Blocking Right

If the setter is a strong end blocker, he should block on his right side. When the attack is from the opponents' strong side, the center blocker can approach from the middle or use a short switch and approach from the right side. If the attack is from the weak side, the middle blocker should attack from the middle so that the set can be approached from the on-hand side.

In recent world competition, the Russian team stationed its setters on the right side to block, even though their setters were noticeably weaker blockers than their spikers. Their diggers always passed the ball to the right side of the court to allow the setter to face two on-hand spikers, which allowed for greater accuracy in the placement of the set.

When the attack is dug from the opponents' strong side, the middle blocker can approach from the on-hand side in the middle or from the sideline (Figure 8–13a). When the attack is dug from the opponents' weak side, the middle blocker should approach from the middle of the court (Figure 8–13b).

Down Block

Teams must be able to make quick adjustments from defense to offense. The serving team must anticipate a good pass, a good set, and then the spike. If the pass is not good and the setter has trouble getting to the ball, or if another player must step in and set the ball, the defense should be ready for a bad set. If the set is good enough to be hit by the spiker at a downward angle, but not sharp enough to block, the blockers yell, "Down!" or "Stay down!" At this call, the blockers drop their arms and the off-blocker and three backcourt players attempt to dig the ball. When a backcourt player digs the ball, it should be directed to the frontcourt setter.

Free Ball

When the defense sees that the offense is going to hit the ball over the net with an

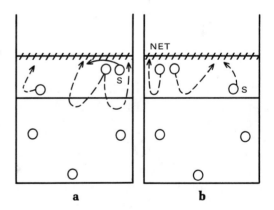

Figure 8–13. *Setter Blocking on the Right.* When the setter is a capable blocker, he should switch to the right side of the court for an easy transition to offense.

Figure 8–14 *Down Block.* When the spiker receives a set that must be hit deep into the defenders' court, "staying down" gives the diggers a clear view of the approaching ball. (Barry Schreiber)

Figure 8–15 *Free Ball.* When a defender sees that the spiker is not likely to receive a good set, he should call, "Free!" Then the blockers can drop away from the net to help their backcourt teammates to field the ball. (Bud Fields)

upward flight or weak spike, it should call, "Free!" and assume a normal serve-reception pattern.

Three-Hitter Attack

The transition from the middle-back defense to the three-hitter attack is a bit more complicated. If the defense does not pass the ball successfully when fielding the attack, it must use the two-hitter offense. When the backcourt setter digs the ball, he should direct it toward the front-court setter so the team can use the conventional two-hitter attack. If another player digs the ball, it normally should be directed about 10 ft from the right sideline, a few feet from the net. The most convenient place for the backcourt

setter to be in order to make a speedy transition to offense is the right-back position (Figure 8–17a). With continued practice, it is possible for the backcourt setter to move under a good dig from any defensive assignment, turn and face the two on-hand spikers, and set the ball.

When the middle blocker is left-handed and a powerful spiker, the setter should play in the left-back position (S in Figure 8–17b). The dig should be directed a few feet from the net and about 10 ft from the left sideline. This allows the setter to play in the power alley, and the left-handed spiker to approach the set from the on-hand side. If a free ball is called, the backcourt setter runs to the net to give the diggers a target to which to pass (No. 29 in Figure 8–16).

Figure 8–16 *Passing a Free Ball.* In good competition, there are at least four or five free balls in a game. Free balls should always be received with the overhand pass because they can be controlled with greater accuracy. A pre-arranged free ball play should be used according to the offensive system in effect. Some teams use a direct set to an attacker who has the option of spiking or setting to another attacker. Other offensive systems call for a low, fast pass to the setter in order to make a quick play before the opponents' defense is set up. When a free ball is converted into a scoring play, the receiving team is given momentum. (Barry Schreiber) *Above*

Figure 8–17 *Changing from the Middle-Back Defense.* ▶ To make this transition, the backcourt setter switches to the right sideline (*a*). The setter switches to the left sideline to allow the left-handed middle spiker to approach from the on-hand side (*b*).

MIDDLE-IN DEFENSE

The middle-in defense is strong against dinks and off-speed hits. Teams with quick, tall blockers can prevent the opposition from attacking the weak zone located in the center of the court beyond the 10-ft line.

The end blocker should line up about 3 ft from the sideline and move the block toward the center of the court in an attempt to encourage the spiker to hit the ball down the line.

If the ball is set near the sideline and close to the net, the end blocker will have to line up on the ball to prevent a straight-down spike that cannot be dug by the defensive player on the line.

Right Back

The right-back player is responsible for spikes hit down the line and for long balls hit off the block that fall on the right side of the court. The right-back player does not take any responsibility for the short dink shot and can concentrate fully on the spiker's line shots. If the right back is a good digger, the end blocker should concentrate on the cross-

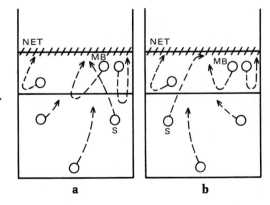

a   b

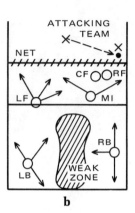

a   b

Figure 8–18 *Middle-In Defense.* Teams are more accustomed to attacking the middle-back defense, so they usually have difficulty adjusting to this defense. (Stan Troutman)

court spike and rely on the right-back player to dig the line shot (No. 10 in Figure 8–20).

Middle-In

Balls looped over the block are covered by the middle-in player who first starts behind the center blocker on the 10-ft line. The middle-in player is not responsible for hard-driven spikes; instead, he concentrates on retrieving dinks, off-speed shots, and block rebounds. He should be able to dive quickly to retrieve balls, and often becomes the setter when the team uses a three-hitter attack.

In Figure 8–21, the middle-in player starts on the 10-ft line behind the blockers and concentrates on the possibility of

a dink shot and his chances of retrieving balls rebounding off the block. If the spiker manages to drive a hard spike through the middle of the block, there is little chance that the middle-in player will field a successful dig at such a close distance.

Left Back

The left-back player should be in line with the ball and the armswing of the spiker. She should start about 5 ft in from the endline and sideline. Although her primary responsibility is to dig spikes hit outside the blocker's left hand, the left-back player is also responsible for balls hit through the block. She must have good lateral movement.

Figure 8–19 *End Blocker Encouraging Spiker to Hit a Line Shot.* The end blocker (No. 7) leaves the line open in the hopes that the spiker will hit to No. 12. Instead, the spiker hits the ball to the open zone in the middle-back court. (Norm Scindler)

In Figure 8–22, No. 2 moves laterally to line up the spike traveling through the block. Although no player is stationed directly behind the block in the middle-in alignment, the better blockers will slow up the spike or force the spiker to hit in a flat trajectory to give the back-court player time to dig the ball.

Off-Blocker

The off-blocker should quickly back off the net to the 10-ft line while watching the setter and remaining blockers (Figure 8–23a). When the ball is set toward the center of the court, he should move close to the sideline. When the middle blocker does not jump or the set is wide, the off-blocker should move toward the center of the court.

Middle Blocker

The middle blocker is responsible for closing any spaces or holes in the block. Because there is no deep middle back-

court player, the middle blocker must slow up or block spikes hit in the center so that the backcourt players have time to move laterally to field the ball. If the spiker dinks, the middle blocker usually lowers his hands below the net to allow the player behind the block to pass an easy ball.

In Figure 8–24, the middle blocker should have shouted, "No!" or "Down!" to warn his teammate not to deflect the ball away from the middle-in player. The player backing up the spiker assumes a full squat position which allows him more time to react to a blocked ball.

STOPPING THE CENTER ATTACK

When a blocker finds himself alone in the block and defending himself against the

Figure 8–20 *Right Back Staying Deep in the Court.* This player should concentrate on digging long spikes and should not rush the net to dig the difficult "straight-down" spike. (Barry Schreiber) *Above*

Figure 8–21 *Protecting Against the Dink Shot.* The middle-in player starts on the 10-ft line from which he must dive to field well-placed dink shots. (Norm Scindler)

middle spiker, he should cover the center of the court. This is particularly important in the middle-in defense because there are no backcourt players behind the block.

In Figure 8–25, the blocker has found herself alone on the block and realizes that she must defend against the middle spiker. She does so by covering the center of the court. Teammates should remember that there are no backcourt

players behind the block in the middle-in defense.

The ideal court coverage for a one-player block is shown in Figure 8–26a. Both off-blockers (LF and RF) drop away from the net about 8 ft to dig a spike hit toward the sideline. The middle-in player lines up off the blocker's right shoulder to cover dink shots. This player "cheats" to the right (moves before the ball is actually contacted) because most dink shots are placed in the same direction as the set. The backcourt players (LB and RB in Figure 8–26a) line up off the outside shoulder of the blocker in

Figure 8–22 *Lining Up the Spike.* The left back in the middle-in defense must dig balls hit over and through the middle blocker as well as sharp spikes hit inside the block. (Barry Schreiber)

Figure 8–23 *Off-Blocker Lining Up the Spike.* The off-blocker is in a perfect position to dig a spike by No. 12. (Dr. Leonard Stallcup)

Figure 8–24 *Middle Blocker Allowing the Dink to Go By.* The middle blocker drops his hands to allow the middle-in player to field the dink shot. (Bob Van Wagner)

order to see the spiker contact the ball and then be able to react to the attack.

On a normal set, or a two-set, two blockers can reach the center spiker. No. 10 in Figure 8–27 is held at the net by the threat of the setter (No. 9) backsetting the ball to the off-hand spiker (not shown). This trapped blocker puts extra pressure on his backcourt teammate to move closer to the net to compensate for his lack of court coverage.

When the end blocker joins the middle blocker to stop the center attack, the middle-in player covers the area vacated by the end blocker (M1 in Figure 8–26*b*) rather than charging the 10-ft line to defend against a possible "straight-down" spike angled inside the left-front blocker. The right back lines up outside the middle blocker's arms to watch the attacker contact the ball. The left-back lines up behind the blockers (LB in Figure 8–26*b*) to dig balls deflected by the block.

Figure 8–25 *Three-Set.* This play often traps blockers at the net. (Dr. Leonard Stallcup)

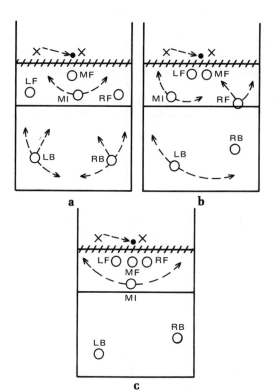

▶ **Figure 8–26** *Center Spiker v. Middle-In Defense.* The middle-in player should stay to the right of a one-player block when the set is coming toward him because most spikers dink away from the direction of the set (*a*). When two players block the middle attacker, the middle-in player must cover the area vacated by the end blocker. In this situation, the off-blocker (RF) must share the responsibility for the dink shot (*b*). When the entire front line blocks, the middle-in player is in serious trouble. He must line up behind the middle blocker and rely on the end blockers to deflect balls dinked toward the sideline.

When all three blockers leave the floor, the three remaining defenders cannot cover the court adequately. The middle-in player must cover the 300 sq ft of court inside the 10-ft line, and the two remaining defenders must divide the 600 sq ft in the backcourt (Figure 8–26c).

MIDDLE-IN DEFENSE TO OFFENSE

The middle-in defense is ideal for the transition to the three-hitter attack when a setter plays behind the block. When the best setter in the backcourt is also the best digger, the strategy may call for the setter to play in the left-back position, where the greatest number of balls are usually hit. Normally, the middle-

Figure 8–27 *Middle Spiker v. Two-Player Block.* No. 9 delivers a quick play that traps the off-blocker at the net. The backcourt player behind No. 10 (not shown) had to move closer to the net to compensate for his lack of coverage. (Bob Van Wagner)

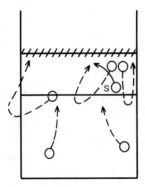

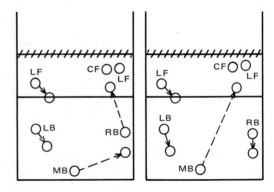

Figure 8–28 *Changing from the Middle-In Defense to Offense.* This can be accomplished smoothly when the setter plays behind the block.

Figure 8–29 *Changing from the Middle-Back to the Middle-In Defense.* This change can be initiated by a verbal command, by the digger's movements on the line (RB, *a*), or by the middle-back player. (MB, *b*).

in player will set the ball if this is the case. When there is an obvious free-ball situation, the setter in the left-back position has ample time to run to the net before the ball is passed.

Free balls passed to the left side of the court are confusing to the opponents' block and are effective if the attacking middle spiker is left-handed.

CHANGING DEFENSES

When a team has mastered both defenses and can play together as a cohesive unit, it is possible to change defenses in the middle of a rally. The opportune moment to change from the middle back to the middle-in defense is when the opposing spiker is off-balance or tired, or when the middle back or line digger expects a dink shot. A verbal signal may be exchanged prior to the switch, or it may be initiated by either backcourt player running in behind the block.

9

Coeducational and Doubles Play

COEDUCATIONAL PLAY

Coed playing rules are the same as those for the regulation game, with the following exceptions:

- There are three males and three females on a team
- The serving order alternates males and females
- When the ball is contacted by more than one player on a team, one of the contacts must be made by a woman
- One backcourt player may also block when there is only one male player in a frontline position

Offense

Coed play should be conducted with an emphasis on equal participation, a high level of sportsmanship, and a spirit of team play. For equal participation and

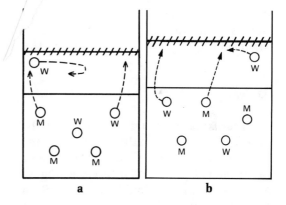

Figure 9–1 *Offense.* A high ball should be passed near the center front of the court so that the setter (LF) can turn and front set the player approaching down the left sideline (*a*). When the setter is on the right side of the court, the ball should be passed 10 ft from the right sideline and a few feet from the net to allow the player to approach from the middle of the court and to attack the ball from the on-hand side (*b*).

enjoyment, the basic M-formation is recommended because it allows every player to become the setter when he or she reaches the middle-front position. When a woman is in the middle-front row, the pass should be directed to her so that she can set the ball to either end spiker. When there is only one man in the front row, he can approach from the left side (if he is right-handed), and the woman on his left can switch to the center of the frontcourt to be in a position to set (*see* Figure 9–1*a*).

On a high pass, the woman should turn to face the man so that she can deliver a front set to him. The woman playing in the right-front position should approach for a back set. If the male spiker is a good passer, he may choose to remain in the center of the court where he can field a greater percentage of the serves. After the pass, he can spike from the center of the court (*see* Figure 9–1*b*).

Defense

It is possible to include two men on the block during the entire game if the woman in the middle front moves away from the net prior to the serve. In Figure 9–3, the man in the middle-back position can switch with the set to the attacker's side line to enable the women to play deeper in the backcourt.

When two women are in the front row, they can block the end with the man blocking the middle, or a man can be brought in from the backcourt to block. When women spikers hit on an 8-ft net, the defense must be ready to call, "Down!" and "Free ball!"

In Figure 9–4, the backcourt man on the sideline can exchange positions with

Figure 9–2 *Setter in the Right-Front Court.* The ball can be passed to the right side of the court when there are two right-handed spikers. (Barry Schreiber)

the frontline women in both the middle-back (*a*) and middle-in defenses (*b*). In the middle-in defense, the remaining backcourt men and women may move toward the center of the court and switch with the set to enable the man to field the more difficult line spikes.

DOUBLES PLAY

Playing rules for doubles in the *Official Volleyball Guide* are the same as those for the regulation game, with the following exceptions:

Each team's court is 30 ft by 25 ft

No substitutions are allowed

The serve should come from the right half of the service area

The game is 11 points, or 5 minutes of ball in play—whichever occurs first

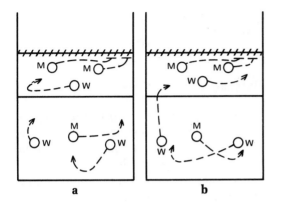

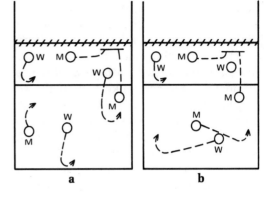

Figure 9–3 *One Woman in the Front Line.* The woman plays the off-blocker position in the middle-back defense (*a*) and the middle-in position in the middle-in defense (*b*).

Figure 9–4 *Two Women in the Front Line.* A 1971 coed rule change allows one backcourt player to block if there is only one male player in a frontline position.

Generally, tournament directors do not use a timer, and the length of the game is increased to 15 points. When doubles are played indoors, the same light, fast regulation ball as that used in the six-man game is in play.

Offense

The server has an advantage when the "short-court" rule is enforced because the serving line is 5 ft closer to the net. This gives the receiver less time to react, especially on fast, low serves directed along the server's sideline. The serve should not be merely a way of putting the ball into play—it should be an offensive tactic to score points.

In doubles volleyball, most of the serving aces are scored in the short middle (within 10 ft of the net), on the boundary lines, or in a seam that lies exactly between the two receivers. Almost all the aces scored in doubles are due to hesitation on the part of the passer. The passer may hesitate because the ball looks as if it is going out of bounds, will hit the net, or be in his partner's receiving area. When a player is tired, the ball should be served deep in the court so the passer will have to run from the back line to the net to spike the set.

The ball should rarely be served to the poor setter because balls set over the net or deep in the setter's court are usually converted into a point for the serving team. The ball should be served repeatedly to a receiver standing in the same position only if a definite weakness has become apparent. The placement, speed, breaking action of the ball, and selection of the receiver should vary to prevent the opposition from falling into a groove.

Occasionally, the ball should be served to the stronger player, particularly if he has a tendency to relax or to cover a weaker partner. When the last serve results in a serving error, the next server should take a little power off the serve to make sure that it lands in fair territory.

Passing, setting, and physical endurance are the keys to attack in doubles. Almost anyone can spike well if the set is placed within a few feet of the net. Excellent spikers who do not have the necessary setting and passing skills do not enjoy great success in doubles volleyball. A poor setter must select an outstanding spiker as a partner to compensate for a lack of precision setting. Spikers must learn to vary their attack and to take advantage of the moving defensive player before the ball is contacted.

Many top players ask their friends for the "book" on their spiking patterns to see if they have become predictable in their attack. More successful players compete with the same player for the entire doubles season to learn where the ball will be passed and set in every situation by that player. There is nothing more satisfying to a spiker than to know that his partner can deliver a set close to the net. Instead of watching the setter and trying to guess where he will place the ball, a spiker who is confident of his partner's setting ability can concentrate on a correct approach and a maximum jump, which are necessary to spike well.

Pinpoint passing is not as crucial in doubles as it is in the six-man game. When the ball is passed high in the air toward the center of the court, the setter should have little difficulty in delivering a good set. The precision setting necessary to help the spiker defeat the two-man block is not absolutely necessary to successful doubles teams. A good spiker should jump high enough to spike the ball down against one blocker and one or two diggers when the ball is set within 3 ft of the net.

Defense

Defenders find it very difficult to dig a good spiker in indoor doubles when the set is right on the net. Most of the time a poor digger should block when defending against a good set in the indoor game. If the spiker can be blocked a few times, the setter will be reluctant to put the set close to the net and the spiker may begin to "be dug" and to commit spiking errors.

The most successful teams also perform well on defense. Better players keep a mental "book" on their opponents and find that certain players usually hit the ball in the same place when they approach the set in what has become a predictable manner. The defense moves into this area before the ball is spiked and, in effect, dares the spiker to alter the attack or to try a shot he does not have in his offensive arsenal.

BEACH DOUBLES

Many experts believe that the long-term national dominance of southern California men's and women's teams stems from the mastery of basic fundamentals that are learned through long hours of practice playing beach doubles.

Official and Unwritten Rules

Many beach doubles' rules are unwritten and vary from those published in the *Official Volleyball Guide*. The following rules and interpretations are in effect for the Southern California Beach Volleyball Tournament Schedule.[1]

Court size is 30 ft by 60 ft as opposed to the 30-ft by 50-ft court used in indoor doubles. Instead of lines, ropes are used to block off the courts. A center rope is placed under the net only if six-man volleyball is played. Stepping across the center of the court below the net is legal if players do not interfere with the opposing team. Players may serve from anywhere behind their end line, as opposed to serving from the right side of the court. The net is placed 7 ft 10 in. above hard-packed sand and 7 ft 9 in. above loosely packed sand (stated in the *Guide*). Net height remains the same for mixed doubles. The antennas on the end of the net are disregarded, and the ball is considered in play if it passes between the wooden posts supporting the net.

The ball has an 18-piece leather cover and is quite heavy in comparison to the indoor ball. This heavier ball is stable in the wind and is always preferred on the beach.

There are no scorers, umpires, timers, or linesmen; the referee keeps score, and there are no time limits on the games. The referee usually sits on a platform attached to one of the volleyball posts. A player on the winning team in the preceding match usually referees the following match. Any player may request a time out when the ball is dead. If, in the referee's opinion, a player has too much sand on his body or in his eyes, an uncharged time out is granted.

Since no substitutions are allowed, players are also granted uncharged time outs for stretching out leg cramps. Players must keep the same serving order throughout the game, but they can change court positions at any time. Because most players are left- or right-side specialists they do not change positions except during prolonged rallies. Teams change sides of the court every four points in 11-point games and every five points in 15-point games. This neutralizes the advantage of serving, setting, and spiking into the wind or sun.

Blocking is permitted by any player, but it is generally considered poor strategy since beach lore forbids the blocker from reaching over the net. Players who contact the net are expected to stop the play immediately and to award the ball to their opponents. It is considered poor form to wait for the referee to call the net foul. For that matter, it is considered a point of honor to call throws or other infractions on yourself if the referee has missed the call.

When a player participates in a block, the ball may be played only once in succession, as opposed to the successive contacts allowed in USVBA rules. It is still considered "bad form" for the setter or digger to place the ball over the net before making a third contact with the ball. However, if one's partner is definitely out of position, "shooting" the ball over on the first or second contact is not frowned upon.

In mixed doubles, the man is expected to hit the ball over the net after the woman contacts it. Since the net is 7 ft 10 in., women do not generally pose much of an offensive threat.

The ball may be hit by any part of the body, including the foot, whereas the

---

[1] For specific details regarding beach doubles' competitions and tournaments in Southern California, readers are advised to write the Santa Monica Recreation Department.

Figure 9–5 *Blocking.* Players are not allowed to block over the net in beach doubles. Wilt Chamberlain, with one foot in the sand, blocks 6-ft 5-in. Miles Papst. (Bob Van Wagner) *Above*

Figure 9–7 *Digging the Spike.* Larry Rundle prepares to overhand dig a spike by Dane Holtzman, Most Valuable Player of the 1970 NCAA Tournament. Hank Bergman moves toward the center of the court to set the dig. (Bob Van Wagner) *Left*

◀ **Figure 9–6** *One-Arm Dig.* A one-arm dig is a popular technique in beach doubles because it gives a player a greater range of court coverage. When a digger is in a good position, the two-hand forearm pass provides greater accuracy. (Bob Van Wagner) *Left*.

▲

Figure 9–8 *Cushioning the Overhand Dig.* The player in the right foreground leans backward to cushion, or give with, the overhand dig of a hard spike in order to keep the ball on his side of the net. (Bob Van Wagner) *Above*

USVBA rules a "dead ball" for contact below the waist. It is considered unsportsmanlike to accept a point if the referee misses the call. Protests are decided on the spot by the referee; in unique cases, the tournament director handles the protests.

Open-hand dinks are automatically "called" throws. The setter is not allowed the freedom of moving his arms across his body to deliver the set. All but the most accomplished setters must squarely face the direction of the in-

a   b

Figure 9–9 *Sky Ball.* The ball is tossed a few feet into the air and contact is made with the heel of the hand. This serve is difficult to field in a high wind or if the sun is directly overhead. (Gary Adams)

tended set. Overhand passing of the serve is frowned upon and scrutinized very closely by the opposition and referee. On the other hand, overhand digging or passing of the spike is interpreted quite leniently, compared to current indoor interpretations.

Beach doubles is weighted in favor of the defense because players cannot jump as high off the sand as they can off the floor and because they are spiking a heavier and slower ball. The block should only be used on a perfect set or by teams that simply cannot dig the ball adequately.

Spikers may *not* follow-through over the net, although they may touch part of the ball on their side of the net. If the sun is directly overhead, the *sky ball serve* should be used. This is an underhand serve that is hit so high it looks as if it is falling out of the sun. It is usually effective against players who are used to playing indoors. When the wind is blowing toward the server, the *overhand spin serve* can have an extraordinary amount of power and still stay in the opponents' court.

10

Volleyball for Children

Power volleyball has been slow to develop in the United States because the basic skills and tactics essential to the sport are not usually taught to children in the elementary schools. Volleyball is much more difficult to teach to older students and adults because they are self-conscious and afraid of looking uncoordinated and generally inept. Volleyball techniques are not easily mastered by people whose sports background has not incorporated similar movements. Children will readily attempt to learn the techniques of the dive and roll, but adults have a well-developed fear of going to the floor to retrieve a ball.

We have strong age-group programs in all of the sports in which our country is successful on an international level. However, the East Europeans and Asians dominate international volleyball because instruction is available at an early age and the interest among young people grows more and more as they mature.

Figure 10–1 *Going to the Floor.* Children should learn the proper techniques of the dive and roll on the mats before playing on hard surfaces (Barry Schreiber)

After the International Volleyball Association developed Mini Volleyball in 1971, the Scientific Research Section of the Committee of Instruction and Popularization of the Japanese Volleyball Association carefully examined its possibilities. The Japanese have ... "taken a leading part in studying the volleyball rules for children and lead-up games that are considered a preceding stage of guidance to Mini-Volleyball" ... [1] The course of study for volleyball in the elementary schools of Japan develops the capacities of catching and throwing as the first step in a progression to the fundamental technique of the overhand pass. The overhand pass is developed by the practice of catching the ball in front of the body and immediately throwing it to a teammate over the net.

The following stages are recommended for teaching volleyball to children by Hiroshi Toyoda, the Chief of Scientific Research of the Japanese Volleyball Association:

1. Throwing and catching the ball.
2. Hitting the ball after bouncing it on the floor.
3. Hitting the ball without bouncing it.
4. A player is not allowed to catch the ball, but the criterion for a held ball is not too severe.
5. The criterion for a legally played ball is almost the same as that for the formal game. [2]

Although there are many stages and styles of individual training for each of the principal lead-up games listed on this page, the main point to stress to children is to move quickly in front of the oncoming ball. When players reach the receiving area, the front foot should hit the floor first and point in the direction of the intended pass. It is very important to maintain a low body position in order to stop with good balance. The stop is made with the lead foot slightly forward and the trailing foot closing to maintain a balanced position. The low body position is illustrated in Figure 10–2 by a fifth grader.

LEAD-UP GAMES

Coordinated kindergarten children can learn to use the forearm pass, and second graders with high abilities are capable of using the overhand serve and putting the ball into the opponents' court 8 out of 10 times at distances up to 30 ft. However, the teacher should be careful not to frustrate children during their initial training period by attempting to teach skills beyond their reach. Unless children feel successful and have fun while they are learning, they will lose interest. Too much drilling without motivating lead-up games and tournaments can quickly turn into drudgery.

The various lead-up games listed below are designed for the elementary and junior high school level.

Throwing and Catching

1. **Net Ball.** The game is played on a regulation court with a net or rope stretched across the center of the court. A team consists of six play-

[1] Hiroshi Toyoda, "Report to the Council of Coaches: FIVB," *Technical Journal* 1 (April 1974): 38–41.
[2] Hiroshi Toyoda, "Volleyball Coaching Seminar," *Technical Journal* 1 (April 1974): 63.

ers or less when working with high ability groups of children; homogeneous groups may play with up to eight on a side. Any player puts the ball into play by throwing the ball over the net from inside the court or behind the court. The ball can be contacted three times; it can be caught, but it must be released quickly. If a player touches the ball two times in succession, he commits a fault. If the ball flies out of the opponents' court or falls on the ground, a fault is called and the op-

ponents' team is awarded a point. Balls that hit the net are always in play. A game is won when a team has scored 21 points.

2. **Newcomb.** This game is played on a regulation court with the height of the net from 5 to 7 ft, depending on the height of the children. The game is played with eight players or less, depending on the abilities of those involved. Many physical education curriculum guides throughout the country list this game, which can be intro-

a

b

Figure 10–2 *Low Body Position.* Children can perform volleyball fundamentals in as technically correct a manner as adults. Here a fifth-grader assumes a low body position by spreading her feet farther than shoulder-width apart, with her lead foot pointed in the direction of the pass. Her knees and hips are bent at about a 90° angle. (Barry Schreiber)

duced in the second grade. Instructors may want to continue this game with low-ability fourth and fifth graders. All balls are allowed to be caught and quickly thrown to a teammate or into the opponents' court. Adult volleyball rules are observed, with the following exceptions:

    a. The server may serve by throwing the ball to put it into play.

    b. The server may stand as close to the net as necessary to complete a successful serve.

    c. A back-row player cannot throw the ball over the net. This rule is not in force when playing with four players or less.

3. **Modified Newcomb.** The rules are the same as Newcomb, but the ball that is returned to the opponents' court must be hit in a legal manner. A freer handling of the ball is allowed. The children line up in the M-formation to receive the serve, and the player who receives the serve may catch it and throw it to the setter in the middle-front court. The setter sets or lobs the ball with two hands in an underhand toss to one of the spikers who hits it over the net using any legal technique. The defense is also allowed to catch the first and second ball as long as the ball is hit into the opponents' court.

Hitting the Ball After Bouncing It

1. **Bounce Volleyball.** The game is played on a regulation court with six players per team. The ball is allowed to bounce and hit once in a regulation manner. The server has two chances to hit the ball over the net, and weaker servers may stand as close as 20 ft from the net.

2. **Option Volleyball.** This is almost the same game as bounce volleyball. A player is allowed to hit the ball with or without bouncing it. The ball may hit the floor once between hits by players on a team, but it must be returned to the opponents' court after three contacts. A game is 15 points with the teams changing sides when 8 points have been scored by one team.

3. **Volley Tennis.** The game is played on a tennis court with a tennis net with a team of six to nine players. The service is made from behind the end line and one assist can be made before the ball crosses over to the opponents' court. Although players are not allowed to catch the ball, they have the option of hitting it on the fly or letting it bounce once before playing it. The ball must be returned to the opponents' court after three contacts. This is a good game to use to emphasize the spike.

Modified Volleyball

1. **Sitting Volleyball.** A team consists of about nine players who all sit or kneel on the floor. A rope or net is drawn across the center of the court. The game can be played on mats and the size of the court is determined by the number of participants. Net height can be varied from group to group, depending on their strength. Service is made from behind the end line, using an overhand pass. Rotation can be used if desired.

2. **Keep It Up.** The game is played on a regulation court with four

Figure 10–3 *Sitting Volleyball.* This is a good game to play when conditions do not permit the use of outdoor facilities. (Barry Schreiber)

teams of three to six players. Each court is divided perpendicularly into two courts so that there are two separate courts on both sides of the net. A front-line player on a team puts the ball into play by using the overhand pass to direct the ball into one of the opponents' courts. If a team returns the ball over the net, the team is awarded one point. When an error is made, the team that made the error serves the next ball. There is no point awarded for serving the ball over the net. Each team is allowed three contacts to return the ball over the net.

3. **Underhand-Serve Volleyball.** The most difficult technique for chil-

dren to master is an accurate pass of a hard overhand serve. To prevent a boring serving contest and to encourage rallys, an underhand serve into a smaller area of the court is used. The ball must be served into the badminton court which seems to be marked inside of every volleyball court in America. This gives the server an area 20 ft wide and 22 ft long to which to serve. The receiving team positions itself in the area of the badminton court for service reception. The percentage of well-placed first passes will increase immediately. Since the first pass is the key to the offense, better sets and spikes also increase significantly. After the serve is received, the boundaries extend back to the 30-ft by 60-ft regulation court. The children play on a net that is lowered until the average child in the game can touch the top of the net with outstretched fingertips from a standing position. The lowered net will encourage spiking. Regulation rules are followed, but the criterion for handling the ball is determined by the abilities of the players.

4. **Bonus Volleyball.** The net height, serve, and criterion for ball handling is the same as in Underhand-Serve Volleyball. Points are awarded in the regulation way, with the following exception: If a team scores using a pass, set, or spike they are awarded 2 points. A game is won when a team scores 21 points.

5. **Spike-It Volleyball.** This game was developed to teach defensive positioning. The ball is put into play by the attacker who hits the ball out of the "Spike-It." Each

Figure 10–4 *Underhand Serve.* Underhand serves are recommended for children because they are so easy to receive successfully, which, in turn increases the length of the rallies and the interest of the children. (Barry Schreiber)

Figure 10–5 *Net Height.* The average student in the group should be able to touch the top of the net with outstretched fingertips. (Barry Schreiber)

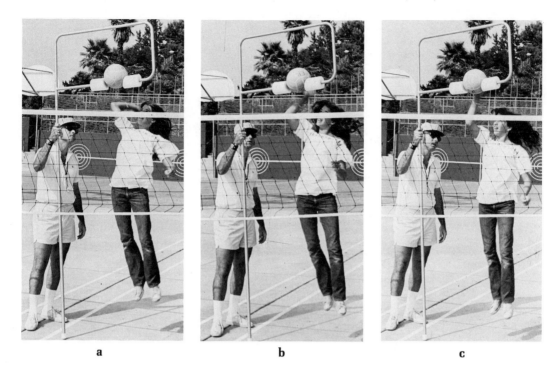

a   b   c

Figure 10–6 *Spike-It.* This teaching aid greatly accelerates the rate at which the spiking technique is learned. (Barry Schreiber)

member of the attacking team hits the ball from the left side of the court before the Spike-It is moved to the center and right side of the court. A point can be scored on each play. The attacking team scores when the defense fails to block or to return the ball over the net. The defense scores a point when the attacker makes an error or when the defenders return or block the spike into the opponents' court.

6. **Triples Volleyball.** The game is played on a badminton court with a lowered net. The underhand serve must be used and all players can block and spike. Two players stay deep in the court to receive the serve and the third player stays at the net in the center of the court to set. Players rotate from the left-back position to setter to the right-back or serving position. To increase the movement of the players and to encourage spiking, the regulation court can be used after the serve is received within the smaller confines of the badminton court. As skill level increases, the standard court can be used with the overhand serve.

An instructor can devise modifications of the lead-up games to place emphasis

a   b

Figure 10–7. *Spike-It Volleyball.* This game is designed to teach defensive positioning. (Barry Schreiber)

on the fundamental techniques that need to be strengthened. It is important not to progress too quickly with games or children will not experience success and will feel that volleyball is too difficult for them.

MINI-VOLLEYBALL

The Trainer Commission Committee on Mini-Volleyball of the International Volleyball Federation developed rules recommended for adoption by all national volleyball associations in 1971.[3] These rules are for children from 9 to 12 years of age and are for games played by two teams of three players each. The rules enable children to grasp the techniques, the elementary tactics and the abilities

[3] Horst Baake, "Mini Volleyball," *Technical Journal* 1 (January 1974): 36–40.

essential to the sport. Children are able to learn all this while they are actually playing. The rules for Mini-Volleyball are based on relevant experiences and on scientific publications of many countries.[4]

Rules

1. A team consists of three players; two substitutions per game are permissible.
2. The height of the net shall be 2.10 meters (about 6 ft 10 in.) for both male and female teams.
3. The players of a team will position themselves within their courts in

[4] FIVB Trainer Commission Committee On Mini Volleyball, *Mini Volleyball Rules for Children From 9 to 12 Years of Age* (Leipzeig, 1971). Translation obtained from Michael Haley, USBVA Chairman of Collegiate and Scholastic Volleyball.

Figure 10–8 *Triples Volleyball.* Three on a team is a good number because players are forced to move quickly and to contact the ball many times during the game. (Barry Schreiber)

such a manner that there will be two "front-line players" and one "back-line player" at the time the ball is served. After serving the ball, the back-line player may not spike the ball from within the attack area or attempt to hit the ball in the attack area, unless the ball is below the height of the net.

4. The players of a team will change their positions upon receiving the ball for service (the right front-line player will become the back-line player and the left front-line player will now be the right front-line player).

5. A team wins the game when it scores at least 15 points and has a two-point advantage over the opponents (15:13; 16:14, etc.).

6. A team wins the match when it has won at least 2 sets of the match (2:0 or 2:1).

7. The match is conducted by a referee. He takes care that the rules are not violated and ensures that the match will be played correctly and in keeping with principles of fair play. In doing this he has a pedagogic function.

8. The playing area shall be 4.5 meters wide and 12 meters long. A net di-

vides the playing area in two equal parts. The spiking line is 3 meters from the center line.[5]

Offense

Because the backline player cannot spike in the official version of the game, it is usually advantageous for the front-row players to receive all the serves and for the back-row players to penetrate to the net in order to set. This allows the offense to be played with two attackers. If players cannot pass accurately, however, this system will not work.

It may be preferable to disregard the rule that does not allow the backcourt player to spike. Instead, a different formation and rotation can be used with two players placed deep in the court to receive all serves.

The third player on the team is placed at the net in the center of the court and has no receiving responsibility. This player's job is to set all passes to one of the other players to spike. All players are allowed to spike and to block, and players rotate from the left-back position to setter to the right-back, or serving, position.

Defense

Most children under thirteen years of age are not capable of executing strong spikes, so it is often best to position all three defenders back in the court to receive the spike. This also leads to long rallies and great concentration and pride in digging techniques by the participants. The enthusiasm that is evident when children complete these long rallies is very stimulating for the participants and spectators. When players are capable of strong spiking, they should be opposed by one blocker.

Mini-Volleyball in East Germany

About 1962, the East German Volleyball Federation began to assign some of their top volleyball coaches to work with children under twelve years of age. They were soon confronted with arguments that power volleyball techniques were too difficult to teach to children because of their insufficient physical development. However, their immediate success caused mini-volleyball to spread throughout Europe. Today volleyball is an integral part of many national physical education programs and it is particularly strong in Eastern Europe and Asia.

Teachers and coaches begin teaching mini-volleyball to children who are eight and nine years old. This experience would be difficult to duplicate in the United States because the overwhelming majority of children do not receive regular instruction from a physical education teacher until they are in the seventh grade. The Chairman of the International Volleyball Council of Coaches, reporting on the East German Mini-Volleyball Championships, stated that "children possess already astonishing technical and tactical achievements, and their enthusiasm is enormous."[6] He gives several

[5] 4.5 m by 12 m is approximately 14 ft 9 in. by 39 ft 5 in. However, since most school volleyball courts have badminton courts marked within their dimensions, it is suggested that badminton courts be used for Mini- and Triples Volleyball. This gives an area of 20 ft by 44 ft with a spiking line 6 ft 6 in. from the center line. Badminton courts can be used for children up to the seventh grade with good results.

[6] Baacke, "Mini Volleyball," pp. 36, 37.

a

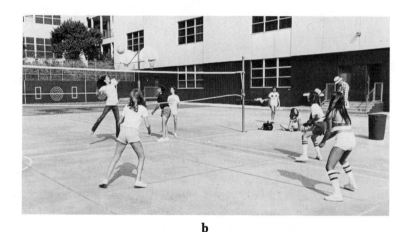

b

Figure 10–9   *No Block.*   This is the defense system to use when opponents cannot spike the ball strongly. (Barry Schreiber)

reasons for the quick and successful development of mini-volleyball: (1) Volleyball techniques are easier to acquire before puberty when the requirements of the game are modified to accommodate the age level. (2) The essential physical qualities of speed, mobility, and agility exist at this age or can be quickly developed. (3) Children are enthusiastic about the game and about competition. (4) The rich emotional content of mini-volleyball provides a strong attraction for children.

Children who train twice a week can learn the fundamental techniques in two or three months. After four or five months of training, they can successfully participate in formal competition. Mini-volleyball matches are decided by win-

a   b

Figure 10–10 *One Blocker.* This block should be used against a strong spiker. (Barry Schreiber)

ning two out of three games, so children can play several matches on the same day without overstraining themselves. "For children, mini-volleyball is a complete, whole game, a struggle full of a sense of joy, an event and at the same time a lesson. It is of paramount importance to stimulate the interest and the enthusiasm, to learn the movements of the game, to develop the physical qualities essential for volleyball both for all mass games of entertainment and the elite volleyball."[7]

JUNIOR HIGH SCHOOL VOLLEYBALL

In a physical education class, intramural program, or extramural program at the junior high level, students should be given an opportunity to learn to set and to attack. Under our present system, players are labeled as setters or spikers

[7] *Ibid.,* p. 37.

and often fail to develop the fundamental techniques required to play the other positions. On our national teams, there are setters who are poor attackers and there are spikers who are poor setters. These players missed the opportunity in their development to become a complete player, capable of performing all techniques and of playing all positions.

At the junior high school level of competition, one position on the court should be designated as the setting position. For example, if a team is using a two-hitter attack, every player who rotates to the middle-front position should set the ball for the side-out attempt. If a team uses a three-hitter attack, the player in the right-back position should set. This six–six system of offense forces all players to develop fundamental volleyball abilities. On defense, the player should also play each of the six positions.

During the summer months, I conduct coeducational volleyball classes which meet daily for two hours for a five- to six-week period. The children are entering grades six through eight, and the first 24 students to sign up for the course are accepted without regard to ability. We usually spend the first 20 minutes of class reviewing the previous day's progress and establishing points of emphasis for the current lesson. I have found that it is best to spend this time in the classroom where the students are not distracted by playground activities. The next 30 minutes are spent on drills with no more than two or three students to a ball. When the players have learned a sufficient number of ball-handling drills, they should be moved from drill to drill very rapidly so that interest does not lag. Spiking and digging drills are introduced last because they are the most satisfying and provide the best motivation.

A 10- to 15-minute break is taken at this point to allow the players to get drinks and a snack if desired. Many students prefer to work with the ball during the break in an unsupervised game of one-on-one or doubles. Others request help with certain techniques, particularly spiking. After the break, I assign the class to various teams covering two to three courts, depending on the content of the daily lesson. Older boys and girls are often invited into the class at this stage to challenge the better players in doubles or mini-volleyball while the majority of the class plays the other modified games.

Because the class plays on the blacktop, the weather is a determining factor in the selection of the activity for the second half of the class. On particularly hot or humid days, the students are divided into three teams so that they can rest between games. We can play three games of Underhand-Serve Volleyball in 50 minutes, which gives every team two games. The more energetic players are allowed to play an unstructured game on the adjoining courts instead of resting. This type of practice is not designed to develop a school team, but rather to teach the fundamental techniques and to instill interest in the sport.

In Eastern Europe and Asia, children twelve to fourteen years old train a minimum of 10 to 12 hours a week after school if they are representing a school team. Studies conducted by a prominent coach in Bulgaria indicate children are capable of playing a five-game match at this age and on the following day are fully rested and ready to play again.[8] I have not been able to find similar studies in the literature, but my experiences with children of this age lead me to concur with the Bulgarian study.

[8] Thomas Chakarov, "Some Questions of the Maximum Possibilities of Playing of Children in Volleyball," *FIVB Bulletin* 49–50 (March 1970): 27–35.

IV

Organization

11

Coaching

PHILOSOPHY

Coaching philosophy is usually determined by the self-image of the coach and his or her analysis of what constitutes a successful season.

The *idealistic* coach is interested in developing the team's best potential. In attempting to achieve excellence, he stresses teamwork, and wants each player to maintain his individuality. Sportsmanship and honor on and off the court are goals of the idealistic coach. He believes that every possible opportunity should be given to players with poorer skills to develop fundamental techniques. Consequently, he does not select a "starting six" until the less-skilled players are convinced that they were selected only after everyone had an equal chance to display their talents.

The idealistic coach divides his attention among all the players and gives substitutes a reasonable chance to try new positions. He allows the poor passer, set-

ter, spiker, server, or digger to play and not be covered or substituted out of the game. He gives every player opportunities to improve weaker skills during game competition, thus building confidence and helping team members become all-around players.

The *realistic* coach is likely to choose and develop a starting line-up early in the season and to concentrate on "starters" during practice sessions. His starting players are usually run through a rigorous conditioning program, and his substitutes are carried on the team as long as they maintain the desire to improve themselves. When they complain about their lack of playing time, they might be told that they should feel free to leave the squad. The realistic coach generally finishes the season with a smaller squad than the idealistic coach.

The realist chooses an offense and defense suited to the abilities of the best players. He is not concerned with developing all-around players and relies on the best talents of each player to develop a winning team.

Poor passers will find themselves under the net when they are in the front row and will find themselves on the end-line when they are in the back row. Poor diggers may find themselves playing the middle-in position behind the blockers during their three rotations across the back row. Setters in the two-hitter attack might not be set unless there is an emergency because their practice time has been devoted to setting. Setters in the three-hitter attack who are less capable spikers than their teammates may be directed to approach for the one-set in the middle from two spiking positions as decoys to hold the middle blocker. Spikers who have not had adequate setting practice may be pushed out of the way by aggressive setters when they have stepped in to set an errant pass. Poor servers and passers may be removed from the backcourt until their skills are perfected in practice sessions.

The *pragmatic coach* may start the game by using an offense and defense that provide for equal participation. If this tactic proves successful, he will maintain this strategy throughout the season. If the team starts to falter during competition, each player will be trained to specialize in a particular role.

The *existentialist coach* might have all the players participate in every fundamental aspect of the game. When every player finds out how they can contribute to the success of the team, they will then be expected to accept the roles of their teammates.

Most coaches develop a unique philosophy that is a blend of the philosophies discussed here.

A coach can be a great teacher, a good organizer, and a thorough conditioner, but if he fails to select the best players to cover the proper positions, makes untimely substitutions, does not use his time outs, and uses the wrong strategy, he will not be successful. Many coaches whose teams fail between the practice session and the game can be classified in several categories.

The *indecisive coach* may have a good game plan with a lot of variables that never become clear to the team. After scouting the opposition and finding a player who cannot pass an easy serve, his instructions may be casually relayed as, "If you get a chance, serve to No. 10." Once the game begins, the indecisive coach may ask the person sitting near him what to do next. The indecisive coach continually has substitutes warming up but can never find the strategic moment to put them in the game. He substitutes only if a player injures himself or asks to be taken out of the game.

The *over-enthusiastic coach* reacts to the play like an ardent fan. He moans, cheers, and yells at the officials, the opposition, and the players. During the time outs, he slaps his players on their backs and is terribly exhausted at the end of the match. He never discusses the game until he sees the charts, and he is so involved with the last play he cannot remember why his team won or lost.

The *morale crusher* is usually a strict disciplinarian and an ardent egotist. Mistakes are not allowed on his team; any offender is immediately removed from the game and given a stern lecture. The morale crusher's teams are characterized by a lack of aggressiveness because players are inclined to avoid the ball so they will not make mistakes.

The *faint heart* cannot bear to watch the action in crucial situations. Overwrought with emotional involvement, the faint heart withdraws by turning away or lapsing into a stupor, while the team captain takes the responsibility of making the judgments when the going gets tough. This approach can be successful when the captain is more knowledgeable than the coach.

The *relaxed spectator* is thoroughly aware of what is happening on the court but believes in predestination. This coach rarely calls a time out or makes a substitution to stop the opponents' momentum because he believes the best team will always win.

The *athlete* is usually a coach who did not quite master the fundamentals of the game in his competitive years but still believes in demonstrating to his players exactly how to play the game. The athlete usually closely supervises all aspects of the team warm-up before the contest and personally sets all of his spikers prior to competition. Of course, setters do not touch the ball for 20 minutes before game time, but the coach gets a chance to maintain "touch" on the ball while giving last-minute encouragement to the hitters. Rival coaches notice that this team's setters always seem to make several errors early in the first game of their match.

Coach Percentage does not seem capable of grasping the psychological aspects of volleyball. Early in the first game, he may send in a serving substitute for a spiker who has just put away seven straight spikes and has sparked the team to a fever pitch. According to Coach Percentage, the spiker may not serve and

pass as well as the substitute, but he is a big part of the team's momentum and should stay in the game. By the time he returns to the game, he may lose his hot streak and be just another hitter. This coach will also take out the substitute who in three backcourt rotations has made three perfect passes and five diving saves while firing the team to great heights. The substitute is made to feel that regardless of how great a job he does in his speciality, he will never be given a chance to play more than a few rotations in a crucial situation.

Successful volleyball coaches who are capable of making the right decisions in competition seem to exhibit an outward calmness and assurance that draws the confidence of their players. All instructions before the game and during time outs are given in a positive, decisive manner, although the coach inwardly may be unsure of himself. Most important, the successful coach learns to blend percentage volleyball with the psychology of the moment. He rarely interrupts or slows down his team's momentum to change strategy, to insert substitutes, or to call time outs. Conversely, he chooses opportune times to slow the momentum of the opposition by substituting players to force the opponent to change successful patterns of attack. Regardless of the situation, the coach can always take a few seconds to speak to the player being substituted out of the game. This habit of speaking briefly to players coming out of the contest often stops morale problems before they develop.

The successful coach knows the capabilities of his players and recognizes their limitations. He realizes that certain players need to be encouraged, whereas others must be calmed down so that rampant emotions do not adversely affect the tactics of the game plan. The successful coach knows that some starting players perform better after a brief rest on the bench, whereas others lose their touch and rhythm. To sum it up, the winning coach knows the capabilities, idiosyncracies, and limitations of his players and helps them to win matches by controlling the tempo of the game and by using their skills to the team's fullest advantage.

PRACTICE SESSIONS

Coach and team must decide upon their goals and aspirations for the coming season. If a team is formed for the recreational value of the sport, it can probably compete well enough to enjoy a low level of competition with one practice a week. The team that aspires to become the national champion must practice longer and harder than the opposition, unless they are substantially physically, technically, and tactically superior to the competition.

The best example of an energetic practice schedule undertaken by amateurs who had to maintain regular working hours was provided in 1964 by the Japanese Women Olympic Volleyball Champions. In Japan, each Olympic team is formed at the members' place of employment. This particular team worked at a company called Nichibo, along with Coach Hirobumi Daimatsu. They kept strict office hours from 8:00 AM to 4:30 PM and practiced only after the completion of the working day. Since their strongest competition was expected to come from a professional Russian women's team,

Coach Hirobumi Daimatsu devised the most rigorous training schedule ever attempted by a group of amateur athletes:

Nichibo Girls' Daily Schedule

8:00 A.M.	Workday begins
4:30 P.M.	Workday ends
5:00 P.M.	Training starts
6:30 P.M.	Snack
6:40 P.M.	Training resumes
11:00 P.M.	Training ends
1:00 or 2:00	Sleep

Coach Daimatsu describes his methods:

We will do what is impossible: We endured the hard training and five hours sleep to win the World Volleyball Championship. When I considered their play insufficient, I made them try over and over again, however late it might be, until they could play sufficiently and completely—that was *my way* of training, though the severity of our training often made by-standers shut their eyes. I cried, "Do you think that you can defeat the Russian team in such a clumsy manner!!!" Many times we practiced until the eastern sky became bright. It was getting late, they could not do what I asked them to do—Even their Captain, Miss Kasai, sometimes protested against me. "Coach! Do you think we can do such a thing?" If I had given into her and softened the hardness of training, all our suffering up to that time, would have come to nothing. I rejected her protest. *"Do what is impossible."*

Orientation Meeting

An orientation meeting for all prospective players should be scheduled prior to the first day of practice. The meeting should begin precisely at the prescribed time and be planned as carefully as any practice session. The following can be covered in 90 minutes:

Completion of player questionnaire (*see* page 259)
Discussion of team standards
Eligibility rules
Playing rules and rule changes
Weight training
Presentation of the basic offense that the team will use
Evaluation of the previous season and expectations for the forthcoming season
Season practice schedule and competitive schedule
Physical examination
Locker room procedure
Reporting for first practice

A clear understanding of team standards is important. The coach must not back himself into a corner by setting standards that are unrealistic for the team. A growing number of athletes resent a coach who places regulations on their grooming habits. However, if long hair interferes with performance, the coach is responsible for pointing out this flaw and the team members must correct it. Team members must also remember that only the coach is authorized to decide who will play.

Complete understanding of eligibility rules for all the competition planned for the upcoming season is imperative. For colleges, this means school, conference, and association eligibility requirements. All technical eligibility questions should be referred to the regular institutional authority on eligibility.

Playing rules and rule changes and their implications should be discussed at the orientation meeting as well as at selected practices throughout the season. More than one match has been lost in national competition because of illegal substitutions and other rule infractions, simply because the team was not aware of current rules.

A film demonstrating the basic fundamentals of the serve, pass, set, spike, dive, and role is valuable (*see* page 281). If the film is not in slow motion, a projector with reverse and stop action should be used to reinforce critical teaching points.

The performance of last year's team should be evaluated and related to expectations for the upcoming season. The coach should give this analysis considerable thought because it can provide the proper motivation for extensive physical conditioning during the early season workouts.

The preparatory and competitive stages of training should be outlined, and the players should understand the emphasis the coach will be placing on physical, technical, and tactical training as the season progresses. Season practice, tournament, and match schedules should be made available to each player.

No player should be allowed to practice until he has had a physical examination. It is recommended that the coach reserve a block of time for physicals and follow through with a *no physical–no practice* rule.

The last items on the agenda should be locker room and equipment procedure and instructions for reporting to the first practice.

SCOUTING AND STATISTICS

The use of charts and statistics contributes to the scouting of team and individual strengths and weaknesses. Experience has shown that in the beginning of the season it is far more valuable to have your own team scouted by assistant coaches, managers, or substitutes than to compile information on opposing teams.

Team Error Charts are particularly valuable to help to determine the amount of time the coach should allocate to the various fundamentals during practice sessions. Errors committed while serving, passing, and setting should be charged to players who mishandle or misdirect the ball. Spiking errors include fouling, hitting out of bounds or into the net, and being blocked for a point or side out.

Because of the amount of subjective judgment necessary to determine whether a spiked ball should have been blocked or allowed to pass over the net, blocking errors are recorded only when the player touches the net or steps over the center line while attempting to block. A position error is charged when the opposition scores a point or side out because of poor court position. The better teams force their opponents to commit errors by serving accurately, blocking well, and keeping the ball in play.

Good physical endurance prevents increased errors during the crucial fifth game of a match. Blocking and positioning errors usually mount up during this period because tired players begin to foul on the block and fail to maneuver into proper court position. Teams that average errors on more than two blocks, two serves, three passes, three sets, or eight spikes per game should devote more practice time to developing these fundamental skills. In average varsity competition, seventeen errors per game is usually the determining point for victory and defeat. In the NCAA Championships, the winning team usually makes less than six errors per game.

Until fundamental skills are satisfactorily developed, the most clever systems of offense and defense will not be executed correctly.

An Individual Error Chart helps to select a starting line-up. An average player commits approximately three errors per game. According to the Individual Error Chart, players A, B, and F played a good match, averaging under two errors per game.

Team Error Chart

Game	Serve	Pass	Set	Spike	Block	Position	Total Errors	Score*
1	2	1	6	5	0	0	14	**15**–12
2	2	3	1	8	1	2	17	**14**–16
3	1	1	3	9	0	0	14	**15**–9
4	1	4	3	10	0	1	19	**7**–15
5	1	4	2	6	3	3	19	**11**–15
Match Totals	7	13	15	38	4	6	83	62–67

*The score of the team being charted appears in bold.

*Individual Error Chart for
Starting Players*

Player	Games Played	Errors	Average Errors
A	4½	7	1.6
B	5	6	1.2
C	5	15	3
D	4	18	4.5
E	5	15	3
F	4	4	1

*Individual Error Chart for
Substitute Players*

Player	Games Played	Errors	Average Errors
G	½	2	4
H	½	2	4
I	½	3	6
J	1	6	6

If a player makes an outstanding number of errors, a separate chart should be maintained on his performance, incorporating the same headings used in the Team Error Chart. The findings should clearly focus on the player's specific areas of weakness; upon seeing his record, he should be motivated to improve his basic skills.

A simple serve-receiving chart that evaluates each player's passes should be kept on *both* teams. The Home Team Receiving Chart (serve-receiving chart) is a compilation of a five-game match. The home team received 85 serves in a 6–2 offensive formation which was used in four of six rotations. During the course of the match, the players passed 27 serves in their four-man receiving pattern, which indicates receiving trouble in that rotation. The four-two offense or two-hitter attack was used in one rotation. The home team only received 16 serves, and the offense was quite successful.

With this information, the next practice session should have been devoted to improving the team's passing and attack in the four-man receiving pattern, with particular attention given to the passing of Kilgour, Irvin, and Becker.

The lightface numbers represent the area of the court in which the player received the serve (see the key at the bottom of the chart). The bold numbers represent the total number of serves received using the particular offensive system noted in the columns.

During the same match, the home team manager charted the passing of the opponents. This chart helped the home team coach decide where the ball should be served during every rotation. For example, in the Opponents' Passing Chart, Floyd passed five balls from the left-back position when his team was in a four-man receiving pattern; three passes were perfect and two could only be set well to one spiker. When he was in the right-back position, he only made one perfect pass out of fourteen attempts and thus was selected as a future serving target the next time the two teams met.

After rating the opposition for a few matches, it should become apparent where serves should be directed. Secondary targets should also be selected if the opposition covers the court for the target or removes the poor passer from the game.

Observe the opponents' outstanding spiker or team leader and note his passing weaknesses. An effective tactic that

Home Team Receiving Chart

Date __4/15__ Home Team Score 15, 12, 15, 13, 15 Rater De Fonseca
         Visitors Score 7, 15, 5, 15, 10 Game 1–5

Serving Order: Player and Number	6–2 Offense +	6–2 Offense 0	6–2 Offense –	4–Man Reception +	4–Man Reception 0	4–Man Reception –	4–2 Offense +	4–2 Offense 0	4–2 Offense –
1. Kilgour	44 1 **4** 3	22 3 **3**	22 **3** 3	111 2 **4**	1111 2 **5**	1 **1**	44444 **5**	4 **1**	—
sub Shirley						11 **2**			
2. Holtzman	4 5 3 2 **4**		22 5 **3**				222 **3**	2222 **4**	
sub									
3. Irvin	5 44 1 **4**	11 44 **4**	4 **1**	222 **3**	2 111 **4**	1 2 **2**			
sub Zajec	5 3 **2**	4 1 **2**	1 **1**		2 **1**	2 **1**			
4. Becker	222222 1111 **10**	22222 555 **14**	22222 11 **10**		33 1 **3**				
Becker		22 1111	222						
5. Machado		33 **2**	3 **1**						
sub Welch						2 **1**			
6. Herring	1 222 3 44 **7**	111 2 **4**	2222 33 **6**				111 **3**		
sub									
Totals	31	29	25	7	13	7	11	5	—

Area of the court where the passer was:

Net

```
    3   4   5
      2   1
```

Net

```
          4
    3         5
      2   1
```

Net

```
    3           5
          4
      2   1
```

+ A pass that can be set into a perfect one-play
0 A pass that can be set to either end spiker
— An ace pass that can be set only to one spiker or a pass that must be set by a spiker

Opponents' Passing Chart

| Date 4/15 | Visitors | | Score 7, 15, 5, 15, 10 | | Rater Doplemore | | | |
| | Home | | Score 15, 12, 15, 13, 15 | | Game 1–5 | | | |

Serving Order: Player and Number	6–2 Offense			4–Man Reception			4–2 Offense		
	+	0	—	+	0	—	+	0	—
1. Floyd	4	11	22 141	1222	3 11	111111 11111 22			
sub Payne	352	22 115	1111 22 223		1	33			
2. Skalecki						333			
sub Stevenson			25			6			
3. Marlowe	1 22	2		2	1	1111			
sub									
4. McFarland	4	21	111122	11222	1122	22222 111 3			
sub Zuelich									
5. Cantor	1 222	1 2222 3 5	2222 22222 346	3	111 3	1112 33			
sub									
6. Carey	11 22	22	1 2 55	122	222	1222			
sub									
Totals	16	19	38	14	16	42			

Area of the court where the passer was:

```
     Net                    Net                    Net
                             4
  3   4   5              3          5           3          5
    2   1                                          4
                       2          1             2    1
```

often pays big dividends is to serve to the star player consistently, hoping that the continuing pressure will cause him to err and destroy his team's confidence in him. Players who cannot withstand pressure should be served to when they begin to cover less court area as the game nears completion.

The most effective spiker on any team can be identified through the formula:

$$E = \frac{U-M}{A},$$

where:

E = spiking efficiency

U = returnable balls that the spiker has attacked for a point or side out

M = errors, or balls blocked for a point or side out and balls hit into the net or out of bounds

A = attempts, or number of balls set to the spiker, balls that the spiker hits or dinks, and balls returned by opponents

The Attack Chart can be used during the match to determine strategy or substitute spikers. The chart on page 227 is a compilation of a five-game match. By analyzing the attack from the left side of the court first, we see that Kilgour received the most sets although he barely had a plus spiking percentage. The opposition had aligned its best blockers against him and the setters should have been instructed to use him as a decoy and set to another spiker opposed by weaker blockers. Although Herring had an excellent percentage from the right side, it is apparent from his minus average that he needed a lot of practice on the left.

The team's middle attack went well, with the exception of Irvin and Zajec.

Both of these men needed much practice on the one-play that is synonomous with the middle attack.

It is important to find a solution to poor spiking efficiency. In Irvin's case, the setter had to give him greater opportunity to attack from the middle position in competition. If the spiker and setter could not perfect the one-play in that rotation, Irvin could not hold the middle blocker and the opposition could mount a two-man block on the end spikers. Zajec still had difficulty coming off the bench to substitute and had to stay warm during the game to regain the effectiveness he had displayed as a starter. Kilgour, Herring, Holtzman, and Becker were almost unstoppable from the right.

Before a league match begins, the spiking statistics of the six leading spikers against four or five of the toughest teams they have faced should be compiled. The Analyzing Attack by Spiking Position chart represents the spiking statistics of a college team against teams that finished the season as the top four finishers in the USVBA National Championships. Statistics are not meaningful when compiled with data from weak competitors.

After reviewing the statistics, the spikers are put in their game positions; the setter delivers balls to them in their weakest position against the best available blockers while the coaching staff evaluates their techniques and spiking tactics.

In Holtzman's case, he was not receiving enough sets on the left side because the setter had lost confidence in his spiking ability. By keeping a spiking diagram with arrows drawn on a scaled court, it was determined that better opponents were continually delivering the line shot to him on his power side and taking advantage of his habit of hitting crosscourt spikes. He worked hard on developing his line shot and finished the season with a .312 percentage on the left side.

Madison and Herring devoted themselves to mastering the one-play in the

Attack Chart

Serving Order: Player and Number	Left +	Left 0	Left —	Middle +	Middle 0	Middle —	Right +	Right 0	Right —
Date 4/5 Game No. 1–5 Home Team / Visitors Score 15, 12, 15, 13, 15 / 7, 15, 5, 15, 10 Rater Event Pelton Match									
1. Machado	3	2	1	3		1	1		
sub									
2. Becker	7	2	2	8		1	10	4	1
sub									
3. Irvin	3	3	1			2	5	2	3
sub Żajec	2	2	1		1	2			3
4. Kilgour	5	4	4	6	5	2	10	1	
sub									
5. Holtzman	6	2	3	4		1	6		
sub									
6. Herring	4	1	5	3		2	8	2	2
sub									
Totals	30	16	17	24	6	11	40	9	9

+ Balls resulting in a point or side out
0 Attempt that does not result in score by either team
— Error, stuff, foul, spike, or dink that allows the other team to score or side out

Analyzing Attack by Spiking Position

Player	Composite	Left	Middle	Right
Kilgour	319/.250	214	356	250
Lee	165/.230	294	250	090
Toyoda	170/.200	180	146	200
Holtzman	123/.182	044	304	203
Madison	200/.180	279	065	180
Herring	208/.158	163	040	178

middle and brought their meager averages in that position up to .307 and .333, respectively, by the end of the season.

By analyzing the attack, it was found that the setters had fallen into a predictable pattern of delivering the set to Kilgour when they were playing against strong competition. His early effectiveness had made this tactic acceptable, but the team attack had become too predictable. The habit of continually setting to the power spiker catches up to a team when the power spiker has an off-day or when the opposing team aligns its two best blockers against the star spiker. Then the setters must deliver the ball to players who have been relatively ignored during the competition.

It is best to move the sets around to keep the attack unpredictable and to give all three attackers the motivation to approach for every spike with the anticipation of receiving the set.

As the season progresses into the competitive stage, more practice time is usually devoted to the finer points of team tactics, at the expense of conditioning. It is particularly important at this stage to chart the spikers' performance in each game to ascertain their endurance at the end of a long match. The Spiker Efficiency by Game chart identifies a tired spiker who should have been substituted out of the fifth game.

An Opponents' Scouting Report (*see* rotations on page 230) can be compiled from passing and spiking charts of the opposition. This report should be discussed with the team during the practice before and immediately prior to the match so that they will understand why defenses are being altered and why serves should be directed at particular areas of the court.

An explanation by the coach must accompany the brief notes on the charts if the game strategy is to be meaningful. The strategy determined from the Opponents' Scouting Report could be presented in this manner on the night before the match:

In Rotation 1, the best place to serve is to B's right, close to the net. B is their best spiker and receives significantly more sets than any other player. Although he is a good passer, he has trouble recovering to spike when he is pulled to his right and close to the net to receive the serve. It is to their advantage to start in this rotation because of B's spiking ability, and we assume they will start there tomorrow night. Therefore, Kilgour will serve to the opponent in this rotation and will

Spiker Efficiency by Game

Game	Unreturn- able Balls	Mis- takes	Balls Re- turned	Total Attempts	Game Average
1	5	2	1	8	.375
2	6	2	–	8	.500
3	5	1	3	9	.444
4	4	1	–	5	.600
5	5	3	2	10	.200
Match Totals	25	9	6	40	.400

practice serving to the three areas indicated in the chart.

C has rarely received a serve when he is in the right-front position and has not passed well from there. If B gets in a groove, we will serve to their right-front player. Be sure to serve very short or B will let the ball go to L, who is an excellent passer. R has trouble in the left-back position when he has to receive balls over B's right shoulder or O's left shoulder. He is an excellent passer if the ball is served directly to him. Becker will block the middle and Herring will block the line against B.

Since B hits very high and deep into our court, we'll attempt to soft block and to deflect the ball to our backcourt diggers. Herring can come off the line more than usual since B doesn't go inside the end blocker but prefers to hit over the block. We'll use the middle-in defense, with Kilgour playing behind our end blocker when B spikes. Do not play outside the end blocker until B hits the line. Irvin will play middle-in although B will not dink unless he is in trouble. We expect Becker to deflect spikes to your area.

Do not attempt to field the hard spike or you'll cut off Holtzman in the right-back position. Holtzman should receive most of B's spikes. Start deeper than usual because most of B's spikes hit a few feet from the backline. He hits with a lot of topspin and rarely hits out. The off-blocker will be Machado. When the set goes to B, get as far off the net as possible before B contacts the ball and then move forward. Machado should get to the 12-ft line near the sideline. Holtzman will be deeper than usual, and Machado will take some of his normal coverage; B will not hit the ball inside the 10-ft line. The set will go to C about one-third of the time. Machado will block the line, even when he's blocking one-on-one. We may "cheat" Becker toward B and end up with several one-on-one situations here.

Irvin, be alert for the middle dink. The rest of the defenders keep normal spacing, but rotate to your left if there is no effective crosscourt attack by C.

The presentation of the defensive scouting report should be handled by the coach subjectively rather than relying on

Opponents' Scouting Report

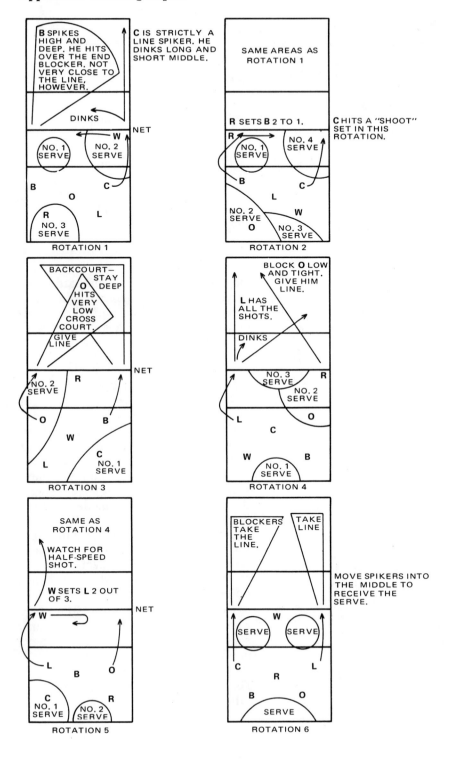

ROTATION 1

B SPIKES HIGH AND DEEP. HE HITS OVER THE END BLOCKER. NOT VERY CLOSE TO THE LINE, HOWEVER.

C IS STRICTLY A LINE SPIKER. HE DINKS LONG AND SHORT MIDDLE.

DINKS

NET

NO. 1 SERVE

NO. 2 SERVE

W

B

O

C

R

NO. 3 SERVE

L

ROTATION 2

SAME AREAS AS ROTATION 1

R SETS B 2 TO 1.

C HITS A "SHOOT" SET IN THIS ROTATION.

R

NO. 1 SERVE

NO. 4 SERVE

B

C

L

NO. 2 SERVE

W

O

NO. 3 SERVE

ROTATION 3

BACKCOURT— STAY DEEP

O HITS VERY LOW CROSS COURT.

GIVE LINE

NET

NO. 2 SERVE

R

O

B

W

L

C

NO. 1 SERVE

ROTATION 4

BLOCK O LOW AND TIGHT. GIVE HIM LINE.

L HAS ALL THE SHOTS.

DINKS

NO. 3 SERVE

R

NO. 2 SERVE

L

O

C

W

B

NO. 1 SERVE

ROTATION 5

SAME AS ROTATION 4

WATCH FOR HALF-SPEED SHOT.

W SETS L 2 OUT OF 3.

NET

W

L

B

O

C

NO. 1 SERVE

R

NO. 2 SERVE

ROTATION 6

BLOCKERS TAKE THE LINE.

TAKE LINE

MOVE SPIKERS INTO THE MIDDLE TO RECEIVE THE SERVE.

W

SERVE

SERVE

C

L

R

B

O

SERVE

scouting charts and statistics. Within one match, a coach can pick out the ineffective blockers and pick up weaknesses in a team's defense. The defense can be easily identified during the match. However, identifying poor diggers and players who are habitually out of position can be done only if the team being scouted has strong opposition.

The best places to evaluate the blockers are above and behind the referee's stand and behind the blocking team's endline in the center of the court. By watching the match from both vantage points, the coach can see if the blocker reaches over the net. Lateral arm movement can also be evaluated. The backcourt setter on defense should be watched. Does he leave his position before the ball is spiked to run to the front row and set when the ball is dug?

Some players are too slow to cover dink shots and have a tendency to compensate by playing too close to the net where they cannot possibly dig a ball. Other players squat low to the floor before the ball is hit or stand flat-footed and do not react fast enough to dive forward to recover a short dink shot.

When scouting the defense, one should observe the following:

The weak blockers
The types or type of defense used
The best areas to dink
The poor diggers

A scoring summary is helpful for the visiting press. If this summary is used by the coach, it should identify individual players rather than describe events in terms of teams.

THE GAME

The team should be taped and in game uniform and sweatsuits at least one hour before game time. Ten minutes should be set aside for reviewing and finalizing the game plan. The coach should be definite and positive in this final recap of game strategy.

If the opposition is strong, the players should know where and to whom they should serve, who are the weak blockers, what is the opponents' defense, and where are best areas to attack. They should be familiar with the spiking habits and patterns of their opponents and be given explicit instructions on how to stop their offense. The starting line-up should be announced and any peculiarities of the officials reviewed.

If the match begins at 8:00 PM, the players should be jogging around the floor by 7:10 PM. The *pre-game warm up* can be directed by the captain or by the coach. The players should jog and then go through a team or individual routine of stretching and warm-up exercises for 15 minutes. By 7:25 PM, they should pair up with two players to one ball and set, pass, and play pepper until about 7:35 PM. The next 15 minutes should be devoted to spiking, serving, and receiving.

While the team is warming up, the manager should check the following:

1. Is the microphone working?
2. Are there towels in the visitors' and home locker rooms and on the benches?
3. Have the locker room doors been secured?
4. Are the referee, umpire, announcer, trainer, scorekeeper, and linesmen all present?

5. Does the referee have the game ball?

The coach can watch the warm up while going over the charting assignments with the staff. Before the first game, teams warm up together until 10 minutes before introductions are made, whereupon each team takes the entire court for five minutes. The referee should gather the captains together about one-half hour before game time for the toss of the coin to decide serve side. The team that wins the serve warms up first.

While both teams are warming up, there may be a few subtleties exchanged among the opponents in the form of bouncing spikes off opposing setters and displays of spiking prowess designed to impress the opposition. This activity is usually exchanged between the younger members of the team, while the veterans concentrate on the percentage shots they intend to use in competition instead of the straight-down, warm-up spikes that are usually blocked for a point.

Some teams are so awed at watching their opponents warming up that they lose the match before it begins. It is a simple matter for the setter to place the ball about a foot over the opponents' court to allow a spiker to drive the ball straight down. Some teams attempt to dominate the shared court by using three setters and a left, center, and right spiking line, which gives the opposition no alternative but to spend its time getting hit or dodging spikes.

The *starting rotation* is very important because of the various match-ups and mismatches that may occur. For example, a player may be convinced that he cannot handle an opponent's serve in the left-back position and will be useless if the

coach matches him up with that server. Some blockers convince certain spikers that they cannot hit the ball past the block, and other spikers simply cannot be stopped by certain blocking combinations.

More than one crucial match has been lost by a coach leaving his line-up form within view of his opponents. As a precaution, line-ups should be personally handed to the scorer about 10 minutes before game time. He will check the line-up for form and record it. There should be no confusion about who will serve first because the referee or umpire should hold the toss of the coin well ahead of the time when line-ups are to be filled out.

It is good practice to jot down the opposition's starting rotation as the umpire lines up the team prior to the start of the game. In the first game, most coaches fall into the habit of either starting their best spiker in the left-front position, regardless of which team wins the serve, or of arranging their line-up so that their best server serves first. If their team wins the serve, the ace server should be in the right-back position; when the opponent serves first, the best server should start in the right-front position and rotate to serve first when the team gets a side out. Other common tactics include placing the best passer in the right-back position or starting a backcourt specialist in the right-back position.

A team is allowed twelve substitutions per game, and each player is allowed three entries in every game, providing the re-entry is to the same position. If a game plan called for dividing one position between a strong spiker in the frontcourt and a strong digger in the backcourt, the player who can make the

USVBA LINE-UP FORM (per Rule 3.62)

Team————   Match No. ———
Please note: Write the players' numbers
in the positions in which they will *start*.
Mark the Captain—C.

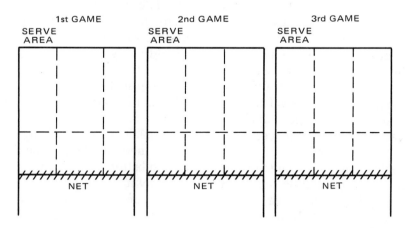

greatest contribution to the team should start on the bench since the third time the player enters the game, he must stay in unless the coach wishes to put another player in that position. DGWS rules do not allow a player to enter the game for the third time; starting the game counts as an entry.

If a coach wins the first game, he usually keeps the same starting line-up or moves the rotation back or forward one position, depending on whose turn it is to serve. When the opposing coach loses badly, he usually starts new players or starts the team in different rotations to try new match-ups. When an opponent has been well scouted, it is always good procedure to have all of the opponents' rotations and your intended match-ups written down so that quick decisions about new line-ups or substitutions can be made.

After team introductions have been made, the entire team should form a pre-game huddle in front of the bench for any last minute instructions and to re-emphasize important points. All players should be included so that everyone is aware of the strategy being used when they enter the game.

Teams should change their strategy during the game to meet the situation. As the opponents' strengths, weaknesses, and strategy become evident, it is wise to make changes in play to take maximum advantage of the situation. Even the best game plans must be changed to counter strong players and alignments and to exploit weak spots of the opposing team. Strong blockers should be switched to positions where they can combat the strong spikes of the opposing team.

If the coach sees that a spiker is scoring by hitting the ball down the line, the blockers must be signaled to block the line and to force the opponent to hit crosscourt. At the same time, the backcourt defense should be realigned so that the best digger is assigned to the area where the block is channeling the hit. Many times an experienced captain can make changes when the ball is dead and prevent incurring charged time out.

Occasionally, a team leader develops with the ability to choose an opportune time to switch defenses during the course of a rally. Most players understand that a change in defense is in order if the opposition is scoring with the present alignment. However, very few players can choose the precise moment to switch from the middle-back to middle-in defense. Usually this moment occurs when the opposing spiker is tiring or out of position for a set and likely to dink or use a half-speed shot.

When the captain is in the front row, the signal for the switch must be verbal. When the defense learns to play together as a cohesive unit, the backcourt can change alignment by letting the center-back player change positions during a rally, with the other backcourt players following his lead. The opposition will not recognize a defensive switch during a rally and will usually direct the ball to an area it has found open earlier in the game—only to have the ball passed by a newly assigned defensive player.

A strong outside blocker who has just blocked his opponent may sense that the spiker will not be set again on the next play. When this situation occurs, the blocker should take the initiative of changing assignments with a weaker teammate in order to align himself with the spiker who is going to receive the set.

Substitutes can be used as messengers

to change offensive and defensive tactics if the coach is not willing to use a time out or has no time outs remaining. While on the bench, the substitute should study the opposing players' assignments so he will be aware of with whom he will be matched. Serving specialists should study the opponents for passing weaknesses. Blocking and spiking specialists should study the opponents' favorite attack patterns and look for weaknesses in the defense. Defensive backcourt specialists should familiarize themselves with the oppositions' spiking habits. If the coach plans a line-up change for the next game, the new player should be inserted as a substitute in the current game, particularly if the present game is one-sided.

As soon as the coach perceives that a player is starting to lose his effectiveness, he should signal the appropriate substitute or substitutes to warm up on the sideline. Substitutes should also share in this responsibility and exercise on the sideline whenever they feel themselves getting cold. A common tactic is to direct the action to the player coming off the bench in an attempt to force errors before the substitute can warm up and get in the groove.

Changing the strategy of the game during a 30-second time out requires a clear explanation of the most important variables in that particular game. The able coach will soon realize which players, if any, can contribute useful suggestions during time outs; he will quickly learn to evaluate and to put into action suggestions that will win games. It is advisable to have the statistician sit next to the coach so that the key statistics influencing the game can be quickly identified before the coach reaches the playing floor. The coach should not chastise a player or players during the time out but rather advise the team in a positive manner on techniques or a change in tactics. Some teams may not develop adequate leadership on the playing floor and must rely totally on signals from the bench to supplement important strategy contrived during the brief time-out period.

When the opponent calls a time out in order to break your momentum, the server should be cautioned to take a little off the first serve to make sure it does not hit the net or go out of bounds.

Then the server can come back with a tough serve after the first point.

The rest period between games is 3 minutes. If the team lost the game, the coach may want to change the line-up to keep his best attacker away from the opponents' strong blockers. There is time to review the opponents' tactics with the team and to decide on any strategy changes for the next game. The winning team often feels relieved and so may relax at the beginning of the next game. The coach should remind a winning team about this factor and encourage them to maintain their momentum in the next

Figure 11–1 *Time Out.* Generally, time outs should be called when a team loses 3 consecutive points; when a player or players is upset; when the coach wants to confer with the referee; when the team is playing poorly; or when a change in tactics is in order. Time outs should never be called when a team has gained momentum. (Stan Abraham)

game. Before three minutes are up, the coach, manager, or captain should give the scorer the written form with the starting players in their starting rotations. Line-ups cannot be changed after the referee has given the signal for the teams to take their positions on the court. If a team or coach is confused about the line-up, positions can be verified with the scorer when the ball is dead.

If conditions allow, the coach should talk briefly to the players being replaced. Many times players do not understand why they are taken out of the line-up, and a quick explanation can often prevent a misunderstanding.

After the match is over, the coach and his team meet in a closed locker room or other private area to talk about the causes of victory or defeat. Pertinent team statistics are discussed, and the coach praises the team if they played up to their potential and lost. The team should also be appraised of poor play if they won. This discussion should be conducted by a composed coach so the players will be in the right frame of mind for the next practice.

12

Conditioning and Training

What is the secret of championship volleyball teams? How do they win year after year?

First, the players' development must be on a constant basis: year-round indoor or outdoor courts must be available so athletes can regularly play under the guidance of experienced players and instructors.

Second, young players must be properly motivated to take up the sport. Tournaments must be held during all seasons to maintain interest. During the warmer months of the year, outdoor doubles tournaments should be held for several classifications of skill.

Third, and most important, championship teams must be systematically conditioned through a well-planned, seasonal training cycle.

CONDITIONING PROGRAMS

The following conditioning programs are applicable to both men and women. Throughout the United States, women are joining men in athletic department weight rooms or, in many cases, building separate weight-training facilities. Although women adjust to conditioning programs as well as men, women have larger stores of adipose tissue that gives them a smaller portion of strength in relation to their body weight. The strength of women is less than that of men because of this larger store of fatty tissue and their smaller heart size in relation to their body weight. Women are capable of training with weights and of gaining considerable strength without showing the marked increase in muscle size found in men because they are replacing fatty tissue with muscle tissue.

Many physiologists and doctors believe that menstruation does not inhibit motor performance; "however, premenstrual fluid retention may cause temporary anxiety and fatigue."[1] The intensity

[1] The Committee on Standards of the Division For Girls and Women's Sports, *Philosophy and Standards For Girls and Women's Sports* (Washington, D.C.: American Association for Health, Physical Education, and Recreation, 1973), p. 19.

of the training should be determined by the woman athlete during her period of menstruation.

GENERAL EXERCISES

Exercises without weights or the ball can develop *flexibility, strength,* and *endurance. Flexibility* is particularly important in preventing muscle tears in the legs and lower back. Players constantly contract the muscles in their back and legs when they are blocking or spiking. This causes them to lose their full range of motion and become subject to muscle tears and strains.

Flexibility Exercises

Flexibility or stretching exercises should be in every practice session and before every match. Before attempting stretching exercises, players should jog and perform jumping jacks to warm up their muscles. Slow stretching is suggested to prevent the player's muscles from tearing during warm up. Explosive stretching exercises before the match begins will cause injuries that show up during competition.

Because muscles strains and pulls in the back and legs are relatively common volleyball injuries, it is recommended that the following exercises be included in workouts and pregame warm ups.

Trunk Twister. Stand with feet spread shoulder-width apart and twist the body from side to side. Do not move the feet.

Alternate Toe-Toucher. Stand with feet spread more than shoulder-width apart and alternately touch toes with fingers on opposite hands.

Groin Stretcher. Spread legs considerably more than shoulder-width apart and alternately squat over one leg while fully extending the other leg.

Crossover Toe Touch. Cross legs in a fully extended standing position. Bending forward slowly from the waist, touch the ground.

Tail Gunner. Position body in a full squat. Hold toes of both feet with the fingers. Without releasing toes, slowly attempt to extend legs fully.

Quadriceps Stretch. Start from kneeling position, with hands on soles of feet. Slowly move the back of the head toward the ground.

Crossover Toe Touch. Lie flat on the back, hands outstretched at right angles to the body. Slowly raise one leg up and over the body to touch the palm of the opposite hand.

Toes Over Head. Lie flat on the ground on the back and slowly raise legs up and over the head until toes touch the ground. Touch toes of both feet to the ground over the left and right shoulder. This is an excellent stretching exercise for preventing the lower back muscles from tightening up.

Exercises to Increase Strength

"The force with which a muscle contracts constitutes a measure of strength. The various strength tests measure the muscle forces acting through the levers of the skeleton rather than the contraction of the muscle per se."[2] Individuals

[2] Richard A. Berger, Chuck Coker, and Harold Zinkin, "Power Makes the Athlete," *Scholastic Coach* (June 1972): 42.

Figure 12–1   *Groin Stretcher.* The USA's Women's Team includes this exercise as part of their pregame warm up. (Barry Schreiber)

may have a high degree of muscle force but poor leverage and, consequently, perform with only moderate strength. The athlete with great muscle force and good leverage will be the strongest. Obviously, nothing can be done about changing the attachment of the muscle to the bone, so the only way to increase strength is to improve the muscle force capacity.[3]

Superior leg strength necessary for satisfactory vertical jumping is paramount to the volleyball player. The strength of the abdominal muscles and, to a lesser degree, of the back muscles, plays a large part in the player's spiking action. Experience has shown that above-average arm strength is not a prerequisite for the successful spiker. Quickness and coordination are crucial to superior spiking. "Research has revealed an inverse relationship between muscle force and speed of movement: As velocity is increased, maximum contraction force is reduced. . . . In fact, where the movement is re-

stricted to the limbs, there may be no difference in speed between strong and weak individuals."[4]

The following exercises are recommended for workouts but in general they are not intended for pregame warmups:

Sit-Ups.
Jackknife Sit-Ups. Lie flat on the back. Simultaneously lift both extended legs and trunk toward each other until outstretched hands touch toes.
Power Sit-Ups. Lie flat on the back, hands clasped behind the neck and legs extended. (A partner holds the ankles.) Touch knees with elbows and return to within a foot of the floor; pause, then repeat. Do not return to the floor until the exercise is completed.
Back-Ups. Lie on the stomach, legs extended and hands clasped behind the neck. (A partner holds the ankles.) Raise the upper part of the body as far off the floor as possible; return to the floor and repeat. Players with strong backs may pause a foot from the floor for a greater overload of the back muscles.
Stomach and Leg Exercise. One player lies on his back and holds ankles of his partner who stands behind him, whose feet are shoulder-width apart. The player on the ground rapidly lifts his extended legs up over his head toward the standing player, who attempts to push the legs back toward the floor. The object of the player on the floor is to prevent his feet from returning to the ground by powerfully contracting his stomach and leg muscles.
Squats. Jump up and down two

[3] *Ibid.*, p. 42.

[4] *Ibid.*, p. 42.

times from a full squat position; jump the third time for maximum height.

Endurance Exercises

Unless a player has good endurance, his muscles will become tired and fail to respond properly during prolonged competition. By observing the height of a player's jump during a long match, it will become evident whether present endurance levels must be increased. An example of a good jumper with poor endurance is the spiker who contacts the ball 30 in. above the net during warm-ups and only 20 in. above the net during the fifth game. Muscular endurance is developed by repetitively working tired muscles. The athlete who has the ability to drive himself after becoming tired will gradually improve his endurance. The team that can remain physically strong throughout a five-game match or tournament can defeat technically superior teams.

Nothing hinders proper endurance faster than being *overweight*. The player who is 10 pounds overweight must jump and lift those 10 pounds hundreds of times during a match. The overweight athlete must train harder than his teammates at proper weight and generally has great difficulty in maintaining proper endurance.

In recent years, overweight athletes have not been seen in international volleyball competition. Players who tend to gain weight out of season and quickly try to get back in shape during the conditioning phase of the season suffer a loss of strength, endurance, and speed which puts them behind their teammates from the beginning. Periodic weight checks throughout the year can motivate athletes to control their weight.

The following endurance exercises are best used at the end of practice sessions:

Elastic Jump. Zigzag a 25-ft length of elastic between 6 to 18 players at a height of 3 ft. The players jump over each length of elastic using a 2-ft take-off similar to the jump used to spike. On the second trip over the elastic, the jumpers go over forward, backward, and forward again. Raise the height and repeat.

Rim Touch. Jump and touch a basketball rim 50 times without resting.

Net Jump. Select partners of the same height and place them on opposite sides of the net. At 5-ft intervals, partners jump and clap their hands over the net. Repeat jump 50 times.

Step Jump. Ascend steps by jumping one or two steps at a time using a 2-ft takeoff.

Mock Spike. Jump and simulate a

Figure 12–2 *Squat and Jump.* A maximum jump with many repetitions should be used to increase strength and endurance. (Barry Schreiber)

spiking action using an approach and 2-ft takeoff. Repeat 25 times in succession.

WEIGHT TRAINING

A discussion of weight-training procedures for increasing the height and quickness of the vertical jump is necessary for players who are new to the team. The athlete who can lift the heaviest weight will not necessarily jump the highest in game competition; a weaker athlete may be able to contract his or her muscles faster. In speed movements, such as jumping to spike or to block a volleyball, the athlete who effects the greatest force in a brief interval achieves the most success. Because it takes about 2.5 seconds to achieve maximum force isometrically,[5] the maximum potential force is rarely achieved by a blocker or by a spiker unless he or she is defending or attacking an extremely high set.

Returning athletes who have been weight training during the post-season period should continue their program in order to maintain their increased "spring" until the end of the competitive season. The coach should provide a copy of weight-training theory and its implications for volleyball for each player.[6]

Serious players lift weights to increase the height of their vertical jump and to sustain maximum jumping ability throughout long matches and tournaments. The low squatting position of backcourt players tends to sap vital leg strength and to decrease the height of the jump in net play—unless the legs are thoroughly conditioned. Untrained athletes should first complete 50 consecutive squats with weights that weigh half of their body weight before training with heavy weights. This procedure will screen players who are not yet safely capable of working with heavier weights. The *theory of specificity* maintains that training is specific to the cells and to the specific structural and functional elements within a cell that are overloaded. Transfer of training occurs only to the extent that the same muscle fibers are recruited and used in a similar manner.[7]

When weight training to increase vertical jumping height for the spike, the player should squat just as low as he would in competition. Slow-motion films may be used to determine knee angle and foot spacing. If the spiker is using the correct technique, the feet should be almost parallel. The legs should be extended as quickly as possible so that the muscle fibers are used as they are in competition. Players with strong backs and arms may add a further refinement by jumping with a barbell held behind their neck above the shoulders. The jump should be made as quickly as possible, and the arms should push against the barbell to prevent the neck from supporting its weight. The back should be kept straight to prevent muscle strain or tear when the athlete lands on the floor. The shock of returning to the floor must be absorbed by a controlled squatting action to prevent damage to the supportive structure surrounding the knee joints and vertebrae.

[5] *Ibid.*, p. 42.
[6] John A. Faulkner, "New Perspectives in Training for Maximum Performance," *The Journal of the American Medical Association* 205 (Sept. 9, 1968): 117–22.

[7] *Ibid.*, p. 119.

The *theory of strength training* contends that lifting weights from one to six times with maximum effort is the most effective method of producing an increase in muscle size and of increasing muscle strength. This training should be carried out through the full range of motion required for the athlete's particular skill.[8] Training to increase the height of the vertical jump may be done every other day. However, "many athletes will experience an additional gain of five to ten percent in vertical jumping height by daily lifts."[9]

The *theory of overload* contends that for skeletal muscle cells to increase in size or functional ability or both they must be taxed to the limit of their present ability to respond.[10]

As additional strength is gained, more weight can be added to the program to ensure continued gains. Increasing the weight gradually is mandatory to prevent excessive stretching of ligaments surrounding the joint. When the muscles become fatigued or weight is excessive, full weight is placed on the ligaments.[11] "Rapid movements should result in the selective recruitment of the faster fibers."[12] Speed training requires the movement of light loads at a high velocity compatible with correct technique.

When training for leg speed, it is suggested that a light weight be used in three sets of ten explosive jumping squats.

The *theory of endurance training* maintains that the "interaction of load, speed, and duration may be successfully resolved by either continuous exercise or intermittent exercise."[13] The important point is to overload the muscle group or groups.

Experience has shown that 50 daily, full-controlled squats using weights that weigh 50 percent of a player's body weight builds the leg endurance necessary to maintain the low defensive backcourt position throughout a long tournament.

Safety Rules and Procedures

All lifts should be done with smooth, rhythmic, powerful motions with full extension of the arms. Lifting for strength and quickness involves a maximum effort in short bursts over an extended period of time. The beginner must use light weights until the proper technique is established. Most coaches use a three-day-a-week program of lifting on alternate days to allow for the removal of waste products from the muscle before strenuous lifting is resumed. Some well-conditioned athletes prefer to lift daily; there may be a slight gain in strength for some individuals following a daily program, as opposed to lifting on alternate days.

The execution of an exercise from the starting position back to the starting

---

[8] *Ibid.,* p. 119.

[9] From a personal interview with David Major, the Pan American Weightlifting Coach, on July 29, 1967.

[10] Faulkner, "New Perspectives in Training for Maximum Performance," p. 117. Emphasis added.

[11] Jay A. Bender, "Some Guidelines for the Development of Exercise Programs," *The Physical Educator* (May 1966): 60–62.

[12] Faulkner, "New Perspectives in Training for Maximum Performance," p. 119.

[13] Faulkner, "New Perspectives in Training for Maximum Performance," p. 120.

position is called a *repetition*. A *set* is a given number of repetitions. There are usually two to three minutes of rest between sets. Warm-up exercises are always performed before weight training to increase circulation, to elevate body temperature, and to stretch the muscle fibers. By increasing the rate of circulation, the muscles are given increased oxygen to perform the heavy tasks and are able to carry away the by-products of the exercise at a faster rate. A rise in body temperature and moderate stretching of the muscles also helps to prevent strains and tears in the muscles and supporting structures.

A few simple safety rules and procedures will prevent injury: 1) always warm up before beginning to train with weights; 2) learn the correct technique from a qualified instructor; 3) never lift a bar without collars; 4) do not train near other objects or people, or walk close to a person who is training; 5) use chalk to keep your hands dry; and 6) always use a spotter on difficult or heavy lifts.

Players with a history of knee problems are not allowed to weight train unless they are allowed to do so by an orthopedic specialist. Many doctors feel that weight training strengthens the muscles around the knee joint and makes it more stable. Their recommendation usually depends on the condition of the player's supporting knee joint structure. Players with a history of back problems are not allowed to weight train unless they are allowed to do so by a neurologist. Some of the better neurologists charge up to sixty dollars for an initial consultation without X-rays. In many colleges, this type of consultation is provided by the Student Health Center. Since tremendous stress is placed on the

back, the student athlete with back problems should not weight train until a written recommendation is received by the coach from the neurologist. All athletes who perform squats should use a weight belt that supports the lower back.

Lifting Techniques

1. Squat as low as required for the specific technique for which you are training. The coach can use slow motion films to decide which angle to use in the block and the spike. Do not squat beyond a 90° knee angle when using heavy weights.

2. Position a bench under your buttocks to prevent dipping below the 90° angle of the half squat. Do not relax when touching the bench if you are performing half squats. Use a power rack, which guides the barbell and prevents injury to the athlete's back.

3. Balance the barbell on the base of the neck and push up hard with the hands to release some of the pressure on the neck.

4. Keep your head up and stare at a point 10 ft up on the wall. Holding the head up during the lift helps to eliminate back strain.

5. Inhale deeply and lower yourself to the desired squat position. Explode or jump to a standing position and exhale.

UCLA Weight-Training Program

At UCLA, the recommended weight-training program for volleyball players emphasizes squatting and jumping movements to increase leg strength, which is so important for a volleyball player. The UCLA program uses the following weight-lifting exercises:

1. To gain additional strength and speed, squat six to ten times with the maximum amount of weight that you can lift in good form. Extend your legs as quickly as possible. Add more weight as soon as your muscles can handle the additional load. Men may squat with as high as 200 to 300 percent of body weight while women may go as high as 150 to 200 percent of body weight.

2. To develop speed and the ability to jump quickly, perform three sets of 10 explosive jumping squats with one half of your body weight.

3. To build and maintain the endurance to stay in a low defensive position, perform 50 consecutive half-squats with 50 percent of your body weight.

Observance of jumping ability at recent international competition clearly shows that the Cuban men are the best jumpers in the world. At a 1974 volleyball coaching seminar, the director of Japanese Volleyball Research outlined the Cuban exercises to a group of Canadian coaches and players:

1. One half-squat at an angle of 90° using a barbell on shoulders and completing 3 sets of 10.

2. Squat jumps at angle of 90° using a barbell weighing 50 percent of the player's body weight and completing 2 sets of 15 .

3. Jumps that are 2 in. less than a player's best vertical jump. The knees are bent at an angle of 90°

for every jump, and 3 to 5 sets of 10 must be completed.

4. Full squat performed 50 times, using a barbell weighing 50 percent of the player's weight.

Dr. Carl McGown, the 1976 USA Olympic Men's Volleyball Coach, stresses that muscle fibers "are incapable of performing various degrees of work; they are either working as hard as possible or not at all." Therefore, it is important to involve all of the muscle fibers in the work, and "the resistance [the weight] must be so heavy that all of the fibers are required to move it."

Dr. McGown advocates ending the set only when it is impossible to move the weight; in other words, exercising to the point of complete failure. He further states that "in the squats, the actual point of failure may be reached when it is impossible to continue without excessive bending of the back. If you find yourself starting to straighten the legs while your back is still bent, that is the time to stop."

Dr. McGown's weight-training program for the USA Men's Team includes half-squats, quarter-squats, and ten other exercises for total body development. The purpose of the quarter squats is to develop the vastus medialis, the muscle that contributes to the last 15° of the vertical jump. He recommends at first using a weight of 200 pounds and one set of 20 repetitions for men on the USA squad.

Technique Conditioning

Technique conditioning involves conditioning that uses fundamental volleyball techniques.

Exerting tired muscles in rigorous drills leads to greater muscular endurance. Experience has shown that the following drills are particularly suited to condition players as they practice techniques:

Jump Set.   Three setters stand 10 ft apart in a straight line along the net and, with a maximum jump, set the ball to one another. The setter in the middle jumps and back sets the ball.

Endurance Spike.   The spiker hits 40

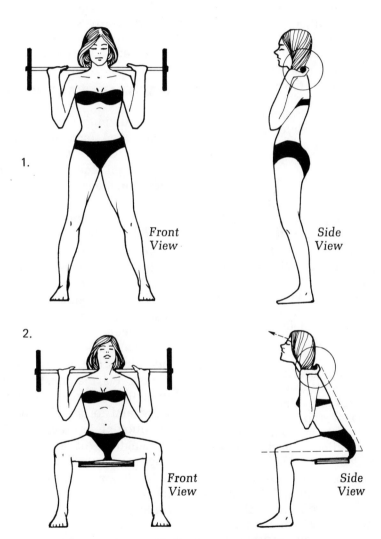

Figure 12–3   *Half Squat.*   The head should be kept up and the back straight during this exercise to prevent muscle strain.

sets in a row as quickly as possible. The rest of the players retrieve the balls to ensure continuous action.

Endurance Blocking. One blocker moves across the net and blocks the left, middle, and right spikers in rotation. The setter delivers a ball to the next spiker as the blocker completes the jump. Ten to fifteen trips across the front row blocking all three positions are usually sufficient.

Running Dig. The player starts on the sideline and runs toward the middle of the backline to dig a spike hit from the net. After diving or rolling to dig the ball, the player returns to the original starting position and repeats the action.

Backcourt Defense. If using the middle-in defense, station a player in each deep corner of the backcourt and a middle-in player in the center of the court on the 10-ft line. Two spikers stand on tables in the left and right spiking positions and maintain a continuous attack directed at the three defenders who attempt to dig and set the ball to targets in the front corners of their court. The rest of the players retrieve balls to ensure no break in the action.

Diving Save. The coach stands on a table and dinks balls over the net to a player in a backcourt defensive position. The player runs and makes a diving pass to a target and returns to the starting position. The drill should then be repeated.

Block Rebounds. The player squats 3 ft from a flat wall and reacts to spikes rebounding off the wall. The spiker stands a few feet behind the player and delivers an assortment of hard and off-speed spikes and dinks against the wall for the player to dig. The player fielding the simulated block rebound should squat at a 90°

to 115° angle to pass the ball straight up into the air.

Backcourt Spiking Game. Three or four players form a team and play a regulation game, with one rule exception: the ball cannot be spiked unless the player leaves the floor from behind the 10-ft spiking line. This game is particularly effective at the end of a long practice when extra motivation is needed to work tired muscles.

SEASONAL TRAINING CYCLE

An individual conditioning program should be commenced before training begins. As the season draws near, the team might meet as a group on Tuesdays and Thursdays and work on individual conditioning programs on Monday, Wednesday, and Friday. The coach should schedule a conference with each player and develop an individualized program that takes into account the age, physical condition, experience, and skill level of each athlete so that the player will have a personalized plan of improvement.

The attitude of the players during the individual conference cannot be overlooked. Players must want to develop strength, endurance, flexibility, and speed and to learn the basic theories of conditioning in order to train effectively. Explanations of the cardiovascular and respiratory systems and principles of strength, endurance, flexibility, and speed training are invaluable to the athlete.

Conditioning Phase

During group workouts, the team should concentrate on strength and flexibility

Seasonal Training Cycle

Month	Training Phase	Physical Training	Technical Training	Tactical Training
1st	Conditioning	70%	25%	5%
2nd	Conditioning	70	25	5
3rd	Conditioning	65	25	10
4th	Preparatory	35	40	25
5th	Competitive	35	35	30
6th	Competitive	30	35	35
7th	Special training cycle for playoffs			

exercises as well as technical training on the approach and jump for the spike. Technical mastery of the dive and roll also should be stressed. During the second half of the two- or three-hour practice, individual and partner ball-handling skills used in the pass, set, dig, dive, and roll should be stressed. These drills should be as rigorous as possible so that the players build up endurance in the muscles used in competition.

To be effective, the conditioning should be gradual and repetitive. To ensure continuous improvement, the intensity and duration should correspond to the strengths and abilities of the team members. Achievement of maximum conditioning within a short period is rarely possible and also may cause injury to the athlete.

After some prospective players are cut from the squad, individual technical training in the block, spike, and serve should be introduced. The final squad cut to 12 players can be made at the last practice. Some teams may choose to carry about 18 players on the squad and to enter two teams in tournament competition in order to give the younger players valuable experience.

During the conditioning program, the players must learn physiological principles that contribute to effective power and endurance development and the proper methods of power and endurance training. Conditioning will not be successful if it is merely thought of as repetitive physical exercise. Coaches must explain the reasons for a particular exercise or drill and how it relates to achieving success in the sport. It is important that players understand the techniques and tactics for which they are developing their capabilities.

Experience has shown that when players acquire the practical and theoretical knowledge of volleyball while developing physical abilities, the morale and will power necessary to build and maintain a high level of conditioning are enhanced.

Some volleyball teams characteristically win tournaments at the beginning of the season, but their achievements decline toward the height of the season. In these cases, perhaps the athletes had a great deal of weight training and running at the beginning of the season but ignored this training aspect during the preparatory and competitive stages. Gradually, the athletes' strength and endurance wane because of the lack of exercise to develop strength, and their performance declines correspondingly.

Preparatory Phase

The volleyball is used in physical training during the preparatory phase. At this stage, the athlete develops thorough technical training in spiking, blocking, and digging. The coach can stand on a table and spike balls just out of the player's effective range of movement. The digger reacts to the spiked ball by running, diving, or rolling to retrieve the spike, rising to his feet, digging the next spike, and so on. When the digger is exhausted, he retrieves balls for the coach while a fresh player takes his place.

On the other court, a player may be spiking 30 or 40 consecutive sets while his teammates quickly retrieve the balls to ensure continuous action. A blocking drill can be formed to build endurance by aligning one blocker against three spikers. As the player completes the block, the next spiker passes the ball and approaches for the set. The blocker must move as quickly as possible from one spiker to another.

It is important that every player participate during these drills, either running balls down or feeding balls to the coach. Players develop a sense of pride by performing as well as possible during the drills. Teammates who endure the same conditioning procedure should yell encouragement and try to motivate the occasional goldbricker to perform with his utmost physical capabilities. The coach should continually alert his players to use correct techniques during these endurance drills to prevent bad habits from being formed.

The preparatory phase of the season may last from four to six weeks. Although practice matches and tournaments may play an important role in the motivation of the athlete during this phase, the emphasis during practice should be on technical execution and conditioning; team tactics of attack and defense should be refined in competition.

During practice matches, many different player combinations and rotations should be used and evaluated subjectively by the coaches and statistically by trained managers who chart serves, passes, sets, spikes, blocks, and digs. Coaches use competition in the preparatory phase in order to evaluate starting

Preparatory Training Cycle

Week	Main Purpose	Intensity of Training
1	Development of techniques	Medium
2	Improvement of techniques	Heavy
3	Development of strength and endurance	Maximum
4	Blending of techniques and tactics	Medium
5	Improvement of tactics	Medium to light

line-ups and to determine the substitutes who react well in pressure situations.

The coaching staff should constantly stress the *what* and *why* of every drill so that the team understands clearly and precisely the problems involved in training. Some players choose to cut their weight training down to twice a week, while other players may prefer to continue daily weight training.

Competitive Phase

The competitive phase begins when standings are kept for league play or selection to regional and national tournaments. For the first time during the season, the team members should know who is in the starting line-up and next to whom they will be playing on offense. Up to one-third of the practice at this stage should be devoted to team tactics, with emphasis on team passing, blocking, and digging.

Individual and team weak points in competition should be worked on in practice. Players should be shown the charts and statistics on their performances, and drills should be developed to minimize their errors. Drills and scrimmages vary according to the imperfections discovered in the last match or tournament. The finer points of team tactics, such as backing up the block and switching from offense to defense, should be stressed.

Physical conditioning should not be isolated from fundamental techniques and playing tactics during the competitive phase. Physical, technical, and tactical training must be developed concurrently for best results. The amount of time allotted to specific areas of training is dependent on the stage of the season and the progress of the individuals and team. The coach must be flexible enough to adjust practice schedules to the progress of the team's development.

During the competitive phase, the substitutes should become *specialists*. Often a single player can fill many specialized roles. The following specialists are needed:

A player who can serve for points in crucial situations

A substitute with the ability to "fire the team up" or to spur them to perform beyond expectation

A journeyman setter with good ball-handling skills

A utility spiker who is also a good all-around performer

An excellent passer and a backcourt defensive specialist

A good hitter and blocker to substitute in the front row

Specialists should not be selected until it becomes obvious that they will not earn a starting position. For example, if a player is too small to spike effectively and cannot handle the ball well enough to set, he can still contribute to his team's success by perfecting his serve, pass, and backcourt defensive skills.

Substitutes should know the positions that they might be required to play and should receive extra practice in their specialties during the competitive phase of the season. This differs from the preparatory phase when all players participate in the same drills.

During the competitive stage of the season, it is important that maximum workouts do not occur the day before the match or tournament. Maximum practice sessions should occur twice a week if a match or tournament is scheduled; three times a week if there is no contest during that week.

Special Phases for Playoffs

Before a championship tournament, it is often helpful to simulate practice sessions with the schedule that will occur in the forthcoming competition. For example, in order to win a championship, a team must play three matches on Friday and two matches on Saturday. Since most teams are accustomed to a light workout on Friday and a heavy tournament schedule on Saturday, they may have difficulty in playing at a high level on both days unless the intensity of prior training is equal to the stress encountered in the championship event.

The coach must constantly be on guard against players *"going stale"* because practices are too frequent and prolonged. If this situation occurs, the coach should vary the drills when planning practice sessions at the conclusion of a long season so the players will be *mentally ready* for important matches or tournaments. Scheduled practices may be cancelled if inadequate or mental fatigue take hold.

Schools and college teams often find that they have lost their momentum after a final exam period because practices where held on a volunteer basis for student athletes who could spare the time from their studies. During the first week after exams, the coach must decide whether to take a long- or short-range view toward planning practices. Should he attempt to regain his players' technical skills through rigorous practice of fundamentals, or should he stress offensive and defensive tactics to use for the

next match? It is best to take the long-range view by emphasizing techniques if the team has a good chance of qualifying for the playoffs.

WEEKLY AND DAILY PRACTICE SCHEDULES

It is best to outline the weekly practice sessions in advance and to develop plans for the next daily session in detail at the conclusion of each practice.

Weekly Practice Schedule

Workouts scheduled for maximum intensity should be followed with practices of less intensity.

Repeated drills are necessary to create a conditioned reaction. For example, if a player has to think about diving to dig a spike, he will move too late to reach the ball. When a player has dived to retrieve balls thousands of times in practice, he will automatically dive for a ball in competition. There is little development or improvement without repetitive conditioning. It is the coach's responsibility to develop varied drills that develop the same technique through repetition.

Daily Practice Schedule

Practice Outline for the Preparatory Phase

1. Warm Up (30 min.)
   Laps and exercises
   Partner drills with emphasis on passing and setting
   Pepper drill

2. Technique (80 min.)
   Drills to correct individual weaknesses
   Setting and attacking
   Blocking
   Digging
   Individual serving and receiving
3. Tactics (40 min.)
   Offense
   Defense
4. Scrimmage and conditioning (20–40 min.)
   Scrimmaging
   Endurance drills

While experienced coaches may prefer to work from a simple practice outline, others may choose a more detailed practice plan. The practices should be evaluated and dated for the coach's reference throughout the season. Whole sections may be omitted from certain practices, particularly during the competitive phase when practice sessions should be used to strengthen weak points that show up in competition.

Detailed Practice Outline for the Preparatory Phase

1. Warm up (30 min.)
   Laps and exercises
   Touch block
   Mock block
   Dives
   Rolls
   Pepper
2. Technique drills (80 min.)
   Attack and setting drills
   Left

Right
Dinks—L, M, R
Deep sets—L, R
4's
3's
1's
Middle 2's
Right 2's
5's
Right x
Tandems
High middle
Blocking
   3 attackers v. 3 blockers
   2 attackers v. 3 blockers
Digging
Serving and receiving
   In frontcourt
   In backcourt
   Team receiving
   In middle-front court
   Middle front
   Pass and hit—1's
Individual skills
   Defense
   Blockers
   Setters
3. Tactics (40 min.)
   Offense
   Defense
   Game preparation
      Back-up spiker
      Free ball
      Down block
      Special
4. Scrimmage and conditioning (20–40 min.)
   Offense and defense scrimmages
   Spike
   Block
   Dig
   Special conditioning

Appendix

SCHEDULING TOURNAMENTS AND MATCHES

The traditional method of conducting local volleyball competition in the United States is to hold a double elimination tournament with a winners' bracket for undefeated teams and a losers' bracket for teams that have lost one match. Teams that lose two matches are eliminated from the tournament. The final competition pits the winner of the winners' bracket against the winner of the losers' bracket. When the team in the losers' bracket defeats its opponent in the final match, a one-game double finals is scheduled to determine the champion. In a double finals playoff, the final match consists of one game. The USVBA uses the double elimination method for its national championships in the men's, women's, senior, and collegiate divisions.

Recently, major regional tournaments have borrowed some aspects of major international or world tournaments by scheduling single round-robin tourna-ments in "pools" or separate brackets. For example, if twenty teams were competing in a tournament, they would be divided into four pools of five teams apiece. The top four teams would be placed in separate pools as well as teams five through eight. The placement of the rest of the teams would depend on their luck in the draw. If the tournament were scheduled to run for one day, the teams would play a two-game round-robin schedule; the top two finishers would compete in a single elimination finals and the rest of the pool would be eliminated. Winners and runners-up would then be seeded into an eight-team single elimination bracket for the championships.

Because volleyball has increased in popularity, and because competitions have become more frequent and more crowded with players and spectators, the present tournament setup has become outmoded and very impractical.

Tournaments in the United States usually start at 9:00 AM and finish late the same night. In other countries, teams

Official Hand Signals

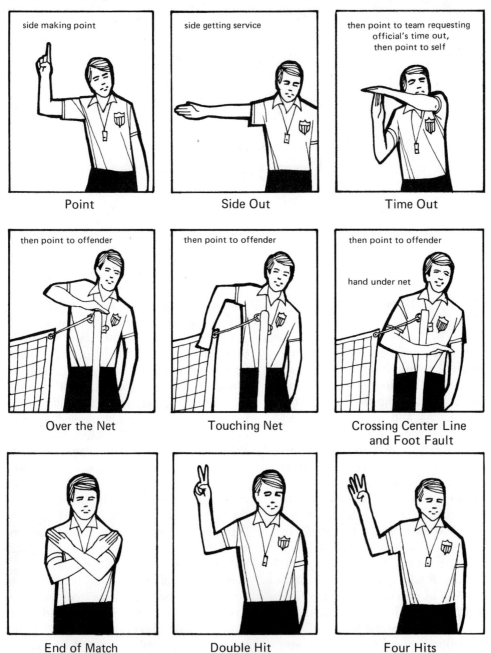

From the *Official Volleyball Guide, 1975*, Marvin D. Veronee, ed. (Berne, Indiana: United States Volleyball Association, 1975). Used with permission.

Official Hand Signals

sweeping motions of arm and hand twice

Thrown Ball

close fingers twice

Held Ball

Lifted Ball

alternately bring hands back and forth toward body

Out of Position

Technical Foul

point thumbs up

Double Foul Or Play Over

rotate hands

Substitution

ball in

ball out

Linesman's Signals

From the *Official Volleyball Guide, 1975,* Marvin D. Veronee, ed. (Berne, Indiana: United States Volleyball Association, 1975). Used with permission.

VOLLEYBALL COURT

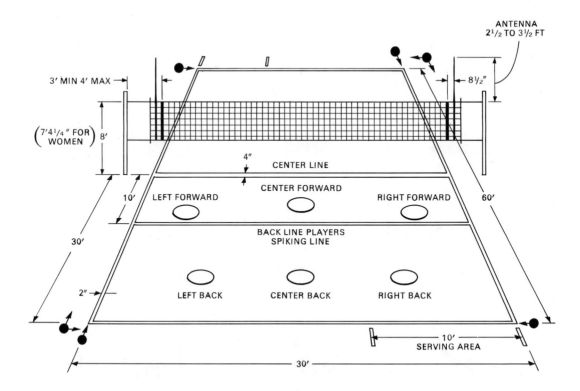

ANTENNA
2½ TO 3½ FT

3′ MIN 4′ MAX

8½″

(7′4¼″ FOR WOMEN) 8′

CENTER LINE

4″

CENTER FORWARD

10′   LEFT FORWARD   RIGHT FORWARD   60′

BACK LINE PLAYERS
SPIKING LINE

30′

2″   LEFT BACK   CENTER BACK   RIGHT BACK

10′
SERVING AREA

30′

NOTE: ALL LINES ARE 2″ WIDE EXCEPT CENTER LINE WHICH IS 4″

INDICATES POSITION OF LINESMAN WHEN FOUR ARE USED

INDICATES POSITION OF LINESMAN WHEN TWO ARE USED

never play more than one five-game match against a single opposing team on the same day. One-day tournaments in the United States develop poor playing habits because players tend to pace themselves so that they will have enough energy to play in the finals. Space is usually at such a premium that play is often held up while players from other courts career into playing areas to retrieve out-of-bounds balls. Referees be-come fatigued and lose their sharpness and ability to control the game. Publicity is virtually nonexistent because the morning paper's deadline has passed before the tournament is completed and newspapers are not interested in printing a story that is a day late.

Most of the players, officials, and fans in the United States are in favor of changing the structure of volleyball competition from tournaments to *leagues.*

COLLEGE VOLLEYBALL QUESTIONNAIRE

If space is insufficient for full answers, please use the reverse side of form.

Name_____ Nickname_____

Campus Address_____ Campus Phone _____

Home Address_____ Home Phone _____

Height _____ Weight _____ Age _____ Date of Birth_____

Married_____ Spouse's Name _____ Children Age(s)_____

Shoe Size_____ Waist Size_____ Jersey Size_____

Month and Year Entered This School _____

College_____ Major _____ Class_____

Organizations _____

Business or Professional Objectives _____

Years of eligibility remaining, including present season _____

When will you graduate? Quarter_____ Year_____

List volleyball experience in high school, clubs, open teams, Armed Services _____ _____

_____

How many seasons of college volleyball have you played?_____

Colleges, universities, and/or junior colleges attended _____

List names, dates, and athletic achievements_____

_____

Prominent relatives in athletics _____

Your biggest thrill in sports _____

_____

Who is the greatest volleyball player you ever played against?_____

_____

_____

Who is the greatest volleyball player you ever saw?_____

Why did you choose this college?_____

_____

Since 1963, the Southern California Intercollegiate Volleyball Association (SCIVA) has been conducting *league matches* between schools in the same area that have relative playing ability. Publicity and attendance at SCIVA matches have improved tremendously over the years. Fans have identified with a college team, and crowds of 4,000 to 5,000 are not uncommon at some of the larger campuses. Local papers publish stories before and after the match and SCIVA standings are publicized.

This collegiate league has drawn excellent athletes, a great number of spectators, and additional money to support the program. Consequently, SCIVA teams are stronger, coaches are better organized, and SCIVA players are selected for national teams. Recently, radio and television have covered the more important matches.

The organization of SCIVA is quite simple. Varsity matches are played at 7:30 PM and consist of three out of five games, with no time limit on their completion. Players go all out and the fans leave at the end of the match in anticipation of the next league contest.

The coaches from the member schools meet once a year to select the commissioner of the league, who draws up the yearly schedule and handles all conflicts that may occur. Eligibility rules do not present a problem because all athletic departments file with the commissioner a certificate of eligibility of their team members, according to NCAA rules and regulations. The commissioner then for-wards a copy of each competing school's eligibility report to member coaches. If an eligibility question arises, the commissioner contacts the athletic director at the involved school.

A head referee is selected to assign officials to all league matches. Each member school pays one fee to the head referee at the beginning of the season and another to the assigned officials during home matches.

As soon as several strong teams have developed in a district, it becomes necessary to hold a district tournament to qualify teams for the national tournament. The initial selection of teams for the district tournament is made by a district advisory committee, which submits its recommendations to the National Volleyball Tournament Committee. The advisory committee uses the following criteria to select teams for the district tournament:

Won—lost record

Strength of schedule

Eligibility of athletes for the National Volleyball Championships

RECORD OF TOURNAMENT WINNERS

For more information concerning the following tables, the reader is referred to Harold T. Friermood's "Cumulative Record of Volleyball Championship Winners" in the *1969 Official Volleyball Guide*.

FIVB Men's World Volleyball Championship Winners

Tourna-ment	Year	Place	Partici-pating Teams	Winner	Runner-Up	USA
1	1949	Prague	10	USSR	Czechoslovakia	–
2	1952	Moscow	11	USSR	Czechoslovakia	–
3	1956	Paris	24	Czechoslovakia	Romania	(6th)
4	1960	Sao Paulo	12	USSR	Czechoslovakia	(6th)
5	1962	Moscow	10	USSR	Czechoslovakia	–
6	1966	Prague	22	Czechoslovakia	Romania	(11th)
7	1970	Sofia	23	East Germany	Bulgaria	(18th)
8	1974	Mexico City	24	Poland	USSR	(14th)

FIVB Women's World Volleyball Championship Winners

Tourna-ment	Year	Place	Partici-pating Teams	Winner	Runner-Up	USA
1	1952	Moscow	8	USSR	Poland	–
2	1956	Paris	17	USSR	Romania	(9th)
3	1960	Sao Paulo	10	USSR	Japan	(6th)
4	1962	Moscow	8	Japan	USSR	–
5	1967	Tokyo	4	Japan	USA	(2nd)
6	1970	Varna	22	USSR	Japan	(11th)
7	1973	Montevideo	10	USSR	Japan	(6th)
8	1974	Mexico City	23	Japan	USSR	(12th)

Pan American Games Men's Volleyball Championship Winners*

Tourna-ment	Year	Place	Winner	Runner-Up	USA
1	1955	Mexico City	USA	Mexico	(1st)
2	1959	Chicago	USA	Brazil	(1st)
3	1963	Sao Paulo	Brazil	USA	(2nd)
4	1967	Winnipeg	USA	Brazil	(1st)
5	1971	Cali, Colombia	Cuba	USA	(2nd)
6	1975	Mexico City	Cuba	Brazil	(4th)

* Volleyball was not included in the first Pan Am Games (1951).

Pan American Games Women's Volleyball Championship Winners*

Tourna-ment	Year	Place	Winner	Runner-Up	USA
1	1955	Mexico City	Mexico	USA	2nd
2	1959	Chicago	Brazil	USA	2nd
3	1963	Sao Paulo	Brazil	USA	2nd
4	1967	Winnipeg	USA	Peru	1st
5	1971	Cali, Colombia	Cuba	Peru	–
6	1975	Mexico City	Cuba	Peru	6th

* Volleyball was not included in the first Pan Am Games (1951).

Olympic Games Men's Zonal Qualification Winners (formerly known as North Central and Caribbean Zone Championship)

Tourna-ment	Year	Place	Partici-pating Teams	Winner	Runner-Up	USA
1	1971	Havana	6	Cuba	USA	2nd
2	1975	Los Angeles	5	Cuba	Mexico	3rd

Olympic Games Men's Volleyball Championship Winners*

Tourna-ment	Year	Place	Partici-pating Teams	Winner	Runner-Up	USA
1	1964	Tokyo	10	USSR	Czechoslovakia	9th
2	1968	Mexico City	10	USSR	Japan	7th
3	1972	Munich	12	Japan	East Germany	**
4	1976	Montreal	10			**

 * Volleyball was not included in the Olympic Games from 1896 to 1960.
**USA team defeated by Cuba in Zonal Qualifications for Olympic Games.

Olympic Games Women's Volleyball Championship Winners*

Tournament	Year	Place	Participating Teams	Winner	Runner-Up	USA
1	1964	Tokyo	6	Japan	USSR	6th
2	1968	Mexico City	8	USSR	Japan	8th
3	1972	Munich	10	USSR	Japan	**
4	1976	Montreal	8			

 * Volleyball was not included in the Olympic Games from 1896 to 1960.
**Did not qualify.

Association of Intercollegiate Athletics for Women Championship Winners

Tournament	Year	Place	Winner	Runner-Up
1	1970	Cal. St. College, Long Beach	Sul Ross St. Univ., Alpine, Texas	UCLA
2	1971	University of Kansas	Sul Ross St. Univ., Alpine, Texas	CSULB
3	1972	Miami Dade CC	UCLA	CSULB
4	1972	BYU	CSULB	BYU
5	1973	College of Wooster	CSULB	Texas Women's University
6	1974	Portland St. Univ.	UCLA	University of Hawaii
7	1975	Princeton	UCLA	University of Hawaii

AIAW Junior College/Community College Championship Winners

Tournament	Year	Place	Winner	Runner-Up
1	1973	Miami Dade CC	Eastern Arizona	Miami Dade CC
2	1974	Kellogg College	Ricks College	Miami Dade CC

National Association of Intercollegiate Athletics Championship Winners

Tournament	Year	Place	Winner	Runner-Up
1	1969	George Williams College	Earlham College	Indiana Tech
2	1970	U.Cal–San Diego, LaJolla	U.Cal–San Diego	Indiana Tech
3	1971	Texas Wesleyan College & University of Dallas	Church College of Hawaii	Indiana Tech
4	1972	Graceland College	Church College of Hawaii	Graceland
5	1973	U.Cal–San Diego, LaJolla	Graceland	George Williams
6	1974	George Williams College	George Williams	Church College of Hawaii
7	1975	Earlham College	Dominquez Hills	BYU West

National Collegiate Athletic Association Championship Winners

Tournament	Year	Place	Winner	Runner-Up
1	1970	Los Angeles	UCLA	CSULB
2	1971	Los Angeles	UCLA	UCSB
3	1972	Muncie, Ind.	UCLA	SDSU
4	1973	San Diego	SDSU	CSULB
5	1974	Santa Barbara	UCLA	UCSB
6	1975	Los Angeles	UCLA	UCSB

National Junior College Athletic Association Championship Winners

Tournament	Year	Place	Winner	Runner-Up
1	1974	Schoolcraft College Livonia, Michigan	Kellogg CC	Schoolcraft College
2	1975	Schoolcraft College	Kellogg CC	San Bernardino CC

United States Volleyball Association Winners Since 1968 Men's Championship

Tourna-ment	Year	Place	Winner	Runner-Up
39	1969	Knoxville	Los Angeles YMCA	San Francisco Olympic Club
40	1970	Honolulu	Chart House of San Diego	Balboa Bay Club, Newport Beach
41	1971	Binghamton	Santa Monica YMCA	Chart House of San Diego
42	1972	Salt Lake City	Chart House Of San Diego	Santa Barbara Volleyball Club
43	1973	Duluth	Chucks Steak House of Southern California	Ski Mart, Long Beach
44	1974	Knoxville	Univ. of California, Santa Barbara	Balboa Bay Club, Newport Beach
45	1975	Reno	Chart House of San Diego	National All Stars
46	1976	Schenectady		

Women's Championships

Tourna-ment	Year	Place	Winner	Runner-Up
21	1969	Knoxville	Long Beach Shamrocks	Hawaiian Women
22	1970	Honolulu	Long Beach Shamrocks	Sul Ross State Univ., Alpine, Texas
23	1971	Binghamton	Los Angeles Renegades	Long Beach Shamrocks
24	1972	Salt Lake City	E. Pluribus Unum, Houston	Region 13 Seniors
25	1973	Duluth	E. Pluribus Unum, Houston	Los Angeles Renegades
26	1974	Knoxville	Los Angeles Renegades	Wilt's Little Dippers
27	1975	Reno	Adidas (Cal.) Volley-ball Club	Santa Monica (Cal.) Dippers
28	1976	Schenectady		

DEVELOPMENT OF VOLLEYBALL RULES

The basic features of the original rules for volleyball, written by William Morgan in 1895, are listed below:

Net height: 6 ft 6 in.

Court dimensions: 25 ft x 50 ft

Any number of participants allowed

Length of game: nine innings; each team allowed three outs per inning

Continuous air dribbling of ball permitted up to a restraining line 4 ft from the net

Unlimited number of hits allowed on each side of court

A served ball could be assisted across the net

A second serve was allowed (as in tennis) if the first serve resulted in a fault

Any ball that hit the net (except on the first serve) was a fault, resulting in a sideout.[1]

Obviously, drastic changes have occurred since Mr. Morgan demonstrated the game to his YMCA associates at Springfield College. The following chronology lists the changes that have taken place and govern the game as it is played in the United States today. Some of these changes were withdrawn for a number of years but were reinstated at a later date:

[1] William T. Odeneal, "A Summary of Seventy-Five Years of Rules," in Martin D. Veronee (ed.), *Official Volleyball Guide, 1970* (Berne, Indiana: United States Volleyball Association, 1970), pp. 149–54.

1912

• 6 players on each team

1915

• Official timer

1916

• Official game: 15 points
• Two out of three games determine a match
• Height of net: 8 ft
• Player rotation: each player serves in turn
• Any serve that touches the net or any outside object to be considered out of bounds
• Ball not allowed to rest in a player's hands
• Playing the ball a second time (unless played by another player) prohibited
  The rules were published in a separate book, *Official Volleyball Rules.*

1920

• Ball may be touched by any part of body above the waist
• Court size: 30 ft by 60 ft
• Before crossing net, ball may be played three times by each team

1922

• The centerline was added to court markings under net
• Official scorer
• Double foul defined and written in rules

1923

• 6 players per team, 12 players per squad

- Players are given numbers
- Player in right-back position serves

1925

- Umpire
- Player must obtain referee's permission to leave court
- Ball must cross net over sideline
- Each team allowed two time outs per game
- Team with a 2-point advantage wins a 14–14 tie game

1926

- Court measurement extended to *outside* edges of boundary lines
- Length of net: 32 ft
- Game forfeited if either team is reduced to less than 6 players

1932

- Centerline extended indefinitely; player allowed outside of court to play the ball
- Vertical tape marker put on net over sidelines

1935

- Players required to wear numbers on shirts
- Touching the net becomes a foul

1937

- If ball is driven into net and causes net to come into contact with player, it is *not* a foul
- Multiple contacts with ball allowed in receiving a hard-driven spike

1942

- Forfeited game score considered 15–0

1948

- Service area: right third of court
- Simultaneous contacts with ball by two players constitute one hit

1950

- Clarification of a held ball stipulates that the ball must be clearly batted

1952

- Players allowed to warm up during time outs

1953

- Substitutes allowed to re-enter game twice

1954

- Players must remain in position until ball is struck for serve

1956

- Players may stand anywhere on court, provided they are in rotation order
- Teams allowed to change courts during third game of a match if the ball has been in play for 4 minutes, or if one team has scored 8 points

1960

- Net height for women: 7 ft 4 1/4 in.

1962

- Players not allowed to grab officials' platform to halt themselves from going over centerline

1965

- Players may cross the extension of

the centerline, if they do not attempt to play the ball
• Illegal to screen receivers from server

1968

• Minimum ceiling height: 26 ft
• Lines added to outline 10-ft serving area on right side of court
• Spiking line moved from 7 1/2 ft to 10 ft back from net; backline spikers allowed to land in front of spiking line, if they jump from behind the line.
• Ball cannot be played with any part of body below waist
• Blockers may reach across net, if they do not contact ball until it has been attacked
• An individual blocker may contact ball twice in succession
• Players may follow-through over the net when returning the ball

1969

• Teams limited to 12 substitutions per game
• Blocking permitted by frontline players only
• If two opponents simultaneously hit ball above net, the player behind the direction of the ball is considered to have touched it last
• If two opponents hold ball simultaneously, it is a double fault and a play-over

1970

• Width of centerline increased from 2 in. to 4 in.
• Umpire's duties increased at discretion of referee
• Injured player must be replaced by a substitute immediately
• No change in line-up allowed after

team has been signaled to take the court
• Ball may or may not be tossed into air before striking it for a serve

1971

• Blocking rules clarified and interpretations refined
• Serve cannot be blocked *across* net
• Any ball, except the served ball, may be played off the ceiling, fixtures, or other obstructions if these intrude on court's height; however, no such ball may rebound into opponents' court
• Ball declared dead if it comes to rest or is wedged in ceiling or other obstruction
• Height of net for elementary school children: no lower than 6 ft
• Coed play: one backcourt player may also block when there is only one male player in a frontline position

1972

• Linesmen can assist in calling contacts with the ball if so instructed by the referee
• Any ball contacted by blocker(s) on the opponents' side of the net is considered to have crossed the net

1973

• Ball is out of bounds when it touches a net antenna or passes over the net not entirely within the net antennas
• Linesmen shall visibly signal the referee when the ball does not cross the net entirely within the net antennas
• A fourth substitution entry shall be refused, and the offending team shall be charged a time out
• When the ball is served, all of the backcourt players in the court must

be completely behind all of the frontcourt players in the court

1974

- Net antenna mandatory
- A player shall not contact any part of the net antenna while the ball is in play
- Five-minute intermission before the fifth game of a match; at this time, a toss of coin shall again be made to determine choice of serve or playing area

1975

- During play any part of a player's body may touch the center line. In addition, only a player's foot or feet may contact the playing area on the opposite side of the centerline, providing that some part of the encroaching foot or feet remains on or above the centerline at the time of such contact

Volleyball Today

The time-consuming ritual of having five players form a screen in front of the server to hide the ball from the receiving team was outlawed in 1965. At one time, screening players were actually allowed to wave their arms in a distracting manner to confuse their opponents. Often the receiver could not see a small server at all—nor could he see the flight of the serve until it came into view just before crossing the net. Naturally, the accuracy of the pass was impaired, which proved to be a great handicap to the few teams that needed a precise pass to use their three-hitter offense.

It was not unusual for a server to change his position from the right to the middle or left of the serving area. Until 1968, this serving area extended across the entire backline. The server often moved the screen about in a comical parade until the chosen receiver was isolated behind a wall of players.

Figure A–1 *The Antenna.* If the spiker hits the ball into the antenna, the ball is declared dead and awarded to the defense. If the ball rebounds into the antenna after touching the block, it is awarded to the offense. (Dr. Leonard Stallcup)

Today's rules call for the server to put the ball into play without undue delay when the referee blows his whistle and calls for the serve. The server must be in the serving area behind the endline in the right third of the court. Players are not allowed to screen or raise their arms to confuse the receiver. Teams now practice receiving the serve from only one area of the court and consequently pass the serve with greater accuracy. This allows the setters to arrive under the ball in position and to watch the approaching spiker and the blockers. Thus, the skilled setter can deliver a variety of "play sets" to deceive the opponents' block.

Allowing the blockers to reach across the net to contact the ball after the offense has attacked it has significantly changed the game. It forces opposing setters to pull the sets back from the net and prevent the blockers from forming a "roof" around the set and stuffing the spike to the floor. Since the spikers must contact the ball farther away from the net, the spike has to travel in a flatter trajectory instead of being hit straight down into their opponents' court. Spikers can no longer jump up and hit the ball as hard as possible to attempt to overpower the block.

Successful spikers learn to place the ball past the blockers using a variety of spiking angles and a change of pace dink shot and/or off-speed spike. The fast and well-coordinated digger has more time to react to spikes which are of necessity hit flatter and deeper into the court. Every good player must learn to dive to recover dink shots and half-speed spikes that fall in front of him.

Individual blockers are now allowed to contact the ball twice in succession instead of standing helpless as their blocked ball drops to the floor. Long rallies are common with the liberalized blocking rules, and the dive and roll have become a common defensive fundamental. Players are no longer cheered when they hit the floor to retrieve a ball; they are expected to do so.

Emphasis on overall conditioning and increasing the vertical jump through weight training have become popular with serious volleyball athletes.

The four-man block that hindered the three-hitter attack was abolished in 1969, and only front-row players are now allowed to block. Teams that can pass the ball accurately usually experience one-on-one blocking situations against their three-hitter attack.

When a backcourt player was allowed to join three frontcourt teammates at the net to block, it was difficult, regardless of the play, for a spiker in a three-hitter attack to isolate himself in a one-on-one situation. Four blockers spaced evenly across the court always enjoyed a tactical advantage at the net. It was feared this rule change would legislate against the small player who, under the previous rulings, could switch to the backcourt to dig and allow a taller player to take his place at the net.

This rule, however, has forced players to become skilled in all defensive aspects of the game. The tall and clumsy player who switched to an end blocking position in all three backcourt positions had to learn to play backcourt defense. The small setter who switched to the backcourt had to learn to block effectively. Smaller players have not vanished from the sport; they have increased their vertical jump by better techniques, weight training, or a combination of both. The tall and slow spiker has either improved his defensive skills or has been relegated to the middle-in position on the middle-in defense where fewer digging skills are needed.

The spiker is allowed to reach over the net when following through after contacting the ball. This relieves the referee of stopping the play every time an offensive player's hand inadvertently flicks across the net.

The referees' whistles were further silenced in 1975 when the defending team was allowed three contacts to return the ball after it was touched or deflected by the block. This rule gives the serving team a better chance to score and shortens the length of the match. In the past, the referee had to call the play dead when a blocker's teammates did not realize that their blocker had contacted the ball and continued to dig, set, and spike for a point or side out.

Effects of International Rule Interpretations

Use of the overhand pass to serve in power volleyball is rare. At recent championships over 99 percent of the serves were passed with the forearms. Coaches no longer teach the overhand pass for service reception, and players only practice this technique for passing slow-moving balls and setting. Before and during the 1964 Olympics, international referees called overhand reception of the serve very tightly. When Olympic players representing the United States returned home, they used the forearm pass exclusively to prevent the officials from calling a thrown ball. Leading coaches reasoned that officials would closely scrutinize the overhand pass but rarely

call a rule infraction on the "bump" or forearm pass. For good percentage plays, the forearm pass and moving players deeper into the court so that they can bump every serve is recommended.

Recent directives from the USVBA and the International Volleyball Federation remind referees and players that overhand service reception is legal. However, current players have perfected the forearm pass until it is possible to bump the ball with such accuracy that there is virtually no advantage in using the overhand pass. The spectators have benefitted also because the referee's whistle is noticeably quieter during service reception.

Upon returning from the 1964 Olympics, United States players, coaches, and referees were astonished at the officials' leniency during the set. At the Olympics, the foreign officials had automatically called every overhand service reception a thrown ball, and then ignored the manner in which the setters delivered the ball. The international setters had learned to set the ball from any body position in any direction. Blockers from the United States were confused by the setters' maneuvers and seemed to be continually late in reaching their blocking assignments.

American setters had been taught to stand with their shoulders at a right angle to the net and to set the ball directly forward or backward. Since the USVBA rules had not yet incorporated the interpretations of the International Volleyball Federation, American setters also had been taught to release the ball with a flick of the wrist, which meant that when they contacted the ball, they released it immediately. Although American players had a good "touch" on the ball, they had not learned to keep the ball in contact with their fingers as long as the foreign setters.

The obvious advantages of a prolonged contact of the ball are increased options of direction and greater accuracy of the set. The foreign setters could maintain prolonged contact by keeping their elbows closer to the sides of their body and by relying on greater arm and hand action to deliver the set. After exposure to the advantageous international style of setting, the better setters from the United States worked to master international techniques, and United States National Officials became more liberal in their interpretations of what constituted a thrown ball.

Although USVBA rules still state that the ball must be clearly hit and cannot visibly come to rest at contact, current interpretation falls between the leniency shown in international play and the pre-1964 competition in the USA:

> For example, the ball does not have to travel in the direction the body is facing as long as there is an immediate contact and release with little or no follow-through by the hands and arms.[2]

In the 1963 Pan American Games, 1964 Olympics, and subsequent international competition, players representing the United States were exposed to half-speed spikes and open-hand dink, or placement, shots. As the international spikers were confronted by opponents reaching over the net to block, they developed these alternate methods of attack to complement the hard spike. These off-speed shots caught the American back-court players flat-footed because they were interpreted as thrown balls in national competition within the United States. Returning Olympians developed these shots as techniques of attack and used them frequently enough to force opposing players to learn to dive and roll to the floor to retrieve off-speed shots.

National officials who would have whistled lesser-known spikers off the court for using open-hand dinks and half-speed spikes with prolonged hand contact, gradually liberalized their interpretation of what constituted a thrown ball during the attack, and these methods soon became accepted practice. Before these techniques of attack became popular, a player went to the floor to retrieve a ball only if he were out of position or had tripped. Today, the spiker may dink the ball with his fingertips and:

> change the course of the ball by directing it across the body, if the change of direction does not come from a break or follow-through of the wrist.[3]

VOLLEYBALL ASSOCIATIONS

United States Volleyball Association (USVBA)

The USVBA, formed in 1928, is recognized by the United States Olympic Committee as the governing body for volleyball in this country. The association has a full-time, paid executive director, 18 volunteer committee chairmen, and 100

[2] Allen E. Scates and Jane Ward, *Volleyball*, 2nd ed. (Boston: Allyn and Bacon, 1975), p. 37.

[3] *Ibid.*

Figure A–2 *Volleyball Camps.* USVBA coaches conduct summer volleyball camps with Olympic Committee funds in many areas of the United States. (Barry Schreiber)

volunteer committee members.[4] The YMCA has supplied integral leadership in this organization. Many volunteers in the association are retired players who wish to stay close to the game and do so by accepting committee or officiating assignments.

The USVBA registers its own players and regulates all eligibility procedures for organizations, teams, and individuals competing in its local, regional and national tournaments. The organization

conducts a double elimination national championship for Open Men's, Open Women's, Men's Collegiate and Senior Men's divisions or at a different site each year. The National YMCA Championship is awarded to the YMCA team that finishes highest in the National Open Championships. The USVBA Championships, which generally accept 80 team entries, are traditionally held Wednesday through Saturday in early May.

The USVBA has a membership of about 13,000, which is very small in comparison with East European and Asian

[4] Veronee (ed.), *1975 Volleyball Guide,* p. 37.

volleyball associations. Czechoslovakia, with a population of 17 million people, has 60,000 members in its volleyball association.

The USVBA publishes an *Official Volleyball Rules and Reference Guide* annually. The association's rules were adopted by the NCAA, NAIA, NJCAA, AAU, and almost every other organization that sponsors volleyball competition in the U.S. With the exception of substitution rules, the USVBA rules are rules followed by every country in the world.

The USVBA holds clinics throughout the country and sends teams abroad to play major international volleyball events. Due largely to the efforts of the USVBA, volleyball has become the greatest participant sport in the U.S., with 60,000,000 participants.[5]

National Collegiate Athletic Association (NCAA)

The NCAA conducts 39 national championships in 17 sports for its 775 colleges, universities, and affiliated associations. Only one national championship is held for volleyball, fencing, hockey, skiing, indoor track, and water polo. These championships are open to all member institutions. Four teams are invited to the NCAA Championships: one team from the West, one from the Midwest, one from the East, and one at-large entry. The Southern California Intercollegiate Volleyball Association (SCIVA); the Midwest Intercollegiate Volleyball Association (MIVA); and the Eastern Collegiate Volleyball League (ECVL) tradi-

tionally supply teams for the NCAA Volleyball Championships.

In 1970 the USVBA Men's Collegiate Championship was discontinued because the NCAA and the National Association of Intercollegiate Athletics (NAIA) colleges were sending teams to their own championship events. The USVBA Collegiate Committee reinstated the Men's Collegiate Division in 1971 primarily for two-year colleges and for unaffiliated four-year colleges.

Division for Girls and Women's Sports (DGWS)

The DGWS is a division of the American Association for Health, Physical Education, and Recreation. It is:

> a nonprofit educational organization designed to serve the needs and interests of administrators, teachers, leaders, and participants in sports programs for girls and women. Active members of the Division are women members of the American Association for Health, Physical Education, and Recreation who are interested in sports for girls and women who participate in the work of the division.[6]

The first intercollegiate national volleyball championships for women were held at California State College at Long Beach in 1970 and were sponsored by the DGWS. Twenty-eight top-ranking teams from states such as California, New Mexico, Oregon, Florida, Ohio, Mississippi, Missouri, Illinois, Utah, and

[5] United States Olympic Committee Newsletter, December 1973, p. 20.

[6] Lynne P. Higgins (ed.), *1973–75 Volleyball Guide* (Washington, D.C.: The Division for Girls and Women's Sports, 1973), p. 5.

Figure A–3 *NCAA Volleyball.* NCAA Championships consistently draw the largest volleyball crowds in the United States. (Stan Troutman)

Texas were represented.[7] Several former Olympians and USVBA All-Americans competed on their college teams. Sul Ross State University in Texas emerged as the first DGWS champion.

Association for Intercollegiate Athletics for Women (AIAW)

The AIAW, established in 1971 by the DGWS, is an "Autonomous organiza-tion, established to provide a governing body and leadership for initiating and maintaining standards of excellence in women's intercollegiate athletic pro-grams."[8] One of its main purposes is "to encourage excellence in performance of participants in women's intercollegiate athletics."[9]

Women are demanding separate teams with a level of administrative support comparable to men's teams. This support will be realized when funding, schedul-ing, practice times, facilities, equipment,

[7] Lyndee Dossey, Publicity Chairman for DGWS National Intercollegiate Volleyball Champion-ships, personal correspondence with the author.

[8] Fact sheet on Association for Intercollegiate Athletics for Women, November 1973.
[9] *Ibid.*

travel, and medical care are equal for men and women.

To encourage excellence in performance, there must be excellence in teaching and coaching. "Discriminatory practices for the past fifty years have taken their toll from the calibre of coaching by women ... Women coaches must now begin to demand specialized training similar to that which has been afforded the male coaches for generations. There must be financial support for the process of 'catching up' to become highly qualified coaches."[10]

Although some women are better performers than some men, the female hormone estrogen inhibits the growth of muscle tissue, imposing limitations on women's performance when competing in activities with men that require strength and speed. Separate teams for men and women are essential to the development of competitive athletics for girls and women. "Any school or district that removes the word 'male' from its regulations and permits participation by girls on previously all-male teams does not prevent discrimination."[11]

Sports programs for girls and women will probably experience rapid growth in the next decade due to the increased emphasis that federal legislation has brought to women's athletics. If schools and colleges are not willing to increase their support of women's programs, the judicial system is a powerful force to which to turn.

The most important piece of legislation pertaining to female athletic programs is Title IX of the U.S. Education Amendment Act of 1972. The Equal Protection Clause of the Fourteenth Amendment; Title VII of the Civil Rights Act of 1964, as amended by the Equal Employment Opportunity Act of 1972; and the Higher Education Act also apply to the status of women in athletics.

The AIAW conducts the women's volleyball championships in four-year and two-year college divisions.

National Association of Intercollegiate Athletics (NAIA)

The first intercollegiate volleyball tournament sponsored by a national collegiate governing body was hosted by George Williams College in Downers Grove, Illinois, in 1969. The seven-team double elimination NAIA volleyball championship "was won by Earlham College, Richmond, Indiana, with Indiana Tech, Fort Wayne, Indiana, finishing second."[12]

The NAIA was officially organized in 1940 and sponsors 17 annual national championships for its 550 member colleges and universities. Its objective is "to champion the cause and promote the interests of the college of moderate enrollment and sound athletic policy and program."[13]

National Junior College Athletic Association (NJCAA)

Kellogg Community College won the first NJCAA Volleyball Championship in

---

[10] Dorothy McKnight and Joan Hult, "Competitive Athletics for Girls: We Must Act," *Journal of Health, Physical Education, and Recreation* (June 1974): 45–46.

[11] *Ibid.*

[12] Jerre McNamara, "Earlham College Wins the National Association of Intercollegiate Athletics National Volleyball Championships," *1970 Official Volleyball Guide*, p. 128.

[13] The *1969–70 National Directory of College Athletics* (Amarillo, Texas: Roy Franks Publishing Ranch, 1969), p. 36.

Figure A–4 *Girls' Volleyball.* Volleyball has been firmly entrenched in high school athletics programs for girls for a number of years. (Barry Schreiber)

Figure A–5. *Boys' Volleyball.* During the last few years, there has been a great increase in the number of varsity teams sponsored by high school boys' athletic departments. (Barry Schreiber)

1974 at Schoolcraft College in Livonia, Michigan. The NJCAA was the last national collegiate governing body to establish a championship event for volleyball.

Amateur Athletic Union (AAU)

The AAU has held over 30 national championships since 1925. It usually holds tournaments a few days before the USVBA Championships and chooses a location near the USVBA site. The AAU tournament attracts a number of teams that desire a final tune-up before the USVBA championships. Teams in this tournament are usually at partial strength because many players are not willing to

take the additional expense and time away from their jobs or schools to compete in both championships.

High School Associations

The National Federation of State High School Athletic Associations conducted a Sports Participation Survey that indicated that there were 1,184 high schools in the U.S. offering intercollegiate volleyball to 21,910 boys.[14] The same report indicated in 1974 that 7,426 high schools

[14] National Federation of State High School Associations, *Official Handbook: 1974–1975*, pp. 86–91.

sponsored girls interscholastic competition in volleyball with 159,535 participants. This was over a 800 percent increase in the total number of boys and girls participating in interscholastic volleyball since 1969. Texas led the nation with a total of 36,000 boys and girls competing in interscholastic volleyball.

United States Olympic Committee (USOC)

The Men and Women's Olympic Volleyball Committee selects players, coaches, managers, and officials to participate in the Pan American and Olympic Games. Up to 30 people serve on this committee, and they are all USVBA members. The president of the USVBA is a member of the USOC Board of Directors and a USVBA Olympian is on the USOC Athletes Advisory Council. There are 130 nations with membership in the International Olympic Committee.

The USOC supplies funds and the USVBA supplies personnel for volleyball development programs in many areas of the United States during the summer months.

Unfortunately, United States Pan American and Olympic Volleyball teams have never achieved their full potential because key members cannot afford to support themselves or their families while training with the U. S. national team. Under a revised eligibility code, the U. S. Olympic Committee can reimburse athletes for a loss of salary, wages, or other income for a period of up to 30 days during an Olympic year as well as reimburse expenses incurred while training for important national or international competition. The U. S. is currently ranked tenth in the Men's World Volleyball Rating and is not likely to progress further until financial aid is provided to allow experienced players to compete and still support their families.

Eight of the ten berths for the Olympic Men's Volleyball competition are filled at least one year ahead of the competition. The host country and the last Olympic champion qualify automatically. The winner of the World Championship and representatives from the continents of Africa, Asia, South America, North and Central America, and the winner of the European championship also qualify. Two nations qualify in a Special Olympic Qualification Tournament held a month before the Olympics. The United States Men's Team must defeat Cuba in the North and Central American zonal qualification to ensure Olympic participation. The United States Women's Team must compete in the same North and Central American Zonal Tournament as the men to ensure Olympic participation.

International Volleyball Federation (FIVB)

One hundred and fifteen to 120 countries maintain membership in the FIVB. Volleyball is a major sport in at least 25 of these countries. Olympic Games, Pan American Games, World Games, international matches, and all competition conducted outside of the United States abide by the playing rules of the International Volleyball Federation. Within the last few years, the USVBA has made several rule changes to bring its rules into alignment with those of the FIVB. In both USVBA and International Rules, the only exception for women is a lowering of the net.

The Federation International Volley Ball (FIVB) competitions are more competitive than the Olympic Games. Since ten men's teams and eight women's teams are allowed to enter the Olympics, many of the world's better teams are eliminated in tough zone competition and fail to earn a berth in the Olympics.

United States Collegiate Council (USCSC)

In 1967 the USCSC was founded by the following organizations:

National Junior College Athletic Association

United States National Student Association

National Association of Intercollegiate Athletics (NAIA)

The National Collegiate Athletic Association (NCAA)

American Association for Health, Physical Education, and Recreation

The primary purpose of the Council is to promote international collegiate sport through increased participation of American student athletes in the World University Games. The World University Games is a major biennial competition sponsored by the IUSF, where membership is represented by over 50 countries. Volleyball competition is held every two years during the summer; full-time students between the ages of 18 and 28 are eligible. The USA Men's team competed for the first time in 1973 in Moscow. There were 24 entries and the USSR won 21 straight games to win the championship. Cuba was second, Korea third, Poland fourth, East Germany fifth, Brazil

sixth; and the United States finished eighteenth.

The USCSC Women's Committee selects players from the AIAW Junior / Community College National Championships, the AIAW National Volleyball Championships, the USVBA National Championships, and the USCSC holds open tryouts at a USCSC Summer Development Camp in even numbered years.

International Volleyball Association (IVA)

Founded by a group of entertainment-oriented entrepreneurs after watching the 1972 Olympics, the IVA is the first professional volleyball league in the world. In 1975 the IVA operated five franchises:

Figure A–6 *International Protocol.* After the introduction at an international match, players always exchange gifts at the net. (Barry Schreiber)

Los Angeles Stars, Southern California (Irvine) Bangers, Santa Barbara Spikers, San Diego Breakers, and El Paso–Juarez Sol. Two women play on the court at all times. The women play in the backline because a designated-player rule allows them to exchange positions with the men. The basic roles of the women are passing, setting, and digging. Several foreign players joined the league, led by Poland's Stan Gosciniak. Gosciniak was the outstanding player in the 1974 World Tournament, won by Poland in Mexico City.

Other Groups

The Mormons have held an annual national volleyball championship since 1950. During the 1968 Olympic year, over 2,500 junior and senior men's teams competed in thirty-seven zones throughout the United States and Canada. Junior and senior zone champions competed in a two-day double elimination tournament in Salt Lake City.[15]

Other groups that hold volleyball championships are the American Turners, Jewish Welfare Board, American Latvian Association, Army, Navy, Air Force, and Marines. The Catholic Youth Organization (CYO) is very active in local competition.

[15] *See* Wayne Mills, "All Church Morman Volleyball Championships," *Official Volleyball Guide, 1969* (Berne, Indiana: United States Volleyball Association, 1969), p. 146.

Bibliography

VOLLEYBALL PUBLICATIONS

Official Volleyball Rules and Reference Guide Marvin D. Veronee, editor. Published annually by United States Volleyball Association. Price: $2.50. Address: USVBA Printer, P. O. Box 109, Berne, Indiana 46711. Presents a complete summary of past season and coming season rules. Much information and many interesting articles are included.

Volleyball Technical Journal for Coaches Lorne Sawula, editor. Published quarterly by Canadian Volleyball Publications. Subscription price: $15.00/year. Address: 78 Tedford Drive, Scarboro, Ontario, Canada.

Volleyball Guide. Published biennially by the Division of Girls and Women's Sports of the American Association for Health, Physical Education and Recreation, 1201 16th Street NW, Washington, D. C. 20036. Price: $1.75. The official DGWS rules, officiating standards and techniques, and accompanying articles on playing, coaching, and teaching volleyball provide up-to-date materials and visual aids for novice and expert volleyball players.

Official Volleyball Rules for Girls and Women: June 1975–June 1977. Published by the Division of Girls and Women's Sports of the American Association for Health, Physical Education, and Recreation, 1201 16th Street NW, Washington, D.C. 20036. Price: $.50.

Volleyball Review Henry C. Murray, editor. Official publication of the United States Volleyball Association. Published bi-monthly. Subscription price: $2.00 annually. Address: Henry C. Murray, U.S. Volleyball Association, P. O. Box 995, San Leandro, California 94511.

FILMS

Volleyball. Official volleyball films of NCAA-AAHPER. Produced by The Ealing Corporation/Sports Illustrated.

Young all-American and Olympic players demonstrate technically flawless volleyball fundamentals. Slow-Motion analysis and freeze-frames are used to help teach critical points. Authored by Allen E. Scates, the set sells for $149.70. Films showing individual techniques can be purchased for $24.95. For further information, contact: NCAA Films, P.O. Box 2726, Wichita, Kansas 67201.

Women's Volleyball Films

Film 1: USA–USSR World Cup Championships of 1973
Film 2: USA–Korea World Cup Championships of 1973
Film 3: USSR–Korea World Cup Championships of 1973
Film 4: Korea–Japan World Cup Championships of 1973
These films are in black and white with sound. Average running time: 33 minutes. Rental price: $25.00 a day. For further information, contact: Schreiber and Company, P.O. Box 24614, Los Angeles, California 90024

VOLLEYBALL TEACHING AIDS

Spike-It Manufactured by Excel Sport Products, P.O. Box 251, Montrose, California 91020. Price: $64.50. The Spike-It allows players to concentrate on correct techniques rather than worry about the placement of the set. The Spike-It can be used to teach the approach, takeoff, armswing, and hand contact before refining setting skills.

Block-It Manufactured by Excel Sport Products, P.O. Box 251, Montrose, California 91020. Price: $72.50. The Block-It is a device that blocks balls into the attacker's court. It is used to teach positioning and technique to back up the spiker. The Block-It is also used to prepare the spiker to hit around the block or over it.

Volleyball Terms

I. OFFENSIVE MANEUVERS: Serving, passing, setting, and attacking

A. Serving

Crosscourt Serve: A serve landing near the opponent's right sideline

Line Serve: A straight-ahead serve landing near the opponent's left sideline

Overhand Serve: A serve performed with an overhand throwing action

Overhand Floater Serve: The overhand floater serve has no spin and moves in an erratic path as it approaches the receiver. The ball is hit with only a momentary point of contact and very little follow-through.

Overhand Spin Serve: The server contacts the lower mid-section of the center of the ball; he or she uses the heel of the hand to initially contact the ball, and then uses the wrist snap to roll the hand over the ball, imparting topspin.

Roundhouse Serve: The arm moves in a windmill action, and the ball is contacted directly over the hitting shoulder.

Sky Ball Serve: An underhand serve that is hit so high it looks like it is falling straight down. It is used for play at large arenas or outdoor courts.

Underhand Serve: A serve performed with an underarm striking action. The ball is usually contacted with the heel of the hand.

B. Passing: The reception of the serve or first contact of the ball. It is an attempt to control the movement of the ball so that the ball reaches another player. A pass of a hard-spiked ball is called a *dig.*

Bump Pass: See Forearm Pass

Elbow Snap Pass: Starting with the elbows in a bent position and then extending them to a locked position just prior to contacting the ball.

Elbow Lock Pass: Arms remain locked before and during contact. Movement of the arms is directed in an arc from the shoulders.

Overhand Pass: Usually a pass executed with two hands in the same direction that the passer is facing.

Forearm Pass: A ball played off the forearms in an underhand manner. It is the best way to pass a serve to the setter. It is also used to dig spikes and play any ball dropping close to the floor.

One-Arm Pass: See One-Arm Dig (Digging).

C. Setting: Passing to place the ball in position for a player to spike. The setter is the player who sets the ball to the spiker.

Back Set: A set made over the head, behind the setter, and usually executed with two hands.

One-Set: An extremely low vertical set delivered from 1 to 2 ft above the net. The spiker contacts the ball while the set is rising.

Slow One-Set: A low vertical set that travels about 2 ft above the net. The spiker attacks the ball after it reaches its peak.

Two-Set: This set usually travels from 3 to 4 ft above the net. It does not require the same split-second timing as the one-set and can be mastered by any good spiker.

Three-Set: A play set delivered low and fast about 10 ft from the left sideline to the middle spiker. It is designed to beat a slow middle blocker.

Slow Three-Set: A play set lobbed 10 ft from the left sideline to the left attacker. It is most effective when the middle attacker can "freeze" the middle blocker with the threat of a quick hit.

Four Set: A play set placed about a foot from the sideline at a height of 1 to 2 ft above the net. This play is very difficult for the middle blocker to cover when the ball travels a distance of 15 to 20 ft from the setter to the spiker.

Five-Set: A back lob to the setter on the right sideline is called a five-set. It is low enough to create a one-on-one situation for the off-hand spiker.

Regular Set: A ball delivered in a high arc that drops about 2 ft from the net, at either corner of the net.

Shoot Set: See Four Set

Lateral Set: A set made to either side of the setter with two hands.

Normal Set: See Regular Set

One Hand Set: Many setters jump-set passes that are going to travel over the net by intercepting the ball with the fingertips of one hand. This works particularly well in the one-set to a quick middle attacker.

Punch Set: When the ball is going to be passed over the net and it is impossible to set the ball with two hands, the backcourt setter may elect to punch set the ball with the knuckles rather than risk the chance of throwing the ball by contacting it with the fingertips.

Jump Set: The player setting the ball jumps to confuse the block or to place himself in a better position to save a long pass that will drop over or hit the net.

D. Attacking: Hitting the ball into the opponents's court.

Crosscourt Spike: A spike directed diagonally to the longest part of the court.

Dink: Usually a one-hand hit in which the tips of the fingers are used to hit the ball to an area of the opponent's court.

Deep Dink: A dink that lands in the opponent's backcourt.

Follow-through: The attacker reaches over the net contacting the ball on his side first.

Line Spike: A spike directed down the sideline closest to the spiker.

Off-Hand Side: The side of the court on which the spiker would contact the ball with the predominant hand before the ball crosses in front of the spiker's body. For example, the right-front corner would be the off-hand side for a right-handed spiker.

Off-Speed Shot: A ball that rapidly loses momentum because of the reduced speed of the striking arm just prior to contact. The off-speed shot is most effective when used infrequently and directed toward a definite weakness in the defense. The ball can be contacted by the hand or fingers.

On-Hand Side: The side of the court on which the spiker would contact the ball with the predominant hand before it crosses in front of his body. For example, the left-front corner would be the on-hand side for a right-handed spiker.

Pre-Jump Takeoff: With his power foot, the spiker hops and lands both feet simultaneously with the heels parallel; next he shifts his weight to the balls of his feet, bends his legs, forceably contracting them, and thereby forcing himself to leave the floor.

Round House Spike: A spike hit with a windmill action of the arm. The ball is usually contacted with the body perpendicular to the net.

Spike: A ball hit forceably with one hand. Backcourt players cannot spike the ball unless they take off from behind the 10 ft spiking line.

Spiker: A player who performs a spike, dink, or off-speed shot.

Step-Close Takeoff: The spiker takes a long last step by jumping forward, contacting the floor with the heel of one foot and then with the heel of the other foot; his weight then rolls from both heels to the toes as he takes off.

Tip: See Dink.

Wipe-Off Spike: A conscious effort to spike the ball laterally off the block into the out-of-bounds area.

II. DEFENSIVE MANEUVERS: Blocking and Digging

A. Blocking

Block: A play by one or more players who attempt to intercept the ball over or near the net. Blocking is permitted by any or all of the players in the front line.

Attack Block: An attempt to intercept the ball before it crosses the net.

Double Block: Two players blocking at the net.

Down Block: Blockers drop their arms when they judge that the ball will not be hit by the spiker at a downward angle.

Key: A term used to describe close observation of opposing players' habits or actions in order to gain a clue to their next moves. For example, many blockers watch or "key" on the setter to see if he arches his back prior to contacting the ball, which usually indicates a back set.

Key on the One Play: The middle blocker jumps with the middle attacker to stop the quick one-set.

One-Hand Block: A technique used when the blocker is out of position. This maneuver gives the blocker greater lateral coverage above the net.

One-on-One Block: Used when only one blocker can reach his assignment.

Single Block: One player blocking at the net.

Soft Block: The forearms are held parallel to the net and the hands are held either tilted backward or parallel to the net.

Triple Block: Three players blocking at the net.

Turning the Ball In: A technique used by the end blocker to prevent the spike from hitting his hand and going out of bounds. He reaches over the net with his outside hand between the boundary line and the ball.

B. **Digging:** Passing a spiked ball while standing, diving, rolling, or jumping.

High Dig: Arms are held parallel to the floor—when the flight of the ball permits—to enable the dig to travel high into the air on the digger's side of the net.

Backhand Dig: Hitting the ball with the back of the hand. During the dive, this technique allows the player to keep his palms close to the floor in anticipation of a quick landing.

Cushioning the Ball: Digging the ball with a backward movement of the arms or body.

Dive: An attempt to recover a ball by going to a prone position on the court.

One-Arm Dig: Used when the ball cannot be contacted using the forearm pass. The ball can be effectively contacted anywhere from the knuckles of the closed fist to the elbow joint.

Roll: A lateral movement that allows a player to go to the floor without injury and return quickly to his feet. Ideally, the ball is contacted just before the thigh and buttocks hit the floor.

III. TEAM DEFENSE

Area Block: Blocking a designated area of the net. Frequently used when good diggers are in the back court.

Blue Defense: See Off-Blocker Defense.

Free Ball: When the defense sees that the offense will hit the ball over the net with an upward flight or weak spike, it calls, "Free!" and assumes a normal serve-reception pattern.

False Weakness: A play used to lure the opposition into spiking to an area that they think is weak. For example, a blocker may leave the area above the net open for a crosscourt shot and then quickly swing his arms to the middle of the net just prior to when the spiker contacts the ball.

Middle-Back Defense: A defensive formation that uses the middle-back player to recover deep spikes.

Middle-In Defense: A defensive formation that uses the middle-back player to recover short dink shots.

Off-Blocker Defense: A defensive formation that uses the off-blocker to recover short dink shots.

Red Defense: See Middle-In Defense

White Defense: See Middle-Back Defense

Zone Block: See Area Block

IV. TEAM OFFENSE

A. Combination: A play that involves two attackers penetrating into a single blocker's zone of the net.

Double Quick: The middle attacker approaches for a one-set and the off-hand attacker approaches for a back one-set. This play usually isolates the middle blocker who must defend against two attackers.

Right Cross: The middle attacker approaches for a one-set and the right attacker crosses behind him for a two-set. The setter watches the middle blocker and sets to the open spiker.

Tandem: The middle attacker approaches for a one-set, and the left attacker follows right behind him for a two-set. The setter watches the middle blocker; if the middle blocker jumps with the first attacker, the setter delivers a two-set to the second man.

Four-Man Reception: Four-man receiving formations are very efficient if four superior passers are receiving the serve. The advantage of this system is that the player approaching for the one-set has a better approach because he starts at the net and has little serve receiving responsibility.

Five-One Offense: This offense uses five hitters and one setter. Consequently, in 50 percent of the rotations, the offense runs with three hitters and in 50 percent of the rotations, it runs with two hitters at the net. One player sets all the good passes.

Multiple Offense: A two- or three-hitter system that uses play sets.

One-on-One Situation: This refers to one attacker spiking against one blocker. Most offenses run their patterns with one-on-one situations as their goal.

Percentage Play: Certain sets can be hit with a better spiking percentage in certain situations. For example, when the ball is passed about 15 ft from the net, the best percentage set is a regular set. The attacker would have a poor spiking average if the setter delivered a quick set on a bad pass.

Play Sets: Sets used to create favorable attack conditions. Plays are called by the setter or the attacker to avoid the block. Play sets vary greatly in height and distance from the setter to the attacker.

Six-Two Offense: An offense that uses three hitters at the net and a back-row setter. Four players are spikers and two are setter-spikers.

Technique Player: Primarily a spiker who sets the ball only when he is in the right-back rotation.

Three-Hitter Attack: The offense used when a backcourt setter is used.

Two-Hitter Attack: The offense used when one of the frontcourt players is a setter.

V. MISCELLANEOUS

Antenna: A pole extending vertically from the bottom of the net to a height of 2 1/2 to 3 1/2 above the net at the sideline.

Contacted Ball: A ball that touches or is touched by any part of a player's body or clothing.

Foul: A failure to play the ball properly as permitted under the rules.

Gather: The act of squatting just prior to jumping.

Netting: Touching the net while the ball is in play. This act terminates play when seen by the referee or umpire. In doubles, the player calls his own nets.

Out of Bounds: The ball is out of bounds when it touches any surface, object, or ground outside the court; touches the net outside the markers on the sides of the net; touches a net antenna; or passes over the net not entirely within the net antennas.

Scoring: A team can only score points when it is serving

Screw Under Step: A technique used by a player to put himself in a more favorable position to play the ball by taking a long step with his lead leg and squatting. His trailing leg is extending as he pivots toward the ball. This technique is used to pass, dig, or set the ball.

Seam: The area directly between two serve receivers or diggers.

Short Court: The official doubles court is 30-ft by 50-ft. This rule is largely ignored by doubles players throughout the country who continue to use the 30-ft by 60-ft court.

Side Out: When the serving team fails to score a point, the ball is given to their opponents; the exchange of service is called a side out.

Thrown Ball: When, in the opinion of the proper official, the ball visibly comes to rest at contact, the player has committed a foul.

INDEX

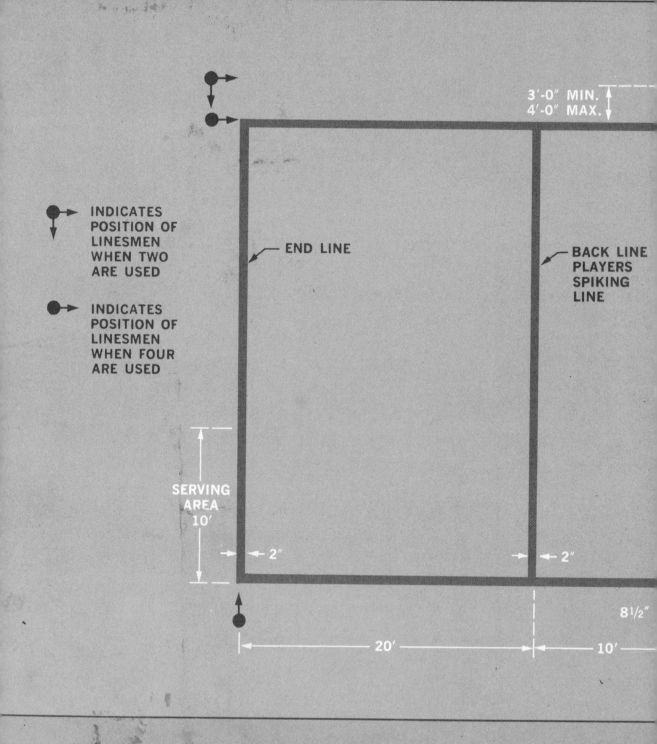

INDICATES POSITION OF LINESMEN WHEN TWO ARE USED

INDICATES POSITION OF LINESMEN WHEN FOUR ARE USED

3'-0" MIN.
4'-0" MAX.

END LINE

BACK LINE PLAYERS SPIKING LINE

SERVING AREA 10'

2"

2"

8½"

20'

10'